HEALTHY FAVORITES

★ FROM AMERICA'S ★

COMMUNITY COOKBOOKS

More Than 200 Delicious, Family-Tested Recipes
Selected by **PREVENTION** Magazine

Edited by Jean Rogers and the
Food Editors of **PREVENTION** Magazine Health Books

Rodale Press, Inc.
Emmaus, Pennsylvania

Front Cover Recipe: Old-Fashioned Strawberry Shortcake (page 256); adapted from: *Albuquerque Academy à la Carte* by the Albuquerque Academy Parents' Association

Library of Congress Cataloging-in-Publication Data

Healthy favorites from America's community cookbooks : more than
   200 delicious, family-tested recipes selected by Prevention magazine /
   edited by Jean Rogers and the food editors of Prevention Magazine
   Health Books.
      p.   cm.
   Includes index.
   ISBN 0–87596–317–X   paperback
    1. Cookery, American.   I. Rogers, Jean, date.   II. Prevention
Magazine Health Books.   III. Prevention (Emmaus, Pa.)
TX715.H3962   1996
641.5973—dc20   96–815

Distributed in the book trade by St. Martin's Press

2   4   6   8   10 9   7   5   3   paperback

OUR PURPOSE

*"We inspire and enable people to improve
their lives and the world around them."*

Healthy Favorites from America's Community Cookbooks
Editorial Staff
Managing Food Editor: Jean Rogers
Editors: Sharon Sanders, Mary Jo Plutt
Contributing Writer: Paula M. Bodah
Copy Editor: Kathy Diehl
Designer: Elizabeth Youngblood
Associate Art Director: Elizabeth Otwell
Studio Manager: Joe Golden
Interior Designer: Joyce Weston
Interior Illustrator: Dorothy Reinhardt
Cover and Layout Designer: Eugenie Seidenberg Delaney
Front and Back Cover Photographer: Becky Luigart-Stayner
Front and Back Cover Food Stylist: Marie Paraino
Recipe Testing: Spectrum Communication Services, Inc.;
    Rodale Test Kitchen: JoAnn Brader
Nutrition Consultants: Linda Yoakam, M.S., R.D.; Anita Hirsch,
    M.S., R.D.
Office Staff: Roberta Mulliner, Bernadette Sauerwine
Production Manager: Helen Clogston
Manufacturing Coordinator: Melinda B. Rizzo

Rodale Health and Fitness Books
Vice-President and Editorial Director: Debora T. Yost
Art Director: Jane Colby Knutila
Research Manager: Ann Gossy Yermish
Copy Manager: Lisa D. Andruscavage

*In all Rodale Press cookbooks, our mission is to
provide delicious and nutritious low-fat recipes.
Our recipes also meet the standards of the
Rodale Test Kitchen for dependability, ease,
practicality and, most of all, great taste. To give us
your comments, call 1-800-848-4735.*

CONTENTS

OUR NUTRIENT GUIDELINES

Every recipe in *Healthy Favorites from America's Community Cookbooks* includes a nutrient analysis to help you plan a healthful diet. We followed these guidelines when analyzing recipes.

• We used the first ingredient listed when an option is given.

• If a quantity range is given (such as two to three tablespoons), we used the first (smaller) amount.

• Ingredients described as optional or designated by "if desired" are omitted from the analysis.

• Ingredients not specifically listed in the recipe are not included, such as salt that the cook might add to the water when preparing pasta or rice.

• Figures given are for cooked meat, poultry and fish, with visible fat and skin removed when specified in the recipe.

• If a range of servings is given, the analysis is for the first number (for example, four servings in a recipe that makes four to six servings).

INTRODUCTION

·················

Sharing and caring. These two words sum up the timeless appeal of America's community cookbooks.

Published recipe collections have long been a fund-raising boon to churches and charities alike, chock-full of the homey dishes people really love to make.

At *Prevention* Magazine Health Books, we care, too—about Americans' well-being. That's why we're sharing our healthful adaptations of more than 200 of the best recipes from dozens of community cookbooks nationwide.

Who doesn't love a makeover?

Just as the fairy godmother made some cosmetic enhancements without changing Cinderella's personality, we executed a nutritional makeover of these appetizing American classics without sacrificing their flavor. Dressed in the most current nutritional standards, these recipes can proudly step out to the Good Health Ball.

Some of the dishes—like Layered Mexican Dip from *Treasures of the Smokies* and Pork Chop Dinner from *Emory Seasons*—are perfect for casual gatherings or family meals.

Others are a bit more sophisticated, yet surprisingly easy to make. Cioppino from *Only in California*, Orange Duck with Wild-Rice Dressing from *Florida Flavors* and Black-Bean and Corn Salad from *Virginia Fare* prove that fine dining and healthful eating can, indeed, share the table.

If you're like many home cooks who crave these nutritional makeovers but lack the time and expertise to execute them, you'll find that we've done the difficult part for you.

When necessary, we trimmed excess fat, calories and sodium from these dishes using many of the wonderful reduced-fat, fat-free and low-sodium products now available in supermarkets.

Sometimes we altered cooking methods. We baked Chinese egg rolls instead of deep-frying them, for instance, to significantly reduce the fat content.

Creative ingredient substitutions—including the use of applesauce and pureed prunes to replace fat in some baked goods and desserts—yield dramatic fat and calorie savings while simultaneously boosting nutrients and fiber.

We scaled down some recipes to yield four to six servings for today's smaller families. We also adjusted the portion sizes to adhere to health experts' guidelines. That means, for instance, serving two to three ounces of cooked protein in a main dish supplemented by complex carbohydrates rich in fiber and vitamins.

Adding value to many of the recipes are our Rodale Test Kitchen tips: user-friendly information nuggets covering advance preparation, storage, serving suggestions and much more. Each recipe is, of course, accompanied by a nutritional analysis.

"Our Cause" boxes share the stories of the nonprofit organizations behind the recipes and are peppered throughout the book. These dedicated groups—such as the Children's Home Society of California, the Omaha section of the National Council of Jewish Women and The Emory University Woman's Club in Atlanta—give so much to their communities that Rodale is giving back, too. A portion of proceeds from *Healthy Favorites from America's Community Cookbooks* will benefit the Children's Miracle Network, which has raised millions of dollars for pediatric hospitals nationwide. You can read more about its inspiring work starting on page 2.

And for all you die-hard fans of community cookbooks, the address directory of participating books beginning on page 285 is a terrific mail-order resource.

The low-fat icing on the cake is our "Sweets and Treats" chapter, the largest in the book. Think of it as an old-fashioned bake sale in print: Elegant Lemon Roll, Chocolate Puffs, Spiced Zucchini Cake, Chocolate-Nut Fingers, Sweet-Potato Pie, Anise Biscotti, Old-Fashioned Strawberry Shortcake, Fresh Peach Ice Cream, Mother's Angel Pie and more—all lightened for your pleasure and health.

The regional flavor of America's best-loved recipes shines in 19 festive menus for holidays and parties. A Gulf-Coast New Year's Day Dinner, Oregon Grilled-Salmon Supper, Chili Bowl for Super Bowl and 16 other menus are entertaining reading indeed.

We'd like to extend a heartfelt thank you to Glen Wimmer and The Wimmer Companies for their participation in this project. As the largest distributor of high-quality community cookbooks in the country, Wimmer supplied us with a cross section of nearly 100 community cookbooks for our unique collection.

Healthy Favorites from America's Community Cookbooks is truly a celebration of good health and good food.

Our Cause

Children's Miracle Network

CHILDREN'S MIRACLE NETWORK

....

A Shining Star of Hope

All of childhood is a miracle. Remember the silent splendor of winter's first snowfall? The breathtaking sparkle of Fourth of July fireworks? A rainbow magically painted across the sky after a scary storm? Everywhere a child turns, it seems, another wonder unfolds.

In children's hospitals throughout the country, miracles are unfolding every day. Children who, just a few years ago, would have had little chance of surviving illness or accidents now live to celebrate birthday after birthday, thanks to the enormous strides in pediatric medicine.

Yet, it can cost a lot of money to save a child's life. Every year legions of children arrive in hospitals, their lives at stake, with no hope of paying for the care they will certainly receive. But now there is a godsend called Children's Miracle Network.

Children's Miracle Network (CMN) started in 1983 when singer Marie Osmond and television star John Schneider hosted a modest television fund-raiser. They broadcast from a small studio in Provo, Utah, to only a handful of television stations. Though small in scale, that first effort raised almost $5 million for 22 hospitals serving children.

Flash forward 13 years. By 1996 CMN raised more than $915 million, which it donated directly to 160 associated hospitals in the United States and Canada. These pediatric facilities are the best in their communities and among the finest in the world. Every year, these hospitals provide care for seven million children—children with cancer, heart disease, birth defects, AIDS and injuries from catastrophic accidents. Their stories are horrifying and, thankfully, often heartwarming.

On a spring morning in 1991, preschooler Brianna Hunter of Louisville, Ohio, woke with a stomachache. Within hours her temperature soared to 104°, and she began to slip into a coma. Doctors at Children's Hospital Medical Center of Akron diagnosed her condition as retractile sclerosing mesenteritis, an extremely rare illness. A hole in her intestine was causing rampant infection, sending her quickly into septic shock . . . and toward death.

For a month Brianna lay in a coma while doctors operated four times to cleanse her infection and to remove blood clots that complicated her condition. At one point doctors gave her a 10 percent chance of survival. That she lived is truly a miracle. Today, she's a healthy eight-year-old—full of life and mischief.

In 1994 Ben Lunsford entered The Children's Hospital at the Medical Center of Central Georgia, where doctors removed a brain tumor discovered by the boy's pediatrician during a routine visit for an ear infection. The first-grader survived the eight-hour operation and today is an active youngster with no trace of the illness that could have stolen his future.

Also in 1994, doctors at Rainbow Babies and Children's Hospital in Cleveland delved deep into research on chronic asthma, trying to determine why the often life-threatening affliction affects urban African-American and Hispanic children more frequently and more seriously than other children. The results of their research enabled 12-year-old Emeri Scott to manage his severe chronic asthma.

In the same year at the Children's Hospital of Geisinger Medical Center in Danville, Pennsylvania, toddler Brynne Harris was rushed into the emergency room with severe cuts from her forehead to her chin caused when she fell into an exhaust fan. Except for some scarring, the tot will grow up with a normal face thanks to the surgeons' meticulous work.

These are the miracles. But there are many more miracles waiting to happen. CMN estimates that seven million children go without adequate health care each year because their families lack the money or the insurance necessary to cover health-care costs.

CMN is working hard to change that, with support from individuals and corporations across North America. Marriott International, for example, encourages employees at all levels to get involved in fund-raising golf tournaments, bake sales, casino nights and celebrity-waiter dinners. Last year, Long John Silver's, the country's largest fast-food seafood restaurant, donated a quarter-million dollars to CMN from sales of holiday crystal votive candleholders. And Wal-Mart Stores, the charity's biggest single benefactor, has raised $47 million for the organization since 1988.

Still, the annual television program is CMN's largest fund-raising effort. The show has expanded to a 21-hour program broadcast live from Walt Disney World in Orlando, Florida, on 200 television stations in the United States and Canada. Hosts Marie Osmond and John Schneider are joined by a cast of big-hearted stars, including

Merlin Olsen, Mary Hart, Mary Lou Retton and Martin Short, for a weekend of laughter and tears, entertainment and information.

Each year, the reigning Miss America acts as Goodwill Ambassador for the Children's Miracle Network. During her tenure, Miss America 1995, Heather Whitestone, talked about the personal formula she used to overcome her own challenges to become the first hearing-impaired Miss America. She called her strategy STARS because of its five points: positive attitude, belief in your dreams, facing your obstacles, working hard and building a support team. Those qualities also define the Children's Miracle Network and explain how it truly does work miracles in the lives of children.

For further information, contact the Children's Miracle Network, 4525 South 2300 East, Suite 202, Salt Lake City, Utah 84117.

ALL-TIME
GREAT APPETIZERS

ZESTY CRAB-AND-ARTICHOKE DIP

Adapted from *Feast of Eden*
JUNIOR LEAGUE OF MONTEREY COUNTY

This robust dip can be prepared ahead of time to cut down on last-minute fuss at party time. Assemble the ingredients and spoon them into the baking dish. Cover the dish and refrigerate for up to 4 hours. To serve, bake the dip for 40 to 45 minutes.

1 large green pepper, chopped
2 cans (14 ounces each) artichoke hearts, drained and finely chopped
1 cup fat-free mayonnaise
1 cup fat-free plain yogurt
⅔ cup grated Parmesan cheese
½ cup thinly sliced scallions
½ cup bottled roasted sweet red peppers, drained and chopped
5 teaspoons lemon juice
4 teaspoons Worcestershire sauce
1 tablespoon seeded and finely chopped pickled jalapeño peppers (wear plastic gloves when handling)
¼ teaspoon celery seeds
1 pound lump crabmeat, picked over and flaked
¼ cup sliced almonds (optional)

Coat a small skillet with no-stick spray. Add the green peppers. Cook and stir over medium heat for 3 minutes, or until tender; let cool to room temperature.

Preheat the oven to 375°. Coat an 8″ × 8″ baking pan with no-stick spray.

In a large bowl, combine the cooked peppers, artichoke hearts, mayonnaise, yogurt, Parmesan, scallions, red peppers, lemon juice, Worcestershire sauce, jalapeño peppers and celery seeds. Gently stir in the crabmeat. Spoon into the prepared baking pan. Sprinkle with the almonds (if using).

Bake for 30 to 35 minutes, or until golden and bubbly.

TEST KITCHEN TIP: If you don't have fresh crab, substitute 2 cans (6 ounces each) crabmeat, drained and flaked, or 12 ounces surimi (imitation crabmeat), chopped.

If halving the recipe, bake it in an 8″ round cake pan for about 25 minutes.

Makes about 5½ cups; 22 servings.

★ PER ¼ CUP: 65 CALORIES, 1.4 G. TOTAL FAT, 0.6 G. SATURATED FAT, 14 MG. CHOLESTEROL, 473 MG. SODIUM

....

PARMESAN PITA CHIPS

Adapted from *River Feast*
JUNIOR LEAGUE OF CINCINNATI

To make these crispy chips more healthful, we replaced butter with butter-flavored no-stick spray and cut the amount of Parmesan cheese in half. These wedges are great with dips, soups or salads.

> 6 pita breads (6″ diameter)
> ¾ cup grated Parmesan cheese

Preheat the oven to 350°. Cut the pita rounds in half crosswise, then split in half. Coat the pieces with butter-flavored no-stick spray; sprinkle with the Parmesan and cut each piece into 4 wedges. Place the wedges in a single layer on a baking sheet. Bake for 12 to 15 minutes, or until crisp and starting to brown.

TEST KITCHEN TIP: For variety, add ¼ teaspoon dried basil or Italian seasoning to the Parmesan.

Makes 96 chips; 16 servings.

★ PER 6 CHIPS: 61 CALORIES, 1.6 G. TOTAL FAT, 0.9 G. SATURATED FAT, 4 MG. CHOLESTEROL, 168 MG. SODIUM

Broccoli and Carrot Crudités

Adapted from *The Best of the South*
NEWTON GENERAL HOSPITAL AUXILIARY

Convenient advance preparation, plus appealing Mediterranean seasonings, makes these crisp vegetables a hit with both cooks and their guests.

CARROTS

>   3 tablespoons white-wine vinegar
>   2 tablespoons olive oil
>   1 clove garlic, crushed
>   ¼ teaspoon seasoned salt
>   1 tablespoon minced fresh parsley
>   8 medium carrots, cut into small sticks

BROCCOLI

>   2 tablespoons olive oil
>   1 clove garlic, crushed
>   ¼ cup lemon juice
>   1 large head broccoli, cut into bite-size florets
>   ¼ cup sliced stuffed olives

TO MAKE THE CARROTS: In a small bowl, mix the vinegar, oil, garlic, salt and parsley. Add the carrots; toss to coat with the dressing. Cover and refrigerate overnight.

TO MAKE THE BROCCOLI: In a medium bowl, mix the oil, garlic and lemon juice. Add the broccoli and olives; toss to coat with the dressing. Cover and refrigerate overnight.

To serve, drain the carrots and broccoli. Discard the dressing.

TEST KITCHEN TIPS: You may substitute mini carrots for regular ones. Use about ½ pound. Leave whole or slice lengthwise as desired.

For an attractive presentation, arrange the broccoli-olive mixture in the center of a serving platter and surround it with the carrots.

Makes 12 servings.

★ PER SERVING: 33 CALORIES, 0.6 G. TOTAL FAT, 0 G. SATURATED FAT, 0 MG. CHOLESTEROL, 49 MG. SODIUM

CREAMY FRESH DILL DIP

Adapted from *Emory Seasons*
EMORY UNIVERSITY WOMAN'S CLUB

Serve this dip with a platter of assorted raw vegetables. If fresh dill is unavailable, use 2 teaspoons dried dill and freshen its flavor with an additional 3 tablespoons fresh chopped parsley.

> 1 cup 1% low-fat cottage cheese
> ¼ cup fat-free plain yogurt
> 3 tablespoons chopped fresh dill
> 2 tablespoons chopped fresh parsley
> ⅛ teaspoon ground black pepper

In a blender or food processor, blend the cottage cheese, yogurt, dill, parsley and pepper until smooth. Cover and refrigerate for at least 1 hour to blend the flavors.

TEST KITCHEN TIP: If you're using a food processor, you can chop the fresh dill and parsley in it before adding the remaining ingredients. Just tear the dill and parsley into small pieces and lightly pack into a tablespoon to measure. Place 3 tablespoons dill and 2 tablespoons parsley into the processor and process with on/off turns until chopped.

Makes about 1 cup; 8 servings.

★ PER 2 TABLESPOONS: 26 CALORIES, 0.3 G. TOTAL FAT, 0.2 G. SATURATED FAT, 1 MG. CHOLESTEROL, 121 MG. SODIUM

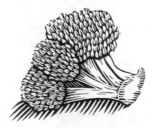

LAYERED MEXICAN DIP

Adapted from *Treasures of the Smokies*
JUNIOR LEAGUE OF JOHNSON CITY

We made this zesty hot dip with ground turkey breast rather than regular ground turkey to guarantee the lowest fat content. Some products labeled "ground turkey" include both skin and dark meat, which make them higher in fat than you'd suspect.

8 ounces ground turkey breast
1 large onion, chopped
2 cans (16 ounces each) fat-free refried beans
1 can (4 ounces) diced green chili peppers, drained
2 cups shredded fat-free mozzarella cheese
1 cup shredded fat-free Cheddar cheese
1 can (10 ounces) diced tomatoes and green chili peppers
1 cup fat-free sour cream

Preheat the oven to 400°. Coat a 13″ × 9″ baking pan with no-stick spray. Set aside.

Coat a medium skillet with no-stick spray. Add the turkey and onions. Cook over medium heat, stirring occasionally, for 5 minutes, or until the turkey is no longer pink. Stir in the refried beans. Spread evenly in the prepared baking pan.

Top with the peppers. Sprinkle with 1 cup of the mozzarella and ½ cup of the Cheddar. Cover with the tomato-pepper mixture.

Bake for 20 minutes. Sprinkle with the remaining 1 cup mozzarella and the remaining ½ cup Cheddar. Bake for 5 minutes, or until heated through.

Cool slightly; spoon the sour cream on top.

TEST KITCHEN TIP: If you're keeping a close watch on your sodium intake, you can eliminate about 135 milligrams per serving by using only 1 cup mozzarella and by replacing the canned chili peppers with ¼ cup chopped fresh jalapeño or serrano peppers and by replacing the canned mixed tomatoes and peppers with 1 cup chopped fresh ripe tomatoes.

Makes about 3 cups; 24 servings.

★ PER 2 TABLESPOONS: 117 CALORIES, 0.2 G. TOTAL FAT,
0.1 G. SATURATED FAT, 6 MG. CHOLESTEROL, 554 MG. SODIUM

WHITE-BEAN AND GARLIC DIP

Adapted from *From Generation to Generation*
SISTERHOOD OF TEMPLE EMANU-EL

Vegetable dippers such as baby carrots, broccoli florets, celery sticks and cherry tomatoes taste fresh and fine with this smooth, lemony dip.

> 2 large cloves garlic
> 1 cup canned cannellini beans (white kidney beans), rinsed and drained
> 2 teaspoons lemon juice
> 1/8 teaspoon hot-pepper sauce
>   Pinch of salt

Place the garlic in a small saucepan and cover with water; bring to a boil. Reduce the heat to medium. Simmer, uncovered, for 5 minutes. Drain and peel the garlic.

In a blender or food processor, blend the garlic, beans, lemon juice, hot-pepper sauce and salt until smooth. (If necessary, stop and scrape down the sides of the container.)

Makes ³⁄₄ cup; 6 servings.

★ PER 2 TABLESPOONS: 29 CALORIES, 0.3 G. TOTAL FAT, 0 G. SATURATED FAT, 0 MG. CHOLESTEROL, 75 MG. SODIUM

Texas Caviar

Adapted from *M. D. Anderson Volunteers Cooking for Fun*
M. D. ANDERSON CANCER CENTER VOLUNTEERS

The black-eyed peas in this versatile vegetable appetizer are low in fat and high in fiber. Set out baked tortilla chips for guests to dip into this colorful combo.

> 2 cans (15 ounces each) black-eyed peas, rinsed and drained
> 2 tomatoes, chopped
> 1 green pepper, chopped
> 1 cup mild picante sauce
> ½ cup chopped onions
> 4 scallions, chopped
> ⅓ cup chopped fresh cilantro or parsley
> 1 clove garlic, minced

In a large bowl, stir together the black-eyed peas, tomatoes, peppers, picante sauce, onions, scallions, cilantro or parsley and garlic. Cover and refrigerate for at least 4 hours to blend the flavors.

Makes 6½ cups; 26 servings.

★ PER ¼ CUP: 32 CALORIES, 0.4 G. TOTAL FAT, 0 G. SATURATED FAT, 0 MG. CHOLESTEROL, 166 MG. SODIUM

SALMON PARTY LOG

Adapted from *RSVP*
JUNIOR LEAGUE OF PORTLAND

*This is a slimmed-down version of a traditional cheese log.
The addition of canned salmon keeps the fat profile lean while
boosting the calcium content. Serve this spread on fat-free wheat
crackers or party-size bread slices.*

> 1 can (14¾ ounces) salmon
> 1 package (8 ounces) light cream cheese, softened
> 2 teaspoons minced onions
> 1 teaspoon prepared horseradish
> 1 teaspoon liquid smoke (optional)
> ⅔ cup finely chopped fresh parsley
> 3 tablespoons chopped walnuts or pecans

Drain the salmon and remove any skin. Place in a medium bowl
and flake with a fork. Use the back of a large spoon to crush any
bones.

Add the cream cheese, onions, horseradish and liquid smoke (if
using); stir to combine. Cover and refrigerate for at least 4 hours to
blend the flavors.

Combine the parsley and walnuts or pecans on a piece of wax
paper. Shape the salmon mixture into an 8"-long log; roll in the pars-
ley-nut mixture. Cover and refrigerate for at least 2 hours before
serving.

Makes 2¾ cups; 22 servings.

★ PER 2 TABLESPOONS: 56 CALORIES, 3.6 G. TOTAL FAT, 1.4 G. SATURATED
FAT, 14 MG. CHOLESTEROL, 168 MG. SODIUM

....

STUFFED CHERRY TOMATOES

Adapted from *Augusta Cooks for Company*
AUGUSTA COUNCIL

A dramatic triple play of savory stuffings makes these tiny toma-
toes a winner for a festive gathering. If you're serving only a few
guests, you can select just one filling to stuff 20 cherry tomatoes.

TOMATOES
    60 large cherry tomatoes

CHICKEN FILLING
    4 ounces cooked chicken breast, ground
    ¼ cup fat-free sour cream
    2 ounces light cream cheese, softened
    2 teaspoons grated Parmesan cheese
    ¼ teaspoon dry mustard
    ⅛ teaspoon ground black pepper
    Finely chopped fresh parsley or paprika

BACON FILLING
    ⅔ cup fat-free mayonnaise
    ¼ cup canned cooked bacon pieces
    6 scallions, finely chopped

CRAB FILLING
    ⅓ cup flaked lump crabmeat, picked over
    3 ounces light cream cheese, softened
    ¼ cup fat-free mayonnaise
    1 tablespoon finely chopped scallions
    ½ teaspoon Worcestershire sauce
    2 drops hot-pepper sauce

TO MAKE THE TOMATOES: Cut a thin slice from the top of each
tomato; carefully scoop out tomato pulp; if desired, reserve pulp for
another use. Invert the shells on paper towels to drain.

TO MAKE THE CHICKEN FILLING: In a small bowl, use an electric
mixer to beat together the chicken, sour cream, cream cheese,
Parmesan, mustard and pepper. Spoon a scant tablespoon of the
mixture into each of 20 tomato shells. Sprinkle with parsley or paprika.

OUR CAUSE

Augusta Council

What do Tom Cruise, Thomas Edison, Whoopi Goldberg and Bruce Jenner have in common? Talent, achievement, fame— and learning disabilities.

Learning disabilities are a "hidden handicap" that can masquerade as lack of intelligence, laziness, even willful misbehavior. Fortunately, organizations such as the Augusta Council of the Georgia Association for Children and Adults with Learning Disabilities help us all to learn that a learning-disabled student is a child with a problem, not a problem child.

Thanks to the organization's work, the special needs of these children can be recognized and overcome. With enlightened help, learning-disabled children can become the well-adjusted, happy, productive citizens they deserve to be.

Proceeds from *Augusta Cooks for Company*, a collection of recipes from the friends and families of learning-disabled youngsters, benefit a scholarship fund to send these special students to colleges and vocational schools.

TO MAKE THE BACON FILLING: In a small bowl, stir together the mayonnaise, bacon and scallions. Spoon about 2 teaspoons of the mixture into each of 20 tomato shells.

TO MAKE THE CRAB FILLING: In a small bowl, stir together the crabmeat, cream cheese, mayonnaise, scallions, Worcestershire sauce and hot-pepper sauce. Spoon a scant tablespoon of the mixture into each of the remaining 20 tomato shells.

Makes 60 tomatoes; 20 servings.

★ PER 3 TOMATOES (1 OF EACH): 53 CALORIES, 2.3 G. TOTAL FAT, 0.9 G. SATURATED FAT, 9 MG. CHOLESTEROL, 256 MG. SODIUM

SKEWERED PASTA AND VEGETABLES

Adapted from Treasures of the Smokies
JUNIOR LEAGUE OF JOHNSON CITY

You can make these innovative appetizer kabobs party pretty by alternating different colored tortellini.

1	teaspoon cornstarch
1	teaspoon sugar
1	teaspoon dried basil
1	teaspoon dried oregano
½	teaspoon dry mustard
¼	teaspoon garlic powder
¼	teaspoon onion powder
	Pinch of salt
⅔	cup water
½	cup cider vinegar
36	plain or colored cheese-filled tortellini, uncooked
1	small green pepper, cut into 24 pieces
12	small whole mushrooms
6	small cherry tomatoes, cut in half

In a small saucepan, stir together the cornstarch, sugar, basil, oregano, mustard, garlic powder, onion powder and salt. Use a wire whisk to gradually stir in the water and vinegar. Cook over medium heat, whisking constantly, until the mixture comes to a boil. Reduce the heat. Cook for 1 minute. Remove from the heat and cool to room temperature.

Meanwhile, cook the tortellini according to the package directions, but without adding salt or fat. Drain and set aside.

Alternate the tortellini, peppers and mushrooms on 12 wooden skewers. Place a cherry tomato half on the end of each skewer. Place the skewers in a 15" × 10" jelly-roll pan; pour the marinade over the kabobs. Cover and refrigerate for 4 hours to allow the vegetables to absorb the marinade; rearrange the skewers after 2 hours. Drain before serving.

Makes 12 servings.

★ PER SERVING: 89 CALORIES, 1.9 G. TOTAL FAT, 0.9 G. SATURATED FAT, 14 MG. CHOLESTEROL, 130 MG. SODIUM

SHRIMP PINWHEELS

Adapted from *Virginia Fare*
JUNIOR LEAGUE OF RICHMOND

Armenian crackerbread rounds can be found in some supermarkets and in specialty food stores. Crisp when purchased, they can be softened to make a moist, pliable flatbread that can be stuffed and rolled in a spiral.

1 Armenian crackerbread (15″ round)
1 package (3 ounces) Neufchâtel cheese with chives, softened
½ teaspoon dried dill
½ teaspoon prepared horseradish
1 package (6 ounces) frozen peeled and cooked shrimp, thawed
1 jar (2 ounces) sliced pimentos, drained
Large romaine leaves, ribs removed

Moisten the crackerbread on both sides by holding it briefly under cold running water; place between damp towels. Cover with plastic wrap to prevent drying out. Let stand about 1 hour, or until softened.

Beat the Neufchâtel, dill and horseradish together in a small bowl. Drain the shrimp and chop finely; stir into the bowl.

Spread the cheese mixture on the crackerbread almost to the edges. Sprinkle with the pimentos.

Arrange romaine leaves evenly over the cheese mixture. Roll up tightly jelly-roll fashion. Press to seal.

Wrap the roll in plastic wrap and chill for 2 to 24 hours.

To serve, cut the roll into ¾″-thick slices.

Makes 20 servings.

★ PER SERVING: 30 CALORIES, 1.3 G. FAT, 0.7 G. SATURATED FAT, 20 MG. CHOLESTEROL, 66 MG. SODIUM

GREEK SPINACH PIE

Adapted from *Holy Smoke*
PEACHTREE ROAD UNITED METHODIST CHURCH

*Phyllo dough is a low-fat parchmentlike Greek pastry that's used
for appetizers, desserts and main dishes. Look for it near the
desserts in your supermarket's frozen-food case. Classic recipes
brush quite a lot of melted butter on the phyllo to keep the layers
separate and to promote crispness. We've achieved the same
results with butter-flavored no-stick spray.*

> 2 packages (10 ounces each) frozen chopped spinach
> 3 egg whites
> 2 eggs
> 2 cups 1% low-fat cottage cheese
> ¾ cup grated Romano cheese
> ½ cup chopped onions
> 1 tablespoon dried dill
> ⅛ teaspoon salt
> 1 package (16 ounces) frozen phyllo dough, thawed
> 2 tablespoons tub-style reduced-calorie margarine, melted

Cook the spinach according to the package directions; drain well
in a colander, pressing out all liquid.

In a medium bowl, beat together the egg whites and eggs; stir in
the spinach, cottage cheese, Romano, onions, dill and salt. Set the
mixture aside.

Coat a 15″ × 10″ baking pan with butter-flavored no-stick
spray. Place 1 sheet of phyllo dough in the pan. (Cover the remaining
sheets of phyllo with a damp cloth to prevent drying out.) Coat the
sheet of dough in the pan with no-stick spray. Repeat layering and
spraying until half of the sheets are layered in the pan.

Spoon the spinach mixture over the phyllo in the pan. Top with
the remaining sheets of phyllo, coating each sheet with no-stick
spray. Cover and chill up to 24 hours.

Preheat the oven to 375°.

Cut the spinach pie into 48 rectangles before baking. Drizzle
with the margarine. Bake for 35 minutes, or until brown. Cool on a
wire rack for 15 minutes before serving.

TEST KITCHEN TIP: To make Greek Spinach Pie ahead, bake
as directed. Let cool, then wrap squares of the pie in aluminum foil

and freeze them. To serve, bake the frozen squares in the foil at 350° for 30 minutes, or until hot.

Makes 48 servings.

★ PER SERVING: 49 CALORIES, 1.1 G. TOTAL FAT, 0.5 G. SATURATED FAT, 11 MG. CHOLESTEROL, 87 MG. SODIUM

SPINACH BALLS

Adapted from *M. D. Anderson Volunteers Cooking for Fun*
M. D. ANDERSON CANCER CENTER VOLUNTEERS

These moist morsels of savory stuffing make a delightful alternative to plain bread on an appetizer buffet.

1 package (10 ounces) frozen chopped spinach
1 cup reduced-sodium herb-seasoned stuffing mix
1 small onion, finely chopped
4 egg whites, lightly beaten
1 egg, lightly beaten
1 tablespoon tub-style reduced-calorie margarine, melted
⅓ cup grated Parmesan cheese
½ teaspoon dried thyme
¼ teaspoon garlic powder
¼ teaspoon ground black pepper

Preheat the oven to 325°. Coat a large baking sheet with no-stick spray.

Cook the spinach according to the package directions; drain well in a colander, pressing out all liquid. Place in a medium bowl. Stir in the stuffing mix, onions, egg whites, egg, margarine, Parmesan, thyme, garlic powder and pepper. Let stand for 5 minutes. Shape into 1½″ balls and place on the prepared baking sheet. Bake for 18 to 20 minutes, or until starting to brown.

TEST KITCHEN TIP: The spinach-bread mixture can be covered and chilled in the refrigerator for several hours before shaping.

Makes 20 balls; 10 servings.

★ PER 2 SPINACH BALLS: 57 CALORIES, 2.3 G. TOTAL FAT, 0.9 G. SATURATED FAT, 24 MG. CHOLESTEROL, 168 MG. SODIUM

EGG ROLLS

Adapted from *Cooks Extraordinaires*
SERVICE LEAGUE OF GREEN BAY

Baking these crispy appetizers makes them leaner—and much less messy to prepare—than traditional deep-fried egg rolls. Serve them with hot mustard and sweet-and-sour sauce.

> 8 ounces ground pork loin
> 1 tablespoon reduced-sodium soy sauce
> 1 teaspoon cornstarch
> 1 teaspoon dry sherry or water
> 8 ounces bean sprouts
> 2 cups finely shredded cabbage
> 1 carrot, shredded
> ½ cup finely chopped scallions
> ½ cup finely chopped celery
> 2 tablespoons all-purpose flour
> 16 egg roll wrappers

Coat a large skillet with no-stick spray; add the pork, soy sauce, cornstarch and sherry or water. Cook over medium heat, stirring, until the pork is broken up and no longer pink. Transfer to a large bowl.

Using the same skillet, cook the bean sprouts, cabbage, carrots, scallions and celery over medium heat until just tender. Drain and add to the pork mixture. Stir in the flour until well-mixed.

Preheat the oven to 375°. Coat a baking sheet with no-stick spray.

Spoon about ¼ cup of the pork mixture diagonally across the center of an egg roll wrapper. Fold one point of the wrapper over the filling and tuck the point under the filling. Fold in the sides of the wrapper; roll up the egg roll. When the roll reaches the remaining point, dampen the point of the wrapper with water and press firmly to seal. Place on the baking sheet.

Repeat with the remaining wrappers and filling. Coat the egg rolls generously with no-stick spray.

Bake for 8 minutes; turn the egg rolls and bake for 4 to 5 minutes, or until light brown and crisp.

TEST KITCHEN TIP: Freeze the baked egg rolls for spur-of-the-moment entertaining. To reheat, wrap the frozen rolls in foil and bake at 350° for 25 to 30 minutes.

Makes 16.

★ PER EGG ROLL: 55 CALORIES, 1 G. TOTAL FAT, 0.3 G. SATURATED FAT, 6 MG. CHOLESTEROL, 65 MG. SODIUM

....

ARTICHOKE SQUARES

Adapted from *Emory Seasons*
EMORY UNIVERSITY WOMAN'S CLUB

For a colorful variation of this savory baked custard, add ¼ cup reconstituted sun-dried tomatoes, cut into strips.

    1 small onion, chopped
    1 clove garlic, minced
    1 cup evaporated skim milk
    4 egg whites, lightly beaten
    2 eggs, lightly beaten
    ½ teaspoon dried oregano
    ⅛ teaspoon hot-pepper sauce
    ⅛ teaspoon ground black pepper
    2 jars (6 ounces each) marinated artichoke hearts, drained
       and finely chopped
    2 tablespoons chopped fresh parsley

Preheat the oven to 325°. Coat a small skillet with no-stick spray. Add the onions and garlic. Cook, stirring, over medium heat for 3 minutes, or until tender.

In a medium bowl, stir together the milk, egg whites, eggs, oregano, hot-pepper sauce and pepper. Stir in the artichokes, onions and parsley. Spoon into an 8″ × 8″ baking pan. Bake for 30 minutes, or until a knife inserted in the center comes out clean. Cut into squares and serve warm.

Makes 16 servings.

★ PER SERVING: 39 CALORIES, 0.7 G. TOTAL FAT, 0.2 G. SATURATED FAT, 27 MG. CHOLESTEROL, 61 MG. SODIUM

APPETIZER POTATO PANCAKES

Adapted from *The Kitchen Connection*
NATIONAL COUNCIL OF JEWISH WOMEN, OMAHA SECTION

Top these earthy delights with a teaspoonful of fat-free sour cream spiked with prepared horseradish, grainy mustard or salsa. For a brunch variation, try a teaspoon of unsweetened applesauce or strawberry jam.

  2 large baking potatoes
  ¼ cup fat-free egg substitute
  1 tablespoon all-purpose flour
  1 tablespoon finely chopped onions
  ½ teaspoon baking powder
  ⅛ teaspoon salt
     Pinch of ground black pepper
  2 tablespoons oil

Scrub the potatoes and shred by hand or in a food processor. In a medium bowl, stir together the potatoes, egg substitute, flour, onions, baking powder, salt and pepper.

Coat a large no-stick skillet with no-stick spray. Pour 1 tablespoon of the oil into the skillet and place over medium heat. Carefully drop half of the potato mixture by tablespoons into the skillet. Fry on both sides until golden brown. Remove and drain on paper towels.

Repeat with the remaining 1 tablespoon oil and the remaining potato mixture.

TEST KITCHEN TIP: To make ahead, fry the pancakes and freeze them separated by pieces of aluminum foil. To serve, preheat the oven to 350°. Wrap a single layer of pancakes in foil. Bake for 20 minutes, or until crisp.

Makes 20 pancakes; 10 servings.

★ PER 2 PANCAKES: 59 CALORIES, 2.8 G. TOTAL FAT, 0.4 G. SATURATED FAT, 0 MG. CHOLESTEROL, 60 MG. SODIUM

National Council of Jewish Women, Omaha Section

When Hannah G. Solomon founded the National Council of Jewish Women in 1893, she never could have imagined that a century later 100,000 members nationwide would celebrate the anniversary of the oldest Jewish women's volunteer organization in the United States. The women of Omaha, Nebraska, wasted no time in signing on with Solomon. The Omaha Section of the council formed just three years later and will celebrate its own centennial in 1996.

The 800 women of the Omaha Section dedicate themselves to a broad array of programs that focus primarily on women, children and families. Among their special projects is the annual Child-Care Fair, a free community-wide event that gives parents the opportunity to shop for day-care options.

Education is important to the National Council of Jewish Women, and the Omaha Section has distributed some $30,000 in the form of mini-grants to public-school teachers for special classroom projects. The group also sends educational materials to underprivileged children in Israel. The recipes in *The Kitchen Connection*, the group's fourth cookbook, were handed down from the mothers and grandmothers of council members.

POTATO SKINS

Adapted from *Cooking with Class*
PARENTS' COUNCIL OF CHARLOTTE LATIN SCHOOL

*You can bake the potatoes up to one day ahead, then scoop out
and prepare the skins just before guests arrive.*

2 large baking potatoes
¼ teaspoon onion salt or garlic salt
¼ teaspoon ground black pepper
⅓ cup shredded reduced-fat Cheddar cheese
¼ cup reduced-fat sour cream

Preheat the oven to 400°. Wash and scrub the potatoes, then pat dry. Prick with a fork. Bake on a baking sheet for 60 to 70 minutes, or until tender.

Let the potatoes stand at room temperature until cool enough to handle. Halve each potato lengthwise, then use a spoon to scoop out the flesh, leaving a shell about ⅛″ thick. Reserve the flesh for another use. (If you leave too much potato, the skins will not be crisp.)

Cut the potato skins into 3″ × 1″ strips.

Coat each strip completely with butter-flavored no-stick spray, then sprinkle lightly with the onion salt or garlic salt and pepper. Sprinkle evenly with the Cheddar.

Place the strips on a large baking sheet. Bake for 15 minutes, or until crisp. Serve with the sour cream.

Makes 4 servings.

★ PER SERVING: 100 CALORIES, 2.1 G. TOTAL FAT, 1.3 G. SATURATED FAT, 4 MG. CHOLESTEROL, 258 MG. SODIUM

Chicken Rumaki

Adapted from *Coastal Cuisine, Texas Style*
JUNIOR SERVICE LEAGUE OF BRAZOSPORT

Classic rumaki is made with chicken livers, but this sleek variation calls for chicken breast instead. To complete the health-ful change, we substituted lean turkey bacon for regular bacon.

  2 boneless, skinless chicken breast halves (8 ounces total)
16 water chestnut slices
¼ cup orange juice or pineapple juice
¼ cup reduced-sodium soy sauce
  2 tablespoons reduced-calorie, reduced-sodium ketchup
  1 tablespoon vinegar
  2 cloves garlic, minced
¼ teaspoon ground black pepper
  4 slices lean turkey bacon
    Brown sugar

Preheat the broiler. Coat the rack of a broiling pan with no-stick spray. Place the chicken on the rack. Broil 4″ from the heat for 5 minutes. Turn the chicken over and broil for 4 to 6 minutes more, or until cooked through. Let stand at room temperature for 15 minutes.

Cut each breast into 6 bite-size cubes. Place in a medium bowl; add the water chestnuts.

In a small bowl, stir together the orange juice or pineapple juice, soy sauce, ketchup, vinegar, garlic and pepper. Pour over the chicken. Cover and marinate in the refrigerator for 4 to 8 hours.

Preheat the broiler. Coat the rack of a broiling pan with no-stick spray. Cut the bacon slices in half lengthwise; cut again to make a total of 16 long strips.

Drain the chicken and water chestnuts. For each appetizer, hold a piece of chicken and a water chestnut in one hand and wrap a piece of bacon around them; secure with a toothpick. Place the brown sugar in a shallow dish. Roll the appetizers in the brown sugar until lightly coated. Place on the broiling rack.

Broil 4″ from the heat for 4 minutes. Turn the appetizers and broil for 4 minutes, or until the bacon is starting to brown.

Makes 16 servings.

★ PER SERVING: 23 CALORIES, 0.9 G. TOTAL FAT, 0.2 G. SATURATED FAT, 8 MG. CHOLESTEROL, 54 MG. SODIUM

ORIENTAL CHICKEN WONTONS

Adapted from *West of the Rockies*
JUNIOR SERVICE LEAGUE OF GRAND JUNCTION

Baking wontons trims fat significantly and eliminates the mess and lingering odor of deep-frying. To serve, dip these zesty tidbits into plum sauce or sweet-and-sour sauce. For variety, replace the chicken with ground pork loin.

8	ounces ground chicken breast
½	cup shredded carrots
¼	cup finely chopped water chestnuts or celery
1	tablespoon reduced-sodium soy sauce
1	tablespoon dry sherry or water
2	teaspoons cornstarch
1½–2	teaspoons grated fresh ginger
30	wonton wrappers

Coat a medium skillet with no-stick spray; add the chicken and cook over medium heat, stirring occasionally, for 5 minutes, or until the chicken is broken up and no longer pink. Transfer to a plate lined with paper towels. Blot the top with additional paper towels.

Transfer the chicken to a medium bowl. Stir in the carrots, water chestnuts or celery, soy sauce, sherry or water, cornstarch and ginger until well-mixed.

Preheat the oven to 375°. Coat a baking sheet with no-stick spray.

Spoon a slightly rounded teaspoon of the chicken mixture onto a wonton wrapper. Lightly brush the edges of the wrapper with water. To shape the wonton, carefully bring two opposite points of the wrapper up over the filling and pinch them together in the center. Carefully bring the two remaining opposite points to the center and pinch together. Pinch the edges together to seal. Place the wonton on the baking sheet.

Repeat with the remaining chicken mixture and the remaining wonton wrappers.

Coat the wontons with no-stick spray. Bake for 8 to 10 minutes, or until light brown and crisp.

Junior Service League of Grand Junction

Dinosaurs once roamed this valley. So did an ancient tribe of agricultural people who remain nameless but still speak to us through petroglyphs painted on canyon walls. The Ute tribe, Spanish colonials and American settlers have all called this home.

Colorado's Grand Valley is truly awe-inspiring. Today, about 100,000 fortunate residents share this region of rugged natural splendor, fertile valley farmland and lush fruit orchards.

The red-rock vertical walls of the Colorado National Monument, Mt. Garfield and the Grand Mesa are but a few of the memorable landmarks in this unforgettable land west of the Rockies.

In 1983 the Junior Service League of Grand Junction formed to enhance life in the valley through support of public radio, the Dinosaur Valley Museum, a school heritage program, hospital rehabilitation and many more worthwhile concerns. Proceeds from their latest effort, *West of the Rockies*, support the Riverfront Project, Young Parents and adult literacy programs.

TEST KITCHEN TIP: If you like, freeze the baked wontons. To serve, take out as many wontons as you need, wrap them in foil and bake at 350° for 15 minutes, or until hot.

Makes 30 wontons; 15 servings.

★ PER 2 WONTONS: 69 CALORIES, 0.3 G. TOTAL FAT, 0.1 G. SATURATED FAT, 6 MG. CHOLESTEROL, 80 MG. SODIUM

Mushroom Caps Stuffed with Crab Imperial

Adapted from *Virginia Fare*
JUNIOR LEAGUE OF RICHMOND

Choose fresh or canned crabmeat for this dish. Frozen crab isn't as good a choice because it can often lose its natural sweetness, becoming tough, watery and less flavorful. If you use canned crab, 2 of the 6-ounce cans will be sufficient.

1 pound lump crabmeat, picked over and flaked
1 jar (2 ounces) sliced pimentos, drained
2 teaspoons dry mustard
1 egg
¼ cup reduced-fat mayonnaise
¼ teaspoon ground black pepper
24 large mushrooms, cleaned and stemmed
   Paprika

Preheat the oven to 350°.

In a medium bowl, mix the crabmeat, pimentos, mustard, egg, mayonnaise and pepper. Spoon the mixture into the mushroom caps. Sprinkle with the paprika.

Place on a baking sheet and bake for 15 minutes, or until the stuffing is hot. Serve hot.

TEST KITCHEN TIP: To clean fresh mushrooms, wipe them with a damp paper towel or quickly rinse them in a colander (don't soak them, or they'll absorb too much water). Another way to clean them is to use a special mushroom brush sold in some specialty cookware stores. The soft bristles are similar to those on an infant's hairbrush.

Makes 24 servings.

★ PER SERVING: 33 CALORIES, 1.3 G. FAT, 0.1 G. SATURATED FAT, 29 MG. CHOLESTEROL, 56 MG. SODIUM

CRISPY SNACK MIX

Adapted from *Delicious Developments*
FRIENDS OF STRONG MEMORIAL HOSPITAL

To make many regular snack mixes, the ingredients are tossed with seasonings and lots of butter or oil. For this sensational snack, egg whites replace the fat to produce a lighter, crispier snack.

2 egg whites, lightly beaten
4½ teaspoons Worcestershire sauce
1 teaspoon garlic powder
2 cups crispy corn- or rice-cereal squares
1½ cups bite-size whole-wheat cereal biscuits
½ cup unsalted peanuts
1 cup reduced-sodium pretzels
1 cup raisins (optional)

Preheat the oven to 300°. Lightly coat a large shallow baking pan with no-stick spray.

In a small bowl, use a fork to beat together the egg whites, Worcestershire sauce and garlic powder.

In a large bowl, combine the corn or rice squares, whole-wheat biscuits and peanuts. Drizzle with the egg-white mixture and stir to coat well. Stir in the pretzels. Spread the mixture in the prepared pan and bake for 40 to 45 minutes, stirring every 15 minutes. Add the raisins (if using) and toss gently; let cool.

Makes about 5 cups; 10 servings.

★ PER ½ CUP: 111 CALORIES, 3.9 G. TOTAL FAT, 0.6 G. SATURATED FAT, 0 MG. CHOLESTEROL, 99 MG. SODIUM

SEASONED OYSTER CRACKERS

Adapted from *Tastes in Plaid*
ALAMANCE COUNTY HISTORICAL MUSEUM

Save this snack for times when the Munchies Monster strikes. Stored in an airtight container, the crackers stay fresh for several weeks.

8 cups oyster crackers
1 envelope reduced-fat buttermilk salad dressing
½ teaspoon dried dill
¼ teaspoon garlic powder
3 tablespoons oil

Place the crackers in a large bowl; coat with butter-flavored nostick spray and stir well. Repeat spraying and stirring twice to evenly coat the crackers.

In a small bowl, stir together the salad dressing, dill and garlic powder. Sprinkle over the oyster crackers. Drizzle with the oil. Toss to evenly coat.

Makes 8 cups; 16 servings.

★ PER ½ CUP: 140 CALORIES, 5.8 G. TOTAL FAT, 0.3 G. SATURATED FAT, 0 MG. CHOLESTEROL, 360 MG. SODIUM

THE BREAD BASKET

ORANGE POPOVERS WITH HONEY BUTTER

Adapted from *Nutbread and Nostalgia*
JUNIOR LEAGUE OF SOUTH BEND

Smooth, creamy honey butter brings out the best in these crispy yet delicate low-fat popovers. Serve them with soup or salad.

ORANGE POPOVERS

    2 egg whites
    1 egg
    1 cup skim milk
    1 cup all-purpose flour
  ⅛ teaspoon salt
1½ teaspoons finely shredded orange rind

HONEY BUTTER

    2 tablespoons honey
    1 tablespoon butter or stick margarine (not reduced-calorie), softened

TO MAKE THE ORANGE POPOVERS: Position one oven rack at the lowest level. Preheat the oven to 450°.

In a small bowl, whisk together the egg whites, egg and milk until smooth.

In a medium bowl, stir together the flour and salt; make a well in the center and pour the egg mixture into it. Add the orange rind. Beat with a wire whisk until well-mixed.

Generously coat five 6-ounce custard cups with no-stick spray. Pour the batter into the cups, filling each cup about two-thirds full.

Place on a baking sheet and bake on the lowest oven rack for 20 minutes. Reduce the heat to 350° and bake for 25 minutes, or until very brown and crusty. Do not open the oven during baking, or the popovers won't rise properly. Remove from the oven and insert a sharp knife in each popover to release steam.

TO MAKE THE HONEY BUTTER: In a small bowl, stir together the honey and butter or margarine. Serve with the hot popovers.

TEST KITCHEN TIPS: Make sure the popovers are very brown and crusty before removing them from the oven or else they will collapse.

OUR CAUSE

Junior League of South Bend

The Junior League of South Bend, Indiana, has printed 49,000 copies of *Nutbread and Nostalgia*, and people are still clamoring for more.

The book, mingling family heirloom recipes with healthy, easy, contemporary fare is a perfect blend of old and new, just like South Bend itself. And more, this popular cookbook has a charming collection of nineteenth-century photos and bits of folk wisdom to remind us of life in a slower, pre-electronic age.

The Junior League members, however, hardly lead quiet lives. This active group is hard at work making a difference for the old and young, homeless and neglected, illiterate and culturally deprived in their community. The group has designated the earnings from this printing of *Nutbread and Nostalgia* to be spent on community projects that help the children of South Bend.

If you have a popover pan, place in the oven until very hot. Remove and coat 5 of the cups with no-stick spray. Add the batter and proceed as above.

Makes 5.

★ PER POPOVER: 222 CALORIES, 6.5 G. TOTAL FAT, 2.9 G. SATURATED FAT, 62 MG. CHOLESTEROL, 166 MG. SODIUM

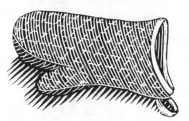

TENDER SCONES

Adapted from *Albuquerque Academy à la Carte*
ALBUQUERQUE ACADEMY PARENTS' ASSOCIATION

Traditional scones are actually a type of biscuit that relies on lots of butter or cream for tenderness. Our version lightens things up with nonfat buttermilk and egg whites.

> 2 cups all-purpose flour
> 2 tablespoons sugar
> 2 teaspoons baking powder
> ½ teaspoon baking soda
> ¼ teaspoon salt
> 3 tablespoons butter or stick margarine (not reduced-calorie), cut into 6 pieces
> ⅔ cup nonfat buttermilk
> 2 egg whites
>   Nonfat buttermilk
>   Sugar

Preheat the oven to 425°. Lightly coat a baking sheet with no-stick spray; set aside.

In a medium bowl, stir together the flour, sugar, baking powder, baking soda and salt. Using a pastry blender, cut in the butter or margarine until crumblike.

In another medium bowl, whisk together the ⅔ cup buttermilk and egg whites. Add to the flour mixture. Stir just until moistened.

Transfer the dough to a lightly floured work surface. Then knead 5 or 6 times. Pat into an 8″ circle. Transfer the dough to the prepared baking sheet. Cut into 8 wedges, but do not separate the wedges.

Brush the wedges with additional buttermilk and sprinkle with additional sugar. Bake for 16 to 17 minutes, or until golden. Serve warm or transfer to a wire rack and cool.

TEST KITCHEN TIP: For variety, stir ⅓ cup currants, raisins, dried cranberries or dried cherries into the flour mixture. If you prefer, you may use a 2″ cutter to cut the dough into rounds. Lightly pat together the scraps to use all the dough.

Makes 8.

★ PER SCONE: 175 CALORIES, 4.6 G. TOTAL FAT, 2.7 G. SATURATED FAT, 11 MG. CHOLESTEROL, 279 MG. SODIUM

Corn Rolls

Adapted from *Florida Flavors*
ENVIRONMENTAL STUDIES COUNCIL

*The only fat in these remarkable rolls comes from the sour cream.
For that reason, you can afford to use regular rather than
reduced-fat or fat-free sour cream. Serve the rolls with your
favorite roast or baked chicken recipe.*

> 1⅓ cups all-purpose flour
> ½ cup yellow cornmeal
> 2 tablespoons baking powder
> 2 tablespoons sugar
> ½ teaspoon salt
> ¾ cup sour cream
> ¼ cup fat-free egg substitute

Preheat the oven to 350°. Lightly coat 2 baking sheets with no-stick spray; set aside.

In a medium bowl, stir together the flour, cornmeal, baking powder, sugar and salt.

In a small bowl, stir together the sour cream and egg substitute. Add to the flour mixture and stir together just until well-mixed.

Transfer the dough to a lightly floured work surface. Roll to ¼″ thickness. Using a 2½″ or 2¾″ round cutter, cut the dough into circles. Fold each circle in half and place on one of the prepared baking sheets, leaving at least 1″ between each. Bake for 15 minutes, or until golden and cooked through.

Makes 18.

★ PER ROLL: 74 CALORIES, 2.2 G. TOTAL FAT, 1.3 G. SATURATED FAT, 4 MG. CHOLESTEROL, 180 MG. SODIUM

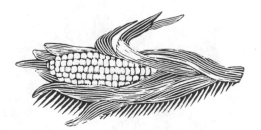

BUTTERMILK CORNBREAD

Adapted from *Cafe Oklahoma*
JUNIOR SERVICE LEAGUE OF MIDWEST CITY

This can't-miss cornbread uses no shortening, butter or vegetable oil, so it's very low in fat. For a hint of sweetness, serve it with honey or pure maple syrup.

1 cup yellow cornmeal
⅔ cup all-purpose flour
1 teaspoon baking powder
½ teaspoon salt
¼ teaspoon baking soda
1 cup 1% low-fat buttermilk
¼ cup fat-free egg substitute

Preheat the oven to 400°. Coat an 8″ × 8″ baking pan with no-stick spray; set aside.

In a large bowl, stir together the cornmeal, flour, baking powder, salt and baking soda.

In a small bowl, stir together the buttermilk and egg substitute. Add to the cornmeal mixture and stir together just until well-mixed.

Evenly spread the batter in the prepared pan. Bake for 15 to 20 minutes, or until lightly browned and a toothpick inserted in the center comes out clean. Cut into squares to serve.

TEST KITCHEN TIP: If you can't find low-fat buttermilk, substitute soured 1% low-fat milk. To make, place 1 tablespoon lemon juice in a glass measuring cup and add enough milk to measure 1 cup. Stir the mixture and let stand for 5 minutes before using.

Makes 9 servings.

★ PER SERVING: 97 CALORIES, 0.8 G. TOTAL FAT, 0.2 G. SATURATED FAT, 1 MG. CHOLESTEROL, 220 MG. SODIUM

PEACHY BRAN MUFFINS

Adapted from *Tastes in Plaid*
ALAMANCE COUNTY HISTORICAL MUSEUM

Peach yogurt gives these bran-and-raisin muffins a mildly fruity flavor.

1 cup all-purpose flour
1 tablespoon baking powder
½ teaspoon ground cinnamon
2 cups whole-bran cereal
1 container (8 ounces) reduced-fat peach yogurt
1 cup skim milk
½ cup raisins
⅓ cup shredded carrots
2 tablespoons packed brown sugar
2 tablespoons oil
2 tablespoons unsweetened applesauce
2 egg whites

Preheat the oven to 400°. Coat twelve 2½″ muffin cups with no-stick spray; set aside.

In a small bowl, stir together the flour, baking powder and cinnamon.

In a large bowl, stir together the cereal, yogurt and ½ cup of the milk. Let stand for 10 minutes to rehydrate the cereal. Stir in the raisins, carrots, brown sugar, oil, applesauce and egg whites until well-mixed. Add the remaining ½ cup milk. Stir in the flour mixture until moistened.

Spoon the batter into the prepared muffin cups, filling each cup about three-quarters full. Bake for 20 to 22 minutes, or until a toothpick inserted in the center comes out clean. Cool the muffins in the pan on a wire rack for 5 minutes, then remove from the pan. Serve warm.

Makes 12.

★ PER MUFFIN: 147 CALORIES, 3.2 G. TOTAL FAT, 0.6 G. SATURATED FAT, 1 MG. CHOLESTEROL, 192 MG. SODIUM

Sweet-Potato Muffins

Adapted from *A Shining Feast*
FIRST BAPTIST CHURCH OF SHREVEPORT

The combination of sweet potatoes, raisins and spices makes these pleasantly sweet muffins perfect for brunch or a salad luncheon.

> 2¼ cups all-purpose flour
> ½ cup sugar
> ¼ cup raisins
> 2½ teaspoons baking powder
> 1 teaspoon ground cinnamon
> ¼ teaspoon ground nutmeg
>   Pinch of salt
> 1 cup skim milk
> 2 tablespoons tub-style reduced-calorie margarine, melted
> 2 tablespoons unsweetened applesauce
> 2 egg whites, lightly beaten
> ¾ cup finely shredded sweet potatoes

Preheat the oven to 400°. Coat twelve 2½″ muffin cups with no-stick spray; set aside.

In a large bowl, stir together the flour, sugar, raisins, baking powder, cinnamon, nutmeg and salt until well-mixed.

In a medium bowl, use a wire whisk to beat together the milk, margarine, applesauce and egg whites. Stir in the sweet potatoes. Add to the flour mixture. Stir just until moistened. (The batter will be lumpy.)

Spoon the batter into the prepared muffin cups, filling each cup about three-quarters full. Bake for 20 minutes, or until a toothpick inserted in the center comes out clean. (Do not overbake.) Cool the muffins in the pan on a wire rack for 5 minutes, then remove from the pan. Serve warm.

Makes 12.

★ PER MUFFIN: 154 CALORIES, 1.3 G. TOTAL FAT, 0.2 G. SATURATED FAT, 0 MG. CHOLESTEROL, 112 MG. SODIUM

....

Chocolate Muffins

Adapted from *Nothin' Finer*
CHAPEL HILL SERVICE LEAGUE

Unsweetened cocoa powder lends rich chocolate flavor, without added fat, to these scrumptious muffins. For an extra treat, serve them with a honey-and-cream-cheese spread (see the Test Kitchen Tip below for a recipe).

    1½ cups all-purpose flour
    ½ cup unsweetened cocoa powder
    ½ cup sugar
    1 tablespoon baking powder
    ⅛ teaspoon salt
    4 egg whites, lightly beaten
    ¾ cup skim milk
    2 tablespoons canola oil
    1 teaspoon vanilla

Preheat the oven to 425°. Lightly coat twelve 2½″ muffin cups with no-stick spray; set aside.

In a large bowl, stir together the flour, cocoa powder, sugar, baking powder and salt.

In a small bowl, whisk together the egg whites, milk, oil and vanilla. Add to the flour mixture. Stir just until moistened.

Spoon the batter into the prepared muffin cups, filling each cup about two-thirds full. Bake for 13 to 15 minutes, or until a toothpick inserted in the center comes out clean. Cool the muffins in the pan on a wire rack for 5 minutes, then remove from the pan. Serve warm.

TEST KITCHEN TIP: To make honey-and-cream-cheese spread, mix together ½ cup fat-free cream cheese and 1 tablespoon honey. Spread on warm muffins.

Makes 12.

★ PER MUFFIN: 127 CALORIES, 2.8 G. TOTAL FAT, 0.2 G. SATURATED FAT, 0 MG. CHOLESTEROL, 133 MG. SODIUM

....

JOHNNYCAKES

Adapted from *A Cook's Tour of the Azalea Coast*
AUXILIARY TO THE NEW HANOVER–PENDER COUNTY MEDICAL SOCIETY

*Johnnycakes were American colonial quick breads—prepared over
an open hearth. Still appealing after all these years, these
cornmeal griddle cakes are wonderful topped with maple syrup
for breakfast or brunch.*

> 1 cup yellow cornmeal
> 2 teaspoons sugar
> ⅛ teaspoon salt
> 1 cup boiling water
> ⅓ cup skim milk
> 2 egg whites, lightly beaten
> 1 teaspoon vanilla

In a medium bowl, stir together the cornmeal, sugar and salt.
Stir in the water and let stand for 5 minutes.

In a small bowl, whisk together the milk, egg whites and vanilla.
Stir into the cornmeal mixture until well-mixed.

Coat a large no-stick skillet with no-stick spray. Place over
medium heat. Drop 1 heaping tablespoon of batter into the hot skillet for each pancake. Cook for 4 to 6 minutes, turning once, until
the johnnycakes are browned and cooked through. Serve warm.

Makes 18.

★ PER JOHNNYCAKE: 30 CALORIES, 0.2 G. TOTAL FAT, 0 G. SATURATED FAT,
0 MG. CHOLESTEROL, 26 MG. SODIUM

Auxiliary to the New Hanover–Pender County Medical Society

The recipes in *A Cook's Tour of the Azalea Coast* should be good for you. After all, they come from the 175 members of the Auxiliary—a group of men and women whose spouses are medical doctors. Many of the recipes are inspired by the bountiful seafood available off North Carolina's lovely Azalea Coast.

The Auxiliary focuses its energies on the medical needs of the community and on health education. That means thousands of hours of volunteer service to hospitals, schools and community health organizations as well as programs in area schools that teach prevention of head and spinal cord injuries. In addition, the Auxiliary was involved in the building of the Hospitality House of Wilmington, a "home away from home" for the families of seriously ill people in local hospitals.

Proceeds from the second edition of the cookbook are earmarked for "Straight Talk," an information and counseling hot line that helps students in the middle and high school grades.

....

LEMON BREAD

Adapted from *Augusta Cooks for Company*
AUGUSTA COUNCIL

This lovely quick bread, enhanced with pecans and a sweet-tart lemon topping, is delightful with a cup of tea. Or toast a slice for breakfast or a snack.

BREAD

- 1 cup sugar
- ¼ cup lemon juice
- 3 tablespoons butter or stick margarine (not reduced-calorie), melted
- 3 tablespoons unsweetened applesauce
- 1 teaspoon lemon extract
- 4 egg whites
- 1½ cups all-purpose flour
- 1 teaspoon baking powder
- ¼ teaspoon salt
- ¼ cup toasted and chopped pecans
- 1½ teaspoons finely shredded lemon rind

TOPPING

- ¼ cup powdered sugar
- 2 tablespoons lemon juice

TO MAKE THE BREAD: Preheat the oven to 350°. Lightly coat an 8″ × 4″ loaf pan with no-stick spray; set aside.

In a large bowl, stir together the sugar, lemon juice, butter or margarine, applesauce and lemon extract. One at a time, whisk in the egg whites.

In a small bowl, stir together the flour, baking powder and salt. Stir into the egg-white mixture. Stir in the pecans and lemon rind.

Spread evenly in the prepared pan. Bake for 45 minutes, or until a toothpick inserted in the center comes out clean. (Do not over-bake.)

TO MAKE THE TOPPING: In a small saucepan, stir together the powdered sugar and lemon juice. Cook over medium heat, stirring, for a few minutes, until the sugar dissolves.

Remove the bread from the oven. Cool in the pan on a wire rack for 15 minutes, then remove from the pan.

Set a wire rack on a piece of foil; place the bread on the rack. Pierce the top of the bread in several places with a thin-bladed knife or the tines of a fork. Pour the topping over the bread. Cool completely. Wrap the bread in foil and allow the bread to stand at room temperature for 24 hours before cutting.

TEST KITCHEN TIP: To toast the pecans, preheat the oven to 350°. Place the pecans in a single layer in a shallow baking pan. Bake, stirring occasionally, for 5 minutes, or until lightly browned.

Makes 1 loaf; 16 slices.

★ PER SLICE: 132 CALORIES, 3.4 G. TOTAL FAT, 1.4 G. SATURATED FAT, 6 MG. CHOLESTEROL, 90 MG. SODIUM

BLUEBERRY BREAD

Adapted from *Cotton Country Cooking*
JUNIOR LEAGUE OF MORGAN COUNTY

Fresh blueberries give this bread the best flavor and color. If they are out of season, use frozen ones that you've thawed and drained. In a pinch, you can use canned blueberries, but be sure to drain them, rinse them thoroughly and pat them dry to avoid having pale blue bread.

BREAD

- ¼ cup water
- 2 tablespoons butter or stick margarine (not reduced-calorie)
- ⅓ cup orange juice
- 1 tablespoon finely shredded orange rind
- 1 cup sugar
- 2 egg whites, lightly beaten
- 2 cups all-purpose flour
- 1 teaspoon baking powder
- ½ teaspoon baking soda
- ¼ teaspoon salt
- 1 cup fresh blueberries

GLAZE

- 1 tablespoon honey
- 2 teaspoons orange juice

TO MAKE THE BREAD: Preheat the oven to 325°. Coat a 9" × 5" loaf pan with no-stick spray; set aside.

In a small saucepan, combine the water and butter or margarine. Bring to a boil over high heat. Remove from the heat and stir in the orange juice and orange rind.

In a large bowl, whisk together the sugar and egg whites until well-combined.

In a medium bowl, stir together the flour, baking powder, baking soda and salt.

Alternately stir the flour mixture and orange juice mixture into the sugar mixture. Fold in the blueberries.

Spread the batter evenly in the prepared pan. Bake for 70 minutes, or until a toothpick inserted in the center comes out clean. (Do not overbake.)

TO MAKE THE GLAZE: In a small bowl, stir together the honey and orange juice.

Cool the bread in the pan on a wire rack for 10 minutes, then remove from the pan and place on a piece of foil.

Spoon the glaze over the top of the warm bread and immediately wrap in the foil. Let stand at room temperature until cooled.

Makes 1 loaf; 16 slices.

★ PER SLICE: 128 CALORIES, 1.6 G. TOTAL FAT, 1 G. SATURATED FAT, 4 MG. CHOLESTEROL, 102 MG. SODIUM

ZUCCHINI BREAD

Adapted from *Cane River's Louisiana Living*
SERVICE LEAGUE OF NATCHITOCHES

Don't be alarmed if a crack forms in the top of this cinnamon-spiced, zucchini-flecked bread. That's typical of quick bread loaves.

> 1 cup sugar
> 3 egg whites, lightly beaten
> ¼ cup oil
> ¼ cup unsweetened applesauce
> 1 teaspoon vanilla
> 1 cup finely shredded zucchini
> 1½ cups all-purpose flour
> ½ teaspoon baking powder
> ½ teaspoon ground cinnamon
> ⅛ teaspoon salt

Preheat the oven to 350°. Coat an 8" × 4" loaf pan with no-stick spray; set aside.

In a large bowl, stir together the sugar, egg whites, oil, applesauce and vanilla. Stir in the zucchini.

In a small bowl, stir together the flour, baking powder, cinnamon and salt. Stir into the zucchini mixture.

Spread the batter in the prepared pan. Bake for 1 hour, or until a toothpick inserted in the center comes out clean.

Cool the bread in the pan on a wire rack for 10 minutes, then remove from the pan and cool completely. Wrap the bread in foil and let stand overnight before slicing.

Makes 1 loaf; 16 slices.

★ PER SLICE: 125 CALORIES, 3.5 G. TOTAL FAT, 0.4 G. SATURATED FAT, 0 MG. CHOLESTEROL, 38 MG. SODIUM

NEW ENGLAND BROWN BREAD

Adapted from *300 Years of Carolina Cooking*
JUNIOR LEAGUE OF GREENVILLE

For a great-tasting low-fat snack or breakfast, spread slices of this rich molasses-flavored bread with fat-free cream cheese and a little orange marmalade.

1 cup low-fat graham crackers crushed to fine crumbs
1 cup all-purpose flour
1¼ teaspoons baking soda
   Pinch of salt
2 tablespoons butter or stick margarine (not reduced-calorie), cut into 4 pieces
1 cup nonfat buttermilk
2 egg whites, lightly beaten
½ cup molasses
1 cup golden raisins

Preheat the oven to 350°. Coat four 10-ounce custard cups with no-stick spray; set aside.

In a medium bowl, stir together the cracker crumbs, flour, baking soda and salt. Using a pastry blender, cut in the butter or margarine.

In a small bowl, stir together the buttermilk, egg whites and molasses. Add to the flour mixture. Stir to combine. Stir in the raisins.

Spoon the batter into the prepared custard cups, filling each cup about three-quarters full. Bake for 40 to 45 minutes, or until a toothpick inserted in the center comes out clean.

Cool in the custard cups on wire racks for 10 minutes, then remove from the cups and cool completely on the wire racks.

Makes 4 loaves; 12 slices.

★ PER SLICE: 151 CALORIES, 2.1 G. TOTAL FAT, 0.4 G. SATURATED FAT, 5 MG. CHOLESTEROL, 157 MG. SODIUM

WHOLE-WHEAT NUT BREAD

Adapted from *The Take Care Cookbook*
MID-FAIRFIELD HOSPICE

If you like, you can use all whole-wheat flour in this hearty quick bread. That will give it a more solid texture and elevate the fiber content.

1½ cups unbleached flour
 1 cup whole-wheat flour
 1 tablespoon baking powder
 ¼ teaspoon salt
 2 egg whites, lightly beaten
 ⅓ cup honey
 2 tablespoons canola oil
 2 tablespoons unsweetened applesauce
 1 teaspoon vanilla
 1 cup skim milk
 ½ cup toasted and chopped walnuts

Preheat the oven to 350°. Coat a 9″ × 5″ loaf pan with no-stick spray; set aside.

In a medium bowl, stir together the unbleached flour, whole-wheat flour, baking powder and salt.

In a large bowl, stir together the egg whites, honey, oil, applesauce and vanilla; stir in the milk until combined. Add the flour mixture and stir just until well-mixed. Stir in the nuts.

Spread the batter evenly in the prepared pan. Bake for 50 minutes, or until a toothpick inserted in the center comes out clean. (Do not overbake.)

Cool in the pan on a wire rack for 10 minutes, then remove from the pan and cool completely.

Makes 1 loaf; 16 slices.

★ PER SLICE: 138 CALORIES, 4.2 G. TOTAL FAT, 0.3 G. SATURATED FAT, 0 MG. CHOLESTEROL, 111 MG. SODIUM

EASY SOUR-CREAM COFFEE CAKE

Adapted from *Florida Flavors*
ENVIRONMENTAL STUDIES COUNCIL

You don't have to sacrifice the convenience of a cake-mix dessert for the sake of better nutrition. We lightened this company-pleasing coffee cake by using egg whites in place of whole eggs, applesauce instead of oil and fat-free sour cream instead of the regular variety.

TOPPING

½ cup sugar
¼ cup toasted and finely chopped nuts
1 tablespoon ground cinnamon

COFFEE CAKE

1 package 2-layer yellow cake mix (without pudding)
1 package (4-serving-size) instant French vanilla pudding mix
8 egg whites
½ cup unsweetened applesauce
1 cup fat-free sour cream

TO MAKE THE TOPPING: In a small bowl, stir together the sugar, nuts and cinnamon.

TO MAKE THE COFFEE CAKE: Preheat the oven to 350°. Coat a 13″ × 9″ baking pan with no-stick spray; set aside.

In a large bowl, use an electric mixer to beat together the cake mix, pudding mix, egg whites, applesauce and sour cream until just combined; beat for 2 to 3 minutes more.

Evenly spread half of the batter into the prepared pan. Sprinkle with half of the topping. Cover with the remaining batter, then the remaining topping.

Bake for 30 to 35 minutes, or until a toothpick inserted in the center comes out clean. Cool in the pan on a wire rack for 10 minutes. Serve warm.

TEST KITCHEN TIP: This coffee cake freezes very well. You can freeze individually wrapped portions for handy brown-bag treats.

Makes 12 servings.

★ PER SERVING: 290 CALORIES, 5.5 G. TOTAL FAT, 1.1 G. SATURATED FAT, 0 MG. CHOLESTEROL, 390 MG. SODIUM

CARAWAY COTTAGE PUFFS

Adapted from *Presentations*
FRIENDS OF LIED CENTER FOR PERFORMING ARTS

The editors of Presentations *describe these rolls as "light and puffy mouthfuls." We certainly agree. Low-fat cottage cheese in the dough keeps the puffs moist and adds calcium, too.*

2⅓ cups all-purpose flour
1 package active dry yeast
¼ teaspoon baking soda
1 cup 1% low-fat cottage cheese
¼ cup water
2 tablespoons sugar
1 tablespoon butter or stick margarine (not reduced-calorie)
¼ teaspoon salt
2 egg whites
2 tablespoons finely chopped onions
2 teaspoons caraway seeds

Place 1⅓ cups of the flour in a large bowl. Stir in the yeast and baking soda.

In a small saucepan, stir together the cottage cheese, water, sugar, butter or margarine and salt. Place over medium heat and stir until just warm (105° to 115°). Pour over the flour mixture.

Using an electric mixer, beat on medium speed until well-combined. Add the egg whites, onions and caraway seeds. Beat for 3 minutes at high speed. Stir in the remaining 1 cup flour.

Coat a clean, dry large bowl with no-stick spray. Spoon the batter into the bowl. Lightly coat the top of the batter with no-stick spray. Cover and let rise in a draft-free place for about 1 hour, or until double in bulk.

Lightly coat twelve 2½″ muffin cups with no-stick spray. Spoon the batter into the cups, filling each cup about half full. Cover and let rise for about 30 minutes, or until nearly double in bulk.

Preheat the oven to 400°. Bake for 11 to 13 minutes, or until golden brown. Cool the rolls in the pan on a wire rack for 5 minutes, then remove from the pan. Serve warm.

TEST KITCHEN TIP: For herbal excitement, substitute 1 tablespoon of either dill seeds, cumin seeds or fennel seeds for the caraway seeds. Toasting the seeds lightly in a small skillet, then crushing them slightly with a mortar and pestle or the flat side of a cleaver will heighten their flavor.

Makes 12.

★ PER PUFF: 124 CALORIES, 1.4 G. TOTAL FAT, 0.7 G. SATURATED FAT, 3 MG. CHOLESTEROL, 147 MG. SODIUM

....

NANCY'S BREADSTICKS

Adapted from *Pass the Plate*
EPISCOPAL CHURCH WOMEN OF CHRIST CHURCH

Take your choice of any of the three different toppers for these soft and chewy breadsticks. They're ideal alongside bowls of soup or salad or served with plates of pasta.

> 3–3½ cups all-purpose flour
> 1 tablespoon sugar
> ½ teaspoon salt
> 2 packages active dry yeast
> 2 tablespoons olive oil or canola oil
> 1¼ cups hot water (130°)
> 1 egg white
> 1 tablespoon water
> Toasted sesame seeds, dried dill or poppy seeds

Place 1 cup of the flour in a large bowl. Stir in the sugar, salt and yeast. Add the oil, then gradually stir in the 1¼ cups water. Using an electric mixer, beat for 2 minutes.

Add 1 cup of the remaining flour and beat until well-combined. Stir in as much of the remaining flour as you can to make a soft dough.

Transfer the dough to a lightly floured work surface. Then knead in enough of the remaining flour to make a dough that is smooth and elastic.

Coat a clean, dry large bowl with no-stick spray. Place the dough in the bowl. Lightly coat the top of the dough with no-stick spray. Cover and let rise in a draft-free place for about 45 minutes, or until double in bulk.

(continued)

Lightly coat 2 baking sheets with no-stick spray. Punch the dough down and divide it into four portions. Roll each portion into a 24″ rope. Cut each rope into 6 sticks. Place the sticks on the prepared baking sheets about ½″ apart. Cover and let rise for about 15 minutes, or until nearly double in bulk.

Preheat the oven to 300°.

In a small bowl, whisk together the egg white and 1 tablespoon water. Brush each stick with the mixture and sprinkle with your choice of sesame seeds, dill or poppy seeds. Bake for 25 to 30 minutes, or until golden brown.

TEST KITCHEN TIP: To make 48 thin, crispy breadsticks, divide the dough into eight portions. Roll each portion into a 24″ rope. Cut each rope into 6 sticks. Let rise and bake as above.

Makes 24.

★ PER BREADSTICK: 71 CALORIES, 1.3 G. TOTAL FAT, 0.2 G. SATURATED FAT, 0 MG. CHOLESTEROL, 47 MG. SODIUM

....

CHOCOLATE CINNAMON ROLLS

Adapted from *Our Country Cookin'*
JUNIOR SOCIAL WORKERS OF CHICKASHA

Because these heavenly rolls are made with cocoa powder rather than melted chocolate, they have lots of wonderful flavor without a lot of fat.

ROLLS

    1 package active dry yeast
    ¾ cup warm water (105°–115°)
    3 tablespoons butter or stick margarine (not reduced-calorie), melted
    1 teaspoon salt
    ⅓ cup + 3 tablespoons sugar
    ¼ cup fat-free egg substitute
    3 cups all-purpose flour
    ⅓ cup unsweetened cocoa powder
    1½ teaspoons ground cinnamon

ICING

  1½ cups powdered sugar
  2 tablespoons skim milk
  1 teaspoon vanilla

TO MAKE THE ROLLS: In a large bowl, dissolve the yeast in the water. Stir in the butter or margarine, salt and ⅓ cup of the sugar. Stir in the egg substitute. Add 1 cup of the flour and the cocoa powder.

Using an electric mixer, beat on medium speed for 2 minutes. Scrape down the sides of the bowl; stir in the remaining 2 cups flour until well-combined.

Coat a clean, dry large bowl with butter-flavored no-stick spray. Place the dough in the bowl. Lightly coat the top of the dough with no-stick spray. Cover and let rise in a draft-free place for about 45 minutes, or until double in bulk.

Lightly coat a 13″ × 9″ baking pan with no-stick spray. Stir the dough down by beating it with 25 strokes. Transfer to a well-floured work surface. Roll into a 12″ × 8″ rectangle.

In a small bowl, stir together the cinnamon and the remaining 3 tablespoons sugar. Coat the dough with no-stick spray; sprinkle with the sugar-cinnamon mixture. Roll the dough up, beginning with a long edge. Pinch the edges together; cut into 12 pieces.

Place the pieces in the prepared pan. Cover and let rise for 1½ hours, or until nearly double in bulk.

Preheat the oven to 375°. Bake the rolls for 20 minutes.

TO MAKE THE ICING: In a small bowl, stir together the powdered sugar, milk and vanilla. Spread on the rolls while they're still hot. Serve warm.

Makes 12.

★ PER ROLL: 230 CALORIES, 3.4 G. TOTAL FAT, 0.6 G. SATURATED FAT, 0 MG. CHOLESTEROL, 221 MG. SODIUM

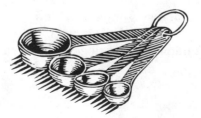

Yogurt Rolls

Adapted from *A Shining Feast*
FIRST BAPTIST CHURCH OF SHREVEPORT

*Light, tender and even-textured, these scrumptious rolls are low
in fat because they use fat-free yogurt, substitute egg whites for a
whole egg and go light on the oil.*

> ½ cup warm water (105°–115°)
> 2 packages active dry yeast
> 1 tablespoon + ½ cup sugar
> 1 cup fat-free plain yogurt
> ¼ cup canola oil
> 3 egg whites, lightly beaten
> 5 cups all-purpose flour
> ½ teaspoon salt

Place the water in a small bowl. Sprinkle with the yeast and 1 tablespoon of the sugar. Cover and let stand for 5 minutes.

In a large bowl, stir together the yogurt, oil and the remaining ½ cup sugar. Add the yeast mixture. Stir in the egg whites.

In a medium bowl, stir together the flour and salt. Stir half of the flour mixture into the egg mixture. Using an electric mixer, beat on medium speed until smooth. Gradually beat in the remaining flour mixture.

Cover the bowl with plastic wrap. Use a rubber band to hold the wrap in place. Refrigerate for 8 hours or overnight.

Coat 2 or 3 large baking sheets with no-stick spray. Transfer the dough to a floured work surface. Mix the dough with your hands until firm enough to knead; knead about 50 times. Roll to ½″ thickness.

Using a 2½″ or 2¾″ round cutter, cut the dough into circles. Transfer the rolls to the prepared baking sheets. Coat the tops of the rolls with no-stick spray. Cover with plastic wrap and let rise in a draft-free place for about 1¼ hours, or until nearly double in bulk.

Preheat the oven to 375°. Remove the plastic wrap from the rolls. Bake for 12 minutes, or until golden brown.

First Baptist Church of Shreveport

It's easy to tell from the pages of *A Shining Feast*, the cookbook put out by the First Baptist Church of Shreveport to mark the church's sesquicentennial, that this congregation has nourished its flock—both spiritually and physically—for all of its 150 years.

The influence the church has had internationally through ministries outside the United States is reflected in recipes from other countries and cultures. Many of the recipes come from the archives of the Baptist Tea Room, a cafeteria once housed in the church basement. The tearoom served lunch to downtown workers in Shreveport for half a century until the church building was relocated. Some of the most special recipes from congregation members are generations old, passed down by great-grandmothers long since departed.

Because the First Baptist Church of Shreveport understands that spiritual hunger cannot be addressed until physical hunger is alleviated, money raised from *A Shining Feast* benefits the church's hunger relief project.

TEST KITCHEN TIP: If you prefer soft-sided rolls, you can bake 12 rolls in a 13″ × 9″ baking pan, 9 rolls in an 8″ × 8″ baking pan or 7 rolls in a 9″ round cake pan.

Makes 28.

★ PER ROLL: 121 CALORIES, 2.2 G. TOTAL FAT, 0.2 G. SATURATED FAT, 0 MG. CHOLESTEROL, 51 MG. SODIUM

HONEY WHOLE-WHEAT BREAD

Adapted from *With Special Distinction*
MISSISSIPPI COLLEGE

To know if the risen bread dough is ready to shape, poke two fingers into it. If the indentation holds, it's time to start shaping.

> 4 cups whole-wheat flour
> ½ cup nonfat dry milk
> 2 packages active dry yeast
> 1 teaspoon salt
> 3 cups water
> ½ cup honey
> 2 tablespoons canola oil
> 3½–4½ cups all-purpose flour

Place 3 cups of the whole-wheat flour in a large bowl. Stir in the milk, yeast and salt.

In a medium saucepan, stir together the water, honey and oil. Stir over medium heat until just warm (105° to 115°). Pour over the flour mixture.

Using an electric mixer, beat on medium speed until well-combined. Stir in the remaining 1 cup whole-wheat flour and 3½ cups of the all-purpose flour.

Transfer the dough to a lightly floured work surface. Knead in enough of the remaining 1 cup all-purpose flour to make a dough that is smooth and elastic.

Coat a clean, dry large bowl with no-stick spray. Place the dough in the bowl. Lightly coat the top of the dough with no-stick spray. Cover and let rise in a draft-free place for about 45 minutes, or until double in bulk.

Lightly coat two 9″ × 5″ loaf pans with no-stick spray. Punch the dough down and divide it in half. Shape into 2 loaves and place in the prepared pans. Cover and let rise for 20 to 30 minutes, or until nearly double in bulk.

Preheat the oven to 350°. Bake for 30 to 35 minutes, or until the loaves sound hollow when tapped with your fingers. Remove the bread from the pans and let cool on a wire rack.

TEST KITCHEN TIP: For variety, substitute 1 cup soy flour for 1 cup of the whole-wheat flour and add ¼ cup wheat germ.

After cooling, one of the loaves can be sliced, placed in a plastic storage bag and frozen. For a quick breakfast or snack, toast 1 slice, then spread with fat-free cream cheese and a sprinkle of ground cinnamon.

Makes 2 loaves; 32 slices.

★PER SLICE: 129 CALORIES, 1.3 G. TOTAL FAT, 0.1 G. SATURATED FAT, 0 MG. CHOLESTEROL, 74 MG. SODIUM

Oatmeal Bread

Adapted from *Amazing Graces*
TEXAS CONFERENCE UNITED METHODIST MINISTERS' SPOUSES ASSOCIATION

Slices of this slightly sweet loaf are delicious toasted for breakfast or a snack. Top them with yogurt cheese or reduced-fat cream cheese.

> 1½ cups boiling water
> 1 cup rolled oats
> 1 teaspoon salt
> 1 package active dry yeast
> ¼ cup warm water (105°–115°)
> ⅓ cup light molasses
> 1½ tablespoons oil
> 4–4½ cups sifted all-purpose flour

In a large bowl, pour the boiling water over the oats. Add the salt; stir and cool to lukewarm.

In a glass measuring cup, dissolve the yeast in the warm water. Add the yeast water, molasses and oil to the oat mixture. Gradually stir in enough flour to make the dough stiff enough to handle.

Turn the dough out onto a work surface. Knead the dough, working in a scant amount of additional flour if needed to prevent sticking, for about 5 minutes, or until smooth and elastic.

Coat a large bowl with no-stick spray. Place the dough in the bowl. Coat the top of the dough lightly with no-stick spray. Cover and let rise in a draft-free place for 1 hour, or until double in bulk.

Coat a 9″ × 5″ loaf pan with no-stick spray. Punch the dough down and knead for a few minutes. Shape the dough into a loaf and place in the pan. Cover and let rise again for 1 hour, or until double in bulk.

Preheat the oven to 375°. Bake for 50 minutes, or until the loaf sounds hollow when tapped with your fingers. Remove the loaf from the pan and let cool on a wire rack.

Makes 1 loaf; 16 slices.

★ PER SLICE: 181 CALORIES, 2.3 G. FAT, 0.3 G. SATURATED FAT, 0 MG. CHOLESTEROL, 135 MG. SODIUM

POTS OF GOLD:
SOUPS AND STEWS

Cool-Cucumber Soup

Adapted from *Sassafras! The Ozarks Cookbook*
JUNIOR LEAGUE OF SPRINGFIELD

You'll be a cool and health-conscious cook when you serve this creamy, chilled, fresh-from-the-garden soup. A serving makes a refreshing opener for a summer dinner party.

> 2 small cucumbers, peeled, seeded and chopped
> 1 cup defatted reduced-sodium chicken broth
> 1 cup fat-free sour cream or fat-free plain yogurt
> ¼ cup chopped onions
> 1½ tablespoons white-wine vinegar
> 1 small clove garlic, minced
> Ground black pepper
> ¼ cup finely chopped tomatoes
> 2 teaspoons finely chopped scallion tops

In a blender or food processor, blend the cucumbers, broth, sour cream or yogurt, onions, vinegar and garlic until smooth. (If necessary, stop and scrape down the sides of the container.) Season with the pepper. Pour into a bowl; cover and refrigerate for several hours or overnight.

Serve sprinkled with the tomatoes and scallion tops.

Makes 4 servings.

★ **PER SERVING**: 92 CALORIES, 0.2 G. TOTAL FAT, 0 G. SATURATED FAT, 0 MG. CHOLESTEROL, 202 MG. SODIUM

CHINESE NOODLE AND MEATBALL SOUP

Adapted from *Simply Simpatico*
JUNIOR LEAGUE OF ALBUQUERQUE

The contrasting shapes, textures and flavors of tiny beef meatballs, fine noodles, fresh mushrooms and spinach leaves make this soup something special.

8 ounces 95% lean ground beef
¼ cup minced scallions
1 teaspoon cornstarch
Pinch of salt
Pinch of ground black pepper
2 cans (13¾ ounces each) reduced-sodium beef broth, defatted
3½ cups water
2 tablespoons dry sherry or 1 teaspoon sherry extract
4 teaspoons reduced-sodium soy sauce
1 teaspoon grated fresh ginger (optional)
4 ounces fine yolk-free egg noodles
1⅓ cups thinly sliced mushrooms
1⅓ cups torn and tightly packed fresh spinach

In a small bowl, mix the beef, scallions, cornstarch, salt and pepper. Shape teaspoonfuls of the mixture into balls and set aside.

In a medium saucepan, combine the broth, water, sherry or sherry extract, soy sauce and ginger (if using). Bring to a boil over medium heat. Add the meatballs and return to a boil.

Slowly stir in the noodles and mushrooms. Gently simmer for 6 to 8 minutes, or until the noodles are just tender and the meatballs are cooked through. Stir in the spinach. Cook for 1 minute, or until the spinach is wilted.

Makes 4 servings.

★ PER SERVING: 262 CALORIES, 7.4 G. TOTAL FAT, 2.6 G. SATURATED FAT, 34 MG. CHOLESTEROL, 730 MG. SODIUM

CREAM OF WINTER-SQUASH SOUP

Adapted from *From Generation to Generation*
SISTERHOOD OF TEMPLE EMANU-EL

This vivid soup, with a dash of curry, makes delicious use of such hard-shell squash as butternut or buttercup, both excellent sources of vitamin A. Acorn squash is also good, but it's not as easy to peel when raw.

1 medium onion, thinly sliced and separated into rings
1 tablespoon reduced-calorie butter blend
1 can (14½ ounces) reduced-sodium chicken broth, defatted
1 small butternut or buttercup squash, peeled, seeded and cut into ¾″ cubes
½ cup cider or apple juice
½ cup evaporated skim milk
1 tablespoon nonfat dry milk
   Pinch of curry powder
   Pinch of ground black pepper
   Finely chopped fresh parsley

Coat a medium saucepan with no-stick spray. Add the onions and butter blend. Cook, stirring, over medium heat for 5 minutes, or until the onion rings are lightly browned.

Add the broth, squash and cider or apple juice. Bring to a boil, then reduce the heat. Cover and simmer for 20 minutes, or until the squash is very tender.

Transfer, in small batches, to a blender or food processor. Blend until smooth. Return the mixture to the saucepan.

Stir in the evaporated milk, dry milk, curry powder and pepper. Cook, stirring, over medium heat until heated through. Serve sprinkled with the parsley.

Makes 4 servings.

★ PER SERVING: 98 CALORIES, 2.7 G. TOTAL FAT, 0.6 G. SATURATED FAT, 1 MG. CHOLESTEROL, 281 MG. SODIUM

OUR CAUSE

Sisterhood of Temple Emanu-El

The accomplishments of the Sisterhood of Temple Emanu-El could hardly be summed up in a book, let alone a paragraph or two. For five generations these spirited, indomitable, generous women have had a profound impact on their community.

The Sisterhood formed in 1875 as the Ladies Hebrew Benevolent Association for the newly formed congregation of Emanu-El of Dallas, Texas. Through two world wars, the Depression, the social unrest of the 1960s and the economic downturn of the past decade, the Sisterhood has been unflagging in its support for, and assistance to, people in every section of Dallas.

The group has supported or created programs to aid the blind, the homeless, immigrants and children. It has also invested in educational, cultural and arts-awareness programs.

Today's Sisterhood draws strength from its diversity. Members are both single and married, young and old, homemakers and career women. The recipes in *From Generation to Generation* reflect both the constancy of the Jewish tradition and the varied life experience of the women of the Sisterhood. Proceeds from the book go toward the group's roster of community projects, including a shelter for homeless children and programs for the blind and the elderly.

CHEESE AND BROCCOLI SOUP

Adapted from *Coastal Cuisine, Texas Style*
JUNIOR SERVICE LEAGUE OF BRAZOSPORT

Eat your vegetables? No problem. Not when the onions, broccoli and carrots are floating in a rich-tasting (yet low-fat) creamy Swiss-cheese base.

1	small onion, finely chopped
1	tablespoon + ¾ cup defatted reduced-sodium chicken broth
1	cup water
1	cup chopped broccoli florets
1	carrot, thinly sliced
1	small clove garlic, minced
⅛	teaspoon ground black pepper
¾	cup skim milk
1–2	tablespoons all-purpose flour
2	tablespoons nonfat dry milk
½	cup finely shredded Swiss cheese
2	slices (¾ ounce each) fat-free Swiss cheese, finely cut up

Lightly coat a medium saucepan with no-stick spray. Add the onions and 1 tablespoon of the broth. Cook, stirring, over medium heat for 5 minutes, or until the onions are tender.

Stir in the water, broccoli, carrots, garlic, pepper and the remaining ¾ cup broth. Bring to a boil, then reduce the heat. Cover and simmer for 5 minutes.

In a small bowl, whisk together the skim milk, flour and dry milk. Using a spoon, slowly stir the milk mixture into the soup. Stir in the shredded Swiss and fat-free Swiss. Cook, stirring, over medium heat for 1 minute, or until the cheese is melted. (Do not boil.)

Makes 4 servings.

★PER SERVING: 130 CALORIES, 4.2 G. TOTAL FAT, 2.6 G. SATURATED FAT, 14 MG. CHOLESTEROL, 389 MG. SODIUM

CREAM OF CAULIFLOWER SOUP

Adapted from *Florida's Finest*
JUNIOR LEAGUE OF SOUTH BREVARD COUNTY

Even small seeds of dietary change can flower into big benefits.
By changing the heavy cream in this soup to whole milk, we
eliminated 19 grams of fat from the recipe.

> 1 cup finely chopped onions
> 2 tablespoons + 2 cups defatted reduced-sodium chicken
>   broth
> 4 cups very small cauliflower florets
> 2 cups whole milk
> 2 tablespoons all-purpose flour
> ¼ teaspoon ground black pepper
>   Chopped fresh parsley or chives

Lightly coat a medium saucepan with no-stick spray. Add the onions and 2 tablespoons of the broth. Cook, stirring, over medium heat for 5 minutes, or until the onions are tender.

Stir in the cauliflower and the remaining 2 cups broth. Bring to a boil, then reduce the heat. Cover and simmer for 7 minutes, or until tender.

In a small bowl, whisk together the milk and flour. Using a spoon, slowly stir the milk mixture into the pan. Cook, stirring, for 2 minutes, or until the mixture slightly thickens. (Do not boil.) Add the pepper. Serve sprinkled with the parsley or chives.

Makes 4 servings.

★ PER SERVING: 136 CALORIES, 4.4 G. TOTAL FAT, 2.6 G. SATURATED FAT,
  16 MG. CHOLESTEROL, 326 MG. SODIUM

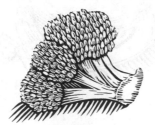

Greek Cucumber-and-Yogurt Soup

Adapted from *Sea Island Seasons*
BEAUFORT COUNTY OPEN LAND TRUST

Fat-free yogurt and skim milk provide a beneficial dose of virtually fat-free calcium in this chilled summer soup.

    2 cups fat-free plain yogurt
    2 large cucumbers, peeled, seeded and coarsely shredded
    1 cup skim milk
    2 tablespoons lemon juice
    2 small cloves garlic, minced
    ¼ teaspoon salt

In a medium bowl, stir together the yogurt, cucumbers, milk, lemon juice, garlic and salt. Cover and refrigerate for 4 to 8 hours to blend the flavors.

TEST KITCHEN TIP: For added flavor, stir a small amount of finely chopped scallions, chives, dill or mint into the soup.

Makes 4 servings.

★ PER SERVING: 118 CALORIES, 1.6 G. TOTAL FAT, 0.8 G. SATURATED FAT, 6 MG. CHOLESTEROL, 388 MG. SODIUM

Yellow-Pepper Soup

Adapted from *Specialties of the House*
KENMORE ASSOCIATION

This sunflower-bright soup can be made in big batches at the end of the summer, when colored bell peppers are a bargain at farm stands. Store it in the freezer for sips of sunshine all winter long.

2 teaspoons tub-style reduced-calorie margarine
2 medium yellow peppers, coarsely chopped
1 medium leek, chopped
1 small onion, chopped
1 stalk celery, chopped
⅛ teaspoon salt
⅛ teaspoon ground black pepper
2 cups defatted reduced-sodium chicken broth

Coat a medium saucepan with no-stick spray. Add the margarine and melt over medium heat. Add the peppers, leeks, onions, celery, salt and pepper. Cook, stirring, for 10 minutes, or until the vegetables are crisp-tender.

Add the broth. Bring to a boil. Reduce the heat to low. Cover and simmer for 20 minutes. Remove from the heat and let stand for 5 minutes to cool slightly.

Transfer to a blender or food processor. Blend until smooth. Return the mixture to the saucepan and heat through.

Makes 4 servings.

★ PER SERVING: 55 CALORIES, 1.2 G. TOTAL FAT, 0.2 G. SATURATED FAT, 0 MG. CHOLESTEROL, 339 MG. SODIUM

Senate Bean Soup

Adapted from *Augusta Cooks for Company*
AUGUSTA COUNCIL

In keeping with cost-cutting measures in Congress, we trimmed the fat in this hearty bean soup, which has been served daily in the U.S. Senate dining room since 1904.

1¼ cups dried navy beans, soaked overnight and drained
4 cups water
12 ounces smoked pork hocks
2 tablespoons minced fresh parsley
1 clove garlic, minced
½ teaspoon dried oregano
½ teaspoon dried basil
½ teaspoon ground black pepper
⅛ teaspoon dry mustard
1 bay leaf
1 small onion, finely chopped
½ cup finely chopped celery

In a large saucepan, combine the beans, water, pork hocks, parsley, garlic, oregano, basil, pepper, mustard and bay leaf. Bring to a boil, then reduce the heat. Cover and simmer for 30 minutes.

Stir in the onions and celery. Cover and simmer for 40 to 60 minutes, or until the beans are tender.

Discard the bay leaf. Remove the pork hocks. Cut the meat from the bones. Discard the bones and fat and stir the meat into the soup.

TEST KITCHEN TIP: For an even heartier soup, stir 2 cups of diced potatoes into the soup during the last 15 to 20 minutes of cooking.

Makes 4 servings.

★PER SERVING: 417 CALORIES, 14.7 G. TOTAL FAT, 5 G. SATURATED FAT, 78 MG. CHOLESTEROL, 801 MG. SODIUM

BARLEY-VEGETABLE SOUP

Adapted from *Cucina Classica*
ORDER SONS OF ITALY IN AMERICA, NEW YORK GRAND LODGE FOUNDATION

Make this soup as summer is winding down and the garden is bursting with tomatoes and zucchini. If nature has been particularly generous, you can prepare several batches for the freezer.

5	cups + 3 tablespoons water
⅓	cup pearl barley
2	cups chopped tomatoes
1	bay leaf
½	teaspoon salt
¼	teaspoon dried sage
¼	teaspoon dried oregano
1	tablespoon olive oil
1	onion, sliced
1	carrot, sliced
1	stalk celery, sliced
2½	cups chopped zucchini

In a large pot, bring 5 cups of the water to a boil. Add the barley, tomatoes, bay leaf, salt, sage and oregano. Reduce the heat; simmer for 30 minutes.

In a large skillet, warm the oil over medium heat. Add the onions and stir for 1 to 2 minutes. Add the carrots and celery; stir for a few minutes more. Add the zucchini and stir again. Reduce the heat. Add the remaining 3 tablespoons water and simmer for 10 to 15 minutes, or until the liquid is almost gone and the vegetables are almost tender.

Add the sautéed vegetables to the barley. Simmer for 10 to 15 minutes, or until the vegetables and barley are tender. Remove and discard the bay leaf before serving.

Makes 4 servings.

★PER SERVING: 135 CALORIES, 4.2 G. TOTAL FAT, 0.6 G. SATURATED FAT, 0 MG. CHOLESTEROL, 294 MG. SODIUM

SAUSAGE AND BARLEY SOUP

Adapted from *Albuquerque Academy à la Carte*
ALBUQUERQUE ACADEMY PARENTS' ASSOCIATION

You can create your own delicious, nutritious lunchtime fast food by packaging this hearty soup in microwaveable containers. The soup is especially good with a little prepared horseradish or Dijon mustard stirred in at serving time.

4 ounces fully cooked turkey kielbasa, cut into ¼″ slices
½ cup chopped onions
1 can (13¾ ounces) reduced-sodium beef or chicken broth, defatted
2¼ cups water
½ cup pearl barley
¼ teaspoon dried oregano
1 can (8 ounces) no-salt-added tomato sauce
1 large carrot, thinly sliced
1 stalk celery, thinly sliced

Lightly coat a large skillet with no-stick spray. Add the kielbasa and onions. Cook, stirring, over medium heat for 10 minutes, or until the onions are tender and the kielbasa is lightly browned.

Stir in the broth, water, barley and oregano. Bring to a boil, then reduce the heat. Cover and simmer for 30 minutes.

Stir in the tomato sauce, carrots and celery. Cover and simmer for 30 minutes, or until the barley and vegetables are tender.

Makes 3 servings.

★ PER SERVING: 237 CALORIES, 3.2 G. TOTAL FAT, 0.9 G. SATURATED FAT, 25 MG. CHOLESTEROL, 646 MG. SODIUM

Albuquerque Academy Parents' Association

To call the Albuquerque Academy exceptional is, perhaps, not to do it justice. This nonprofit middle-through-secondary school is widely regarded as one of the finest schools in the nation, with instructional facilities that rival those of many small colleges. There's no question that the 41-year-old academy is academically rigorous. Only one in four applicants is accepted each year, with 100 percent of graduates going on to college. It's not unusual for students to receive college credit for course work completed at the Academy.

But high academic standards are just one component of this unique private institution. If you could tour the school's 312-acre campus, with stunning vistas of Rocky Mountain foothills and desert mesas, you would meet a diverse student body. Here, 51 percent of the students are girls, 38 percent are students of color, and 40 percent receive financial aid. The admissions process is blind to everything except academic achievement. The school is dedicated to the philosophy that talented students admitted to the Academy should not be denied the ability to matriculate because of limited financial resources.

Albuquerque Academy à la Carte, published by the Parents' Association, benefits the school's scholarship fund.

SIRLOIN AND VEGETABLE SOUP

Adapted from *With Special Distinction*
MISSISSIPPI COLLEGE

The lean cut of beef used here makes this soup substantial without overdoing the fat. Choosing fresh mushrooms instead of canned and opting for lower-sodium canned tomatoes and broth keep sodium within healthful guidelines.

8 ounces boneless beef sirloin steak, cut ¾" thick and trimmed of all visible fat
3 cups defatted reduced-sodium beef broth
2 small carrots, thinly sliced
¾ cup sliced mushrooms
1 can (8 ounces) no-salt-added stewed tomatoes (with juice), cut up
1 stalk celery, sliced
¼ cup chopped onions
¼ teaspoon dried thyme
Pinch of ground black pepper
3 medium potatoes, peeled and cubed
Chopped fresh parsley

Preheat the broiler. Coat the rack of a broiling pan with no-stick spray. Place the beef on the rack. Broil 3" from the heat for 3 minutes on each side, or until the surface is browned. Drain the beef, then pat with paper towels and cut into ¾" cubes.

In a 6-quart Crock-Pot or other slow cooker, combine the beef, broth, carrots, mushrooms, tomatoes (with juice), celery, onions, thyme and pepper. Cover and cook on the high heat setting for 3½ hours.

Add the potatoes and stir well. Cover and cook on the high heat setting for 1½ to 2½ hours more, or until the vegetables are tender.

To serve, ladle the soup into bowls. Sprinkle with the parsley.

Makes 6 servings.

★ PER SERVING: 157 CALORIES, 3.6 G. TOTAL FAT, 1.4 G. SATURATED FAT, 25 MG. CHOLESTEROL, 277 MG. SODIUM

SPICY OYSTER-ARTICHOKE SOUP

Adapted from *Carolina Blessings*
CHILDREN'S HOME SOCIETY OF NORTH CAROLINA

You'll probably be too busy appreciating the flavor of this luscious soup to note that the oysters provide more iron than a comparable portion of beef round steak.

2 pints fresh oysters
1 cup chopped shallots or onions
1 bay leaf
½ teaspoon red-pepper flakes
Pinch of dried thyme
2 tablespoons butter or stick margarine (not reduced-calorie)
2 cans (14½ ounces each) reduced-sodium chicken broth, defatted
4 tablespoons instant-blending flour
½ cup cold water
2 cans (14½ ounces) artichoke hearts, drained and coarsely chopped
4 tablespoons chopped fresh cilantro
Pinch of salt
½ teaspoon hot-pepper sauce
1 cup evaporated skim milk

Drain the oysters and reserve the liquid. Chop the oysters and set aside.

In a medium saucepan, sauté the shallots or onions, bay leaf, red-pepper flakes and thyme in the butter or margarine until the shallots or onions are tender. Add the oyster liquid and broth.

In a cup, stir together the flour and water until smooth. Add to the saucepan, whisking constantly until the liquid thickens slightly. Simmer, whisking occasionally, for 15 minutes. Remove and discard the bay leaf.

Stir in the oysters, artichoke hearts, cilantro, salt and hot-pepper sauce. Simmer for 12 minutes, or until the oysters are cooked. Stir in the milk and heat briefly.

Makes 4 servings.

★ PER SERVING: 448 CALORIES, 12.8 G. TOTAL FAT, 2.8 G. SATURATED FAT, 138 MG. CHOLESTEROL, 1,046 MG. SODIUM

CIOPPINO

Adapted from *Only in California*
CHILDREN'S HOME SOCIETY OF CALIFORNIA

Sodium tends to be high in this traditional California seafood stew. By using salt-free products, we brought down the sodium considerably.

1 teaspoon olive oil
¾ cup chopped onions
½ cup chopped celery
¼ cup chopped green peppers
1 clove garlic, chopped
1 can (16 ounces) no-salt-added tomatoes (with juice), cut up
1 can (8 ounces) no-salt-added tomato sauce
½ cup dry red wine or nonalcoholic red wine
½ cup water or clam juice
½ teaspoon dried basil
½ teaspoon dried thyme
½ teaspoon dried oregano
¼ teaspoon salt (optional)
¼ teaspoon ground black pepper
8 ounces skinless firm white fish, cut into 1" cubes
4 ounces crabmeat
4 ounces scallops or peeled and deveined shrimp, halved lengthwise

Coat a medium saucepan with olive oil no-stick spray. Add the oil and place over medium heat. Add the onions, celery, green peppers and garlic. Cook, stirring, for 3 minutes, or until the onions are tender.

Add the tomatoes (with juice), tomato sauce, wine, water or clam juice, basil, thyme, oregano, salt (if using) and black pepper. Bring to a boil, then reduce the heat. Cover and simmer for 30 minutes.

Add the fish, crabmeat and scallops or shrimp. Cover and simmer over medium-high heat about 10 minutes, or until the fish flakes easily when tested with a fork.

Children's Home Society of California

There's no place quite like California. What other state has sizzling deserts and snow-covered mountains; expansive swaths of sandy beach and turbulent stretches of rocky coast; vineyards, forests and fruit trees; cosmopolitan cities and sun-baked one-horse towns—all within its borders?

With obvious pride in its state, the Children's Home Society of California named its cookbook *Only in California* in celebration of the fascinating variety that characterizes California and its people. Variety, in fact, is something of a key word for the society.

This private, nonprofit child-welfare agency is one of the most diverse in the country, helping more than 10,000 children every year from one end of the Golden State to the other. Since the cookbook's first printing in 1989, the sale of some 65,000 copies has raised money for adoption, foster care, group-home care, family support and shelter-care services for California's children in need. A second book, *Celebrating California*, also helps provide funds for the agency's good works.

TEST KITCHEN TIP: If desired, you can make the soup ahead up through the point where it's simmered for 30 minutes. Cover and refrigerate for 1 to 2 days. To finish the soup, bring it back to a boil, add the seafood and continue with the recipe.

Makes 4 servings.

★ PER SERVING: 207 CALORIES, 2.8 G. TOTAL FAT, 0.4 G. SATURATED FAT, 70 MG. CHOLESTEROL, 359 MG. SODIUM

Spicy Shrimp-and-Corn Chowder

Adapted from *Cane River's Louisiana Living*
SERVICE LEAGUE OF NATCHITOCHES

For more shrimp flavor, you can use the shells from the shrimp to make a simple stock that will greatly enhance this chowder. (See the Test Kitchen Tip below.) Use it to replace the vegetable broth.

⅔ cup finely chopped onions
½ cup finely chopped celery
¼ cup finely chopped green peppers
¼ cup finely chopped carrots
2 cups reduced-sodium vegetable broth
1 cup peeled and diced potatoes
1 can (8½ ounces) reduced-sodium cream-style corn
¼ teaspoon ground black pepper
⅛–¼ teaspoon ground red pepper
1 bay leaf
2 tablespoons all-purpose flour
1 can (5 ounces) evaporated low-fat milk
12 ounces small shrimp, peeled and deveined
Hot-pepper sauce
2 slices turkey bacon, finely cut, cooked and drained

Lightly coat a large saucepan with no-stick spray. Add the onions, celery, green peppers, carrots and 3 tablespoons of the broth. Cook, stirring, over medium heat for 8 minutes, or until the vegetables are tender.

Stir in the potatoes, corn, black pepper, red pepper, bay leaf and the remaining broth. Bring to a boil, then reduce the heat. Cover and simmer for 10 minutes, or until the potatoes are just tender.

Place the flour in a small bowl. Gradually whisk in the milk. Stir into the saucepan.

Add the shrimp. Cook, stirring, for 1 to 3 minutes, or until the shrimp turn pink and the mixture begins to slightly thicken. Remove and discard the bay leaf. Season with the hot-pepper sauce.

Serve sprinkled with the bacon.

TEST KITCHEN TIP: To make shrimp stock, place the shells from 12 ounces of shrimp in a 4-quart saucepan. Add 2 cups water, 2 tablespoons chopped onions, 1 small carrot (chopped), 1 small stalk celery with leaves (chopped), 1 sprig fresh parsley, 1 sprig fresh thyme, 1 bay leaf, 2 teaspoons lemon juice and 4 black peppercorns. Bring to a boil, then reduce the heat. Cover and simmer for 20 minutes. Strain, discarding the solids. Store in the refrigerator for up to 2 days or freeze. Makes about 2 cups.

Makes 4 servings.

★PER SERVING: 226 CALORIES, 3.2 G. TOTAL FAT, 0.8 G. SATURATED FAT, 136 MG. CHOLESTEROL, 444 MG. SODIUM

....

NEW ENGLAND CLAM CHOWDER

Adapted from *Pass the Plate*
EPISCOPAL CHURCH WOMEN OF CHRIST CHURCH

The natural briny flavor of fresh clams swims through clearly in our lightened chowder base. Turkey bacon replaces salt pork, while evaporated skim milk stands in for the usual cream.

        2–3 cups chopped chowder clams
         ½ cup chopped onions
          4 slices turkey bacon, finely cut up
          2 medium potatoes, peeled and diced
            Pinch of dried thyme
            Pinch of ground black pepper
        1⅓ cups whole milk
          1 can (5 ounces) evaporated skim milk

Drain the clams and place the liquid in a 2-cup glass measuring cup. Add enough water to the liquid to make 2 cups. Set both the clams and the liquid aside.

In a medium saucepan over medium heat, sauté the onions and bacon for 5 minutes, or until the bacon is almost crisp.

Add the clam liquid, potatoes, thyme and pepper. Bring to a boil, then reduce the heat. Cover and simmer for 10 minutes, or until the potatoes are just tender.

Stir in the clams, whole milk and evaporated milk. Cook, stirring, just until heated through. (Do not boil.)

Makes 4 servings.

★PER SERVING: 295 CALORIES, 6.9 G. TOTAL FAT, 2.6 G. SATURATED FAT, 75 MG. CHOLESTEROL, 177 MG. SODIUM

SHRIMP GUMBO

Adapted from *The Plaid Platter*
GREENWICH ACADEMY

*A Louisiana gumbo's rich flavor depends on a dark roux, flour
that is browned with oil in a skillet. We cut calories while keeping
authentic flavor by browning the flour in the oven, without oil.*

  3 tablespoons all-purpose flour
  2 stalks celery with leaves, chopped
  ¼ cup chopped green peppers
  ¼ cup chopped onions
  2 tablespoons + 2½ cups water
  2 cans (13¾ ounces each) reduced-sodium beef broth,
    defatted
  1 can (16 ounces) cut okra, drained
  1 can (8 ounces) no-salt-added tomatoes (with juice), cut up
  3 tablespoons minced fresh parsley
  ¼ teaspoon dried thyme
  1 tablespoon Worcestershire sauce
3–4 drops hot-pepper sauce
  2 bay leaves
  ¼ teaspoon ground black pepper
  1 pound medium shrimp, peeled and deveined
2½ cups hot cooked rice

Preheat the oven to 400°. Place the flour in a pie plate. Bake,
stirring every 5 minutes, for 15 minutes, or until the flour turns
caramel in color. Set aside.

Lightly coat a large saucepan with no-stick spray. Add the celery,
green peppers, onions and 2 tablespoons of the water. Cook, stirring,
over medium heat for 8 minutes, or until the vegetables are tender.

Sprinkle with the browned flour. Then stir in the broth, okra,
tomatoes (with juice), parsley, thyme, Worcestershire sauce, hot-pepper sauce, bay leaves, black pepper and the remaining 2½ cups water.
Bring to a boil. Reduce the heat and simmer for 50 to 60 minutes.

Add the shrimp. Simmer for 1 minute, or until the shrimp turn
pink. Serve over the rice.

Makes 5 servings.

★ PER SERVING: 279 CALORIES, 1.5 G. TOTAL FAT, 0.4 G. SATURATED FAT,
  139 MG. CHOLESTEROL, 539 MG. SODIUM

TEXAS COWBOY STEW

Adapted from *The Authorized Texas Ranger Cookbook*
TEXAS RANGER MUSEUM AND HALL OF FAME

Hi ho, Silver! The Lean Ranger rides again in this rustic repast.
Serve it with a salad of mixed greens or tender spinach leaves.

1 small onion, chopped
¼ cup chopped green peppers
2 slices turkey bacon, finely cut up
12 ounces 95% lean ground beef
1 clove garlic, minced
2 medium potatoes, cubed
1 can (16 ounces) no-salt-added tomatoes (with juice),
   cut up
1 cup water
2 teaspoons chili powder
¼ teaspoon salt
   Pinch of ground black pepper
1 cup frozen whole-kernel corn

Lightly coat a large skillet with no-stick spray. Add the onions, green peppers and bacon. Cook, stirring, over medium heat for 5 minutes, or until the onions are tender.

Add the beef and garlic. Cook, stirring occasionally, until the beef is browned. Drain in a strainer or colander, then transfer the mixture to a large plate lined with paper towels. Blot the top of the mixture with additional paper towels.

Wipe out the skillet with paper towels and return the beef mixture to the skillet. Add the potatoes, tomatoes (with juice), water, chili powder, salt and black pepper. Bring to a boil, then reduce the heat. Cover and simmer for 10 minutes.

Stir in the corn. Cover and simmer for 15 minutes, or until the potatoes are tender.

Makes 4 servings.

★ PER SERVING: 279 CALORIES, 7.7 G. TOTAL FAT, 2.5 G. SATURATED FAT, 62 MG. CHOLESTEROL, 199 MG. SODIUM

Molasses Beef Stew

Adapted from *Beyond the Bay*
JUNIOR SERVICE LEAGUE OF PANAMA CITY

You can have your beef and eat it, too. This stew originally called for 1½ pounds of beef. We kept 1 pound for flavor and substituted chick-peas for the remainder. This change dramatically increased fiber while reducing both total fat and saturated fat.

¼ teaspoon ground ginger
¼ teaspoon celery salt
  Pinch of ground black pepper
1 pound top round steak, cut ¾" thick and trimmed of all visible fat
2 small onions, thinly sliced
1 can (8 ounces) no-salt-added tomatoes (with juice), cut up
1¼ cups water
¼ cup molasses
3 tablespoons red-wine vinegar
4 medium carrots, thinly sliced
1 cup rinsed and drained canned chick-peas
¼ cup raisins
3 cups hot cooked rice

In a cup, stir together the ginger, celery salt and pepper. Sprinkle half of the mixture on each side of the steak and rub it in well. Cut the meat into ¾" cubes.

Lightly coat a large skillet with no-stick spray. Add the beef. Cook, stirring, over medium-high heat for 5 minutes, or until the cubes are browned but not cooked through.

Add the onions, tomatoes (with juice), water, molasses and vinegar. Stir until combined. Bring to a boil, then reduce the heat. Cover and simmer for 20 minutes.

Stir in the carrots. Cover and simmer for 15 to 20 minutes, or until the carrots are tender. Stir in the chick-peas and raisins. Cover and simmer for 2 minutes. Serve over the rice.

Makes 6 servings.

★ PER SERVING: 355 CALORIES, 3.8 G. TOTAL FAT, 1.1 G. SATURATED FAT, 47 MG. CHOLESTEROL, 249 MG. SODIUM

White-Bean Chili with Turkey

Adapted from *What's Cooking in Delaware*
AMERICAN RED CROSS IN DELAWARE

Hot corn tortillas make a fine accompaniment to this Southwestern-style stew. To heat the tortillas, place an ungreased heavy skillet over medium-high heat and toast the tortillas for 1 to 2 minutes on each side. Keep them warm in a covered soufflé dish or bowl.

CILANTRO YOGURT

> 1 container (8 ounces) reduced-fat plain yogurt
> 2–3 tablespoons minced fresh cilantro
> 3 tablespoons minced fresh parsley

CHILI

> 1½ cups chopped onions
> 1 can (14½ ounces) reduced-sodium chicken broth, defatted
> 1 can (4½ ounces) diced green chili peppers, drained
> 2¼ teaspoons chili powder
> 2¼ teaspoons ground cumin
> 2¼ teaspoons dried oregano
> ½ teaspoon ground red pepper
> 4 large cloves garlic, minced
> 2 cans (15½ ounces each) Great Northern beans, rinsed and drained
> 1 can (11 ounces) tomatillos, coarsely chopped
> ½–¾ cup chopped fresh cilantro
> 2 cups cooked and cubed turkey breast
> ½ cup thinly sliced scallions
> 2 tablespoons fresh lime juice
> ¼ teaspoon ground black pepper
> Finely shredded reduced-fat Cheddar cheese (optional)

TO MAKE THE CILANTRO YOGURT: In a small bowl, stir together the yogurt, cilantro and parsley. Cover and refrigerate for at least 6 hours before serving to blend the flavors.

TO MAKE THE CHILI: Lightly coat a Dutch oven or large saucepan with no-stick spray. Add the onions and 2 tablespoons of the broth. Cook, stirring, over medium heat for 5 minutes, or until the onions are tender.

(continued)

Add the chili peppers, chili powder, cumin, oregano, red pepper and garlic. Cook, stirring, for 5 minutes.

Stir in the beans, tomatillos, cilantro and the remaining broth. Bring to a boil. Add the turkey, scallions, lime juice and black pepper. Heat through, stirring occasionally.

Serve topped with dollops of the cilantro yogurt. Sprinkle with the Cheddar (if using).

TEST KITCHEN TIP: This is a large-quantity recipe that can also suit the needs of smaller families. Package small portions of the chili in freezer containers that are microwave-safe and freeze. Then, for a last-minute dinner or lunch, simply thaw and reheat the chili in the microwave.

Makes 6 servings.

★ PER SERVING: 298 CALORIES, 2.1 G. TOTAL FAT, 0.4 G. SATURATED FAT, 32 MG. CHOLESTEROL, 462 MG. SODIUM

MEAT: THE MAIN DISHES
....

Deep-Dish Taco Squares

Adapted from *Cooks Extraordinaires*
SERVICE LEAGUE OF GREEN BAY

When buying ground beef, choose the leanest available. Most supermarkets carry 95% lean, and sometimes you can even find 97% lean. If your market labels the beef by the cut (for example, ground round), ask someone in the meat department to help you select the leanest type.

8 ounces 95% lean ground beef
½ cup fat-free sour cream
½ cup shredded reduced-fat Cheddar cheese
⅓ cup fat-free mayonnaise
1 tablespoon finely chopped onions
¼ teaspoon garlic powder
⅛ teaspoon ground cumin
1 cup reduced-fat all-purpose biscuit mix
¼ cup cold water
1–2 medium tomatoes, thinly sliced
½ cup chopped green peppers
Paprika

Preheat the oven to 375°. Lightly coat an 8″ × 8″ baking pan with no-stick spray; set aside.

Crumble the beef into a large skillet. Place over medium heat. Cook, stirring, until the beef is browned. Drain in a strainer or colander, then transfer the beef to a large plate lined with paper towels. Blot the top of the beef with additional paper towels.

In a small bowl, stir together the sour cream, Cheddar, mayonnaise, onions, garlic powder and cumin. Set aside.

In another small bowl, stir together the biscuit mix and water until a soft dough forms. Using floured fingers, pat the dough into the prepared pan, pressing it ½″ up the sides. Spread the beef evenly over the dough. Top with the tomatoes, then the peppers.

Spoon the sour cream mixture over top. Sprinkle with paprika. Bake for 25 to 30 minutes, or until the edges of the dough are golden.

Makes 6 servings.

★ PER SERVING: 185 CALORIES, 4 G. TOTAL FAT, 1.4 G. SATURATED FAT, 28 MG. CHOLESTEROL, 657 MG. SODIUM

....

HEADQUARTERS HASH

Adapted from *The Authorized Texas Ranger Cookbook*
TEXAS RANGER MUSEUM AND HALL OF FAME

*Historically, Texas Rangers were required to ride, shoot and cook
so they could be self-sufficient. No need for home cooks to meet
rigorous Rangers' criteria. This recipe is so easy you can whip it
up quickly, then just eat and enjoy.*

> 1 pound 95% lean ground beef
> 3 medium onions, sliced
> 1 large green pepper, chopped
> 1 can (14½ ounces) no-salt-added tomatoes (with juice),
>   cut up
> 1 cup water
> ½ cup long-grain white rice
> 2 teaspoons chili powder
> ½ teaspoon salt
> ¼ teaspoon ground black pepper

Preheat the oven to 350°. Lightly coat a 2-quart casserole with
no-stick spray; set aside.

Crumble the beef into a large skillet. Place over medium heat.
Cook, stirring, until the beef is browned. Use a slotted spoon to remove the beef from the skillet and place it on a large plate lined with
paper towels. Blot the top of the beef with additional paper towels.

Using the same skillet, cook the onions and green peppers for 10
minutes, or until the vegetables are tender; drain well.

Wipe out the skillet with paper towels and return the beef and
vegetables to the skillet. Stir in the tomatoes (with juice), water, rice,
chili powder, salt and black pepper. Heat through. Spoon the beef
mixture into the prepared casserole. Cover and bake for 1 hour, or
until the rice is tender, stirring twice during this time.

Makes 6 servings.

★ PER SERVING: 208 CALORIES, 4.1 G. TOTAL FAT, 1.3 G. SATURATED FAT,
   48 MG. CHOLESTEROL, 233 MG. SODIUM

ROMA MEAT ROLL

Adapted from *Cajun Men Cook*
BEAVER CLUB OF LAFAYETTE

We based this recipe on lean pork top loin and ground it ourselves. You can use either an old-fashioned hand-cranked meat grinder or a food processor to grind the pork.

　　1　can (8 ounces) no-salt-added tomato sauce
　1⅛　teaspoons dried oregano
　　1　pound 95% lean ground beef
　　8　ounces boneless pork top loin, ground
　½　cup finely chopped onions
　⅓　cup low-sodium saltine crackers crushed to fine crumbs
　¼　cup fat-free egg substitute
　½　teaspoon salt
　¼　teaspoon ground black pepper
　　1　cup shredded reduced-fat mozzarella cheese

Preheat the oven to 350°.

In a small bowl, mix ¾ cup of the tomato sauce and ⅛ teaspoon of the oregano. Set aside.

In a medium bowl, combine the beef, pork, onions, cracker crumbs, egg substitute, salt, pepper, the remaining tomato sauce and the remaining 1 teaspoon oregano until well-mixed.

On a piece of foil about 14″ long, form the meat mixture into a 12″ × 10″ rectangle. Spread the mozzarella on top of the meat, keeping it ½″ from the edges. Beginning from a short side, gently lift the foil to roll up the meat and cheese, jelly-roll fashion, into a tight roll. Press the ends together to seal in the cheese.

Lightly coat a 13″ × 9″ baking pan with no-stick spray. Carefully transfer the meat roll, seam side down, to the dish. Cover with foil and bake for 30 minutes.

Remove the foil. Pour off any excess fat. Spoon the remaining tomato sauce over the meat roll and bake for 30 minutes, or until the meat is no longer pink. Let stand for 5 minutes before slicing.

Makes 6 servings.

★ PER SERVING: 244 CALORIES, 8.8 G. TOTAL FAT, 2.1 G. SATURATED FAT, 72 MG. CHOLESTEROL, 397 MG. SODIUM

MUSHROOM SWISS STEAK

Adapted from *Country Treasures*
VIRGINIA FARM BUREAU

It was easy to trim fat without trimming flavor from this homestyle dish. We used minimal oil to brown the meat and opted for cream of mushroom soup that was 97% fat-free instead of the regular version of the soup.

1 boneless beef round steak (1¼ pounds), cut ½" thick and trimmed of all visible fat
1 teaspoon olive oil
¼ teaspoon ground black pepper
6 slices onion
1 can (10¾ ounces) low-fat, reduced-sodium condensed cream of mushroom soup

Preheat the oven to 350°.

Using a meat mallet, pound the beef until about ¼" thick; cut it into 6 equal pieces.

In a large no-stick skillet over medium heat, warm the oil. Add the beef and cook for 2 minutes. Turn the pieces over and cook for 2 minutes more, or until browned.

Transfer the beef to an 11" × 7" baking pan. Sprinkle with the pepper. Top each meat piece with an onion slice. Spoon the soup over the meat. Cover and bake for 50 to 60 minutes, or until the meat is tender.

TEST KITCHEN TIP: For a colorful garnish, sprinkle a little chopped fresh parsley over each serving of meat.

Makes 6 servings.

★ PER SERVING: 173 CALORIES, 6.1 G. TOTAL FAT, 1.6 G. SATURATED FAT, 62 MG. CHOLESTEROL, 254 MG. SODIUM

FILET CHARLEMAGNE

Adapted from *A Taste of Aloha*
JUNIOR LEAGUE OF HONOLULU

For a healthful menu, start with 4 ounces of uncooked beef tenderloin per person and serve this entrée with generous portions of steamed asparagus and a wild rice pilaf.

SEASONED STEAKS
¼ teaspoon salt
¼ teaspoon dried rosemary
¼ teaspoon dried thyme
¼ teaspoon ground black pepper
4 beef tenderloin steaks (4 ounces each), cut ½″–¾″ thick

CHARLEMAGNE SAUCE
1½ teaspoons tub-style reduced-calorie margarine
8 ounces small mushrooms, quartered
¼ cup dry white wine or nonalcoholic white wine
1 tablespoon lemon juice
1 tablespoon cornstarch
¼ cup skim milk
1 can (5 ounces) evaporated skim milk
⅛ teaspoon salt
Pinch of ground black pepper

TO MAKE THE SEASONED STEAKS: Preheat the broiler.

In a cup, stir together the salt, rosemary, thyme and pepper. Sprinkle evenly over both sides of the steak pieces and rub in well.

Coat the rack of a broiling pan with no-stick spray. Place the steaks on the rack. Broil 4″ from the heat for 5 minutes. Turn the steaks over and broil for 5 minutes for rare doneness. If necessary, cover the steaks to keep them warm while preparing the sauce.

TO MAKE THE CHARLEMAGNE SAUCE: While the steak is cooking, melt the margarine in a medium saucepan. Add the mushrooms, wine and lemon juice. Cook over medium-high heat, stirring occasionally, for 5 minutes, or until the mushrooms are tender. Using a slotted spoon, remove the mushrooms, reserving the cooking liquid, and set aside.

In a small bowl, whisk together the cornstarch and skim milk. Slowly stir the mixture into the liquid remaining in the skillet. Stir in the evaporated milk.

Junior League of Honolulu

When most of us think of Hawaii, we daydream about sunshine, jagged volcanic mountains rising from crystal-clear water and the fragrance of exotic flowers on a warm breeze. The women of the Junior League of Honolulu appreciate those beautiful facets of Hawaii just as much as visitors do. But after the visitors have gone home, the steadfast women of the League turn their attention to the many people in their community who need help.

It may be hard to imagine that there is suffering in such a paradise as Honolulu. But this active Junior League has a firm grip on reality and uses proceeds from the sale of its book to support programs to end domestic violence and to promote positive parenting.

Since 1983, the League has sold nearly 125,000 copies of *A Taste of Aloha*, which salutes the diversity of those who make Hawaii their home. Recipes feature all the fresh seafoods, vegetables and fruits of the islands, of course. But the book is liberally sprinkled with Asian, European and even Yankee influences as well.

Cook, stirring, over medium heat until the mixture begins to thicken and just comes to a boil. Reduce the heat to low. Cook, stirring, for 2 minutes.

Stir in the mushrooms, salt and pepper. Serve the sauce over the steaks.

Makes 4 servings.

★ PER SERVING: 233 CALORIES, 8.7 G. TOTAL FAT, 3 G. SATURATED FAT, 66 MG. CHOLESTEROL, 315 MG. SODIUM

POT ROAST WITH APPLE CIDER

Adapted from *Cooking in the Litchfield Hills*
PRATT NATURE CENTER

Originally, this recipe, like most pot roast recipes, called for browning the meat in 2 tablespoons oil. Instead, we broiled the meat to caramelize the savory juices without adding a drop of fat.

  1   boneless beef chuck pot roast (2 pounds), trimmed of all visible fat
  1   large onion, sliced
  8   whole cloves
  1   piece (1″ thick) fresh ginger, peeled and sliced
  2   cinnamon sticks
  ½   teaspoon salt
  2   cups cider or apple juice
8–10   small red or white potatoes
  1   bag (16 ounces) frozen baby onions
 16   baby carrots

Place the pot roast, onion slices, cloves, ginger, cinnamon sticks and salt in a large resealable plastic bag. Pour in the cider or apple juice. Seal the bag, place in a large bowl and refrigerate for 12 to 24 hours, turning the bag over once. Remove the meat from the bag, reserving the marinade and onions. Pat the meat dry with paper towels.

Preheat the broiler. Coat the rack of a broiling pan with no-stick spray. Place the roast on the rack. Broil 4″ from the heat for 5 minutes. Turn the roast over and broil for 5 minutes, or until the surface is browned. Transfer to a Dutch oven.

Add the reserved marinade. Bring to a boil, then reduce the heat to medium-low. Cover and cook for 40 minutes. Add the potatoes, baby onions and carrots. Cover and cook for 50 minutes, or until the meat and vegetables are tender.

Remove the meat and vegetables to a warm platter. Bring the pan juices to a boil; cook and stir until reduced by about half.

Thinly slice the meat. Serve with the pan juices.

Makes 8 servings.

★ PER SERVING: 340 CALORIES, 8.4 G. TOTAL FAT, 3.1 G. SATURATED FAT, 82 MG. CHOLESTEROL, 207 MG. SODIUM

MARINATED FILET MIGNON

Adapted from *Family Creations*
GLADNEY FUND VOLUNTEER AUXILIARIES

If you're eating less beef these days, why not treat yourself to the best when you do indulge? Lean tenderloin fits the bill perfectly. Here, it's enhanced with an herb-and-mustard vinaigrette.

1 beef tenderloin (3 pounds), trimmed of all visible fat
1 onion, thinly sliced
⅓ cup dry red wine or nonalcoholic red wine
¼ cup chopped fresh basil
2 tablespoons olive oil
1½ tablespoons ground black pepper
1½ tablespoons dried thyme
1 tablespoon Dijon mustard
2 large cloves garlic, minced

Place the beef in a long, shallow casserole or dish.

In a medium bowl, combine the onions, wine, basil, oil, pepper, thyme, mustard and garlic. Pour over the beef. Cover with plastic wrap and refrigerate for at least 3 hours (or up to 24 hours), turning and basting several times.

Preheat the oven to 400°.

Remove the beef from the marinade and place in a roasting pan; discard the marinade. Roast for 35 minutes, or until the beef reaches an internal temperature of 140° for rare meat; turn and baste the beef in its own juices several times as it roasts. (If desired, continue roasting to an internal temperature of 160° for medium.)

Remove from the oven and let stand for 15 minutes before slicing.

Makes 8 servings.

★ **PER SERVING:** 254 CALORIES, 12 G. TOTAL FAT, 4.4 G. SATURATED FAT, 96 MG. CHOLESTEROL, 81 MG. SODIUM

MEATBALL STROGANOFF

Adapted from *A Place Called Hope*
JUNIOR AUXILIARY OF HOPE

Here's a streamlined version of an old family favorite.

> 1 pound 95% lean ground beef
> ½ cup reduced-fat cracker crumbs
> ¼ cup reduced-sodium ketchup
> ¼ cup finely chopped onions
> ½ teaspoon salt
> ½ teaspoon pepper
> 1½ cups evaporated skim milk
> 3 teaspoons reduced-sodium Worcestershire sauce
> 2 tablespoons all-purpose flour
> 1 tablespoon canola oil
> 1 can (10¾ ounces) low-fat, reduced-sodium condensed cream of mushroom soup
> 1 tablespoon vinegar
> 4½ cups hot cooked no-yolk egg noodles

In a medium bowl, combine the beef, cracker crumbs, ketchup, onions, salt, pepper, ½ cup of the milk and 2 teaspoons of the Worcestershire sauce. Shape the mixture into 18 meatballs. Place the flour in a shallow dish; roll the meatballs in the flour to coat.

Coat a large no-stick skillet with no-stick spray. Add the oil and place over medium heat. Add the meatballs and cook, turning them occasionally, for 10 minutes, or until browned on all sides.

In a medium bowl, whisk together the soup, vinegar, the remaining 1 cup milk and the remaining 1 teaspoon Worcestershire sauce. Add the mixture to the skillet. Cook until the sauce is hot; do not boil. Serve the meatballs and sauce over the noodles.

Makes 6 servings.

★ PER SERVING: 453 CALORIES, 13.9 G. TOTAL FAT, 3.9 G. SATURATED FAT, 87 MG. CHOLESTEROL, 644 MG. SODIUM

Apple-Orchard Pork Chops

Adapted from *Cooks Extraordinaires*
SERVICE LEAGUE OF GREEN BAY

The pork you buy today is more than 30% lower in fat than the pork that was available a decade ago. Pork sirloin chops are the leanest choice for this recipe, but if you can't find that cut, choose pork loin chops. They will add slightly more than 1 gram of additional fat per serving.

　4　boneless pork sirloin chops (about 4 ounces each), trimmed of all visible fat
　　Ground black pepper
⅔　cup cider or apple juice
　2　tablespoons Dijon mustard
　2　tart cooking apples, cored and sliced ¼" thick
½　cup raisins
½　cup thinly sliced scallions
　3　tablespoons cold water
　2　teaspoons cornstarch

Coat a large skillet with no-stick spray. Place over medium-high heat. Add the pork and brown on both sides. Sprinkle with the pepper.

In a small bowl, stir together the cider or apple juice and mustard; pour over the pork. Cover and cook over low heat for 5 minutes.

Add the apples, raisins and scallions to the skillet. Cover and cook for 5 minutes. Use a slotted spoon to transfer the pork and apples to a serving platter; keep warm. Leave the skillet on the heat.

In a small bowl, stir together the water and cornstarch. Add to the skillet, raise the heat to medium and bring to a boil, stirring constantly. Reduce the heat and cook for 2 minutes. Serve over the pork chops and apples.

Makes 4 servings.

★ PER SERVING: 261 CALORIES, 8.2 G. TOTAL FAT, 2.6 G. SATURATED FAT, 51 MG. CHOLESTEROL, 144 MG. SODIUM

SWEET-AND-SOUR PORK

Adapted from *Cotton Country Cooking*
JUNIOR LEAGUE OF MORGAN COUNTY

The secret to stir-frying with no-stick spray instead of oil is to keep the food in perpetual motion. Use a wooden spoon or a metal stir-fry spatula to gently toss the pieces during cooking.

1 can (20 ounces) pineapple chunks (packed in juice)
¼ cup packed brown sugar
2 tablespoons cornstarch
¼ teaspoon ground ginger
¼ cup vinegar
2 tablespoons reduced-sodium soy sauce
1½ pounds boneless pork top loin, trimmed of all visible fat
2 green peppers, thinly sliced
1 large onion, thinly sliced
¼ cup water
3 cups hot cooked rice

Drain the pineapple, reserving the juice.

In a small bowl, stir together the sugar, cornstarch and ginger. Stir in the vinegar, soy sauce and the reserved pineapple juice. Set aside.

Thinly slice the pork against the grain into bite-size pieces.

Coat a wok or large skillet with no-stick spray. Place over medium-high heat. Add the pork and stir-fry for 2 minutes. Add the peppers, onions and water; stir-fry for 3 minutes, or until the pork is no longer pink and the vegetables are crisp-tender.

Give the soy mixture a stir, then add it to the pan. Cook, stirring, just until thickened. Stir in the pineapple chunks. Heat through. Serve with the rice.

Makes 6 servings.

★ PER SERVING: 390 CALORIES, 7.8 G. TOTAL FAT, 2.6 G. SATURATED FAT, 51 MG. CHOLESTEROL, 223 MG. SODIUM

Junior League of Morgan County

Since the early 1940s the women of the Junior League of Morgan County have been helping people in their corner of northern Alabama. Children, particularly, hold a special place in their hearts. The members have originated or sponsored numerous programs for children and families over the years. One of their greatest achievements is Parents and Children Together, a county-wide child-abuse-prevention program.

For its latest fund-raiser, *Cotton Country Cooking*, the League wisely focuses on its wealth of local culinary traditions. This heart-of-the-South cooking heritage is captured in the "Southern Hospitality" chapter, which features recipes from talented professional and home cooks of this fertile Tennessee River Valley.

By sharing their delicious ways in *Cotton Country Cooking*, the League raises funds for HANDS (Home for Adolescents in Need of Direction and Supervision), a program that will open a residence for preadolescent and teenage girls in need of short-term shelter from a neglectful or abusive home.

PORK CHOP DINNER

Adapted from *Emory Seasons*
EMORY UNIVERSITY WOMAN'S CLUB

Peeled navel oranges, sliced with a serrated knife, make a refreshing garnish for this family-style casserole.

4	boneless pork sirloin chops (about 4 ounces each), trimmed of all visible fat
¾	cup long-grain white rice
1	can (10¾ ounces) low-fat, reduced-sodium condensed cream of chicken soup
1½	cups water
¼	cup chopped fresh parsley
¼	teaspoon ground black pepper
2	cups sliced mushrooms
½	medium onion, sliced

Preheat the oven to 350°. Coat an 8″ × 8″ baking pan with no-stick spray; set aside.

Coat a large skillet with no-stick spray. Place over medium-high heat. Add the pork and brown on both sides. Transfer to the prepared baking pan.

In a medium bowl, stir together the rice, soup, water, parsley and pepper. Pour over the pork. Top with the mushrooms and onions. Cover and bake for 60 to 65 minutes, or until the rice is tender.

Makes 4 servings.

★ PER SERVING: 386 CALORIES, 12.8 G. TOTAL FAT, 3.9 G. SATURATED FAT, 79 MG. CHOLESTEROL, 386 MG. SODIUM

OUR CAUSE

Emory University Woman's Club

If the Emory University campus in Atlanta, Georgia, can be compared with a stately oak tree, it was a mere acorn back in January 1919, when the Emory University Woman's Club formed.

The club established itself to foster social interaction among the faculty and provide service to the university. In the 77 years since, the club has exceeded expectations, growing with the school to contribute to scores of diverse projects. It established a wildflower trail to help fund university libraries, donated Christmas gifts to Children's Medical Services of Georgia and, in 1984, endowed a scholarship called the Emory Woman's Club Memorial Award in Graduate Research.

The scope of club projects mirrors the diversity of Emory University, which welcomes students, staff and faculty from 90 countries. That diversity deliciously repeats itself in *Emory Seasons*, the club's collection of recipes. Menus were developed by Epicurean, an on-campus caterer housed in the historic Houston Mill House, which was, not surprisingly, refurbished by the Woman's Club. The club plans to donate profits from the cookbook to the university's endowment fund.

Stir-Fried Pork with Broccoli and Sesame

Adapted from *The Summerhouse Sampler*
HISTORIC WYNNTON SCHOOL

Pork tenderloin is not only the leanest pork cut available in the market but also the most convenient. Use a Chinese cleaver or a heavy chef's knife to cut it up for stir-frying.

2 tablespoons cornstarch
1 can (14½ ounces) reduced-sodium chicken broth, defatted
1 tablespoon reduced-sodium soy sauce
1 tablespoon canola oil
1 pork tenderloin (1 pound), trimmed of all visible fat and cut into bite-size pieces
4 scallions, sliced
1 clove garlic, minced
1 head broccoli, cut into bite-size pieces
2 tablespoons sesame seeds
4 cups hot cooked rice

In a 2-cup glass measuring cup, whisk the cornstarch with ¼ cup of the broth until smooth. Stir in the soy sauce and the remaining broth. Set aside.

In a wok or large skillet, warm the oil over medium-high heat. Add the pork, scallions and garlic; stir-fry for 3 to 4 minutes, or until the pork is browned and no pink remains. Transfer the pork mixture to a dish and set aside.

Add the broccoli to the pan. Stir-fry for 2 to 3 minutes, or until the color deepens. Add the broth mixture. Cook, tossing occasionally, for 2 to 3 minutes, or until the broccoli is crisp-tender.

Return the pork mixture to the pan. Cook until heated through. Sprinkle with the sesame seeds. Serve with the rice.

Makes 4 servings.

★ PER SERVING: 509 CALORIES, 7.6 G. TOTAL FAT, 2 G. SATURATED FAT, 81 MG. CHOLESTEROL, 453 MG. SODIUM

CHERRY-SAUCED PORK CHOPS

Adapted from *Bay Leaves*
JUNIOR SERVICE LEAGUE OF PANAMA CITY

Team this tasty pork dish with hot cooked brown rice. You'll have plenty of the tart-sweet sauce to serve over both the chops and the rice.

- 1 can (16 ounces) tart red cherries
- ¼ cup packed brown sugar
- 2 tablespoons cornstarch
- 6 boneless pork sirloin chops (about 4 ounces each), trimmed of all visible fat
- ¼ teaspoon salt
- ¼ teaspoon ground black pepper

Drain the cherries, reserving the juice. Add enough water to the juice to make 1 cup.

In a medium saucepan, stir together the brown sugar and cornstarch. Stir in the cherry juice. Cook, stirring, over medium heat until the mixture begins to thicken and just comes to a boil. Stir in the cherries. Set aside.

Coat a large skillet with no-stick spray. Place over medium-high heat. Add the pork and brown on both sides. Sprinkle with the salt and pepper. Spoon the cherry mixture over the chops. Bring to a boil. Reduce the heat to low. Cover and cook for 5 to 6 minutes, or until the pork is no longer pink in the center when tested with a sharp knife.

Makes 6 servings.

★ PER SERVING: 207 CALORIES, 7.4 G. TOTAL FAT, 2.6 G. SATURATED FAT, 51 MG. CHOLESTEROL, 136 MG. SODIUM

Marinated Pork Loin

Adapted from *Cranbrook Reflections*
CRANBROOK HOUSE AND GARDENS AUXILIARY

*Don't be put off by the long cooking time for this delicious roast.
Because all the prep work is done the night or morning before,
the roast takes care of itself at dinnertime, freeing you for other
activities.*

> 2 cloves garlic, minced
> 2 tablespoons chopped fresh parsley
> 1 tablespoon Dijon mustard
> 1 tablespoon water
> 2 teaspoons dried thyme
> 2 teaspoons dried basil
> 2 teaspoons sugar
> 1 teaspoon vinegar
> ¼ teaspoon salt
> ⅛ teaspoon ground red pepper
> 1 boneless pork top loin roast (2 pounds), trimmed of all
>   visible fat

In a small bowl, stir together the garlic, parsley, mustard, water, thyme, basil, sugar, vinegar, salt and pepper.

Place the pork in a pie plate. Spread evenly with the garlic mixture. Cover and refrigerate for 12 to 24 hours.

Preheat the oven to 325°. Coat a roasting rack with no-stick spray and place the rack in a roasting pan. Place the roast on the rack.

Roast for 1 hour, or until a meat thermometer inserted in the center registers 160°. Transfer the pork to a cutting board; cover with foil and let stand for 15 minutes before slicing.

Makes 6 servings.

★ **PER SERVING:** 192 CALORIES, 10.1 G. TOTAL FAT, 3.4 G. SATURATED FAT, 68 MG. CHOLESTEROL, 176 MG. SODIUM

Cranbrook House and Gardens Auxiliary

In 1904 George Gough Booth, publisher of the *Detroit Evening News,* and his wife, Ellen, bought a neglected farm in Bloomfield Hills, Michigan. The Booths, patrons of the Arts and Crafts Movement, filled Cranbrook House (as they named their home) with sculptures, weavings and other works of fine artisans and craftspeople. The rambling house was beautiful enough, but it was the 40 acres of land with gardens like a fantasy that gave the estate its fame.

The Booths passed away in the late 1940s, and the house and grounds fell into disrepair. In 1971 Henry Scripps Booth, the youngest of the Booths' five children, formed the Cranbrook House and Gardens Auxiliary, a volunteer organization dedicated to the restoration and preservation of the Booth home and gardens. That's when the estate began its journey back to its glory days.

Today, the house and gardens are open to the public through tours, special events and community gatherings. Visitors can enjoy the estate's beauty year-round, from the colorful spring blooms to the snow-covered winter landscape. Especially impressive is Daffodil Hill, planted by the Booths' grandchildren on the couple's 50th wedding anniversary.

The Auxiliary's creation, *Cranbrook Reflections*, is as much a coffee-table book as it is a cookbook. Along with the recipes featuring Michigan-grown foods, it is a treasury of color photographs of the estate. Proceeds from sales of the book help continue the work of the Auxiliary.

LAMB CURRY

Adapted from *West of the Rockies*
JUNIOR SERVICE LEAGUE OF GRAND JUNCTION

This spicy Indian recipe calls for celeriac, which is another name for celery root. If you don't have any, substitute ¾ cup chopped potatoes.

       1 large onion, chopped
    1½ pounds boneless leg of lamb or lamb loin, trimmed of all
          visible fat and cut into 1" cubes
       2 tablespoons curry powder
       2 cans (14½ ounces each) reduced-sodium chicken broth,
          defatted
       4 ounces celeriac, peeled and diced
       4 tomatoes, peeled, seeded and diced
       3 tart cooking apples, peeled, cored and chopped
      ⅓ cup + 1 tablespoon all-purpose flour
       1 cup fat-free sour cream
       2 cups hot cooked rice
          Chutney

Coat a Dutch oven with no-stick spray. Place over medium heat. Add the onions and cook, stirring, for 3 minutes.

Raise the heat to medium-high. Add the lamb. Cook, stirring, until browned. Stir in the curry powder. Add 1 can of the broth, ¾ of the celeriac and ¾ of the tomatoes. Bring to a boil, then reduce the heat to low. Cover and simmer for 1 hour, or until the lamb is tender.

Stir in ⅔ of the apples, the remaining celeriac and the remaining tomatoes. Cover and cook for 2 minutes.

In a medium bowl, stir together the remaining 1 can broth and ⅓ cup of the flour. Stir into the lamb mixture. Cook, stirring, until the mixture begins to thicken. Cook, stirring, for 1 minute more.

In a small bowl, stir together the sour cream and the remaining 1 tablespoon flour. Then stir the sour cream mixture into the lamb mixture. Cook, stirring, just until heated through.

Serve with the rice, chutney and the remaining apples.

Makes 4 servings.

★ PER SERVING: 552 CALORIES, 9 G. TOTAL FAT, 2.9 G. SATURATED FAT,
86 MG. CHOLESTEROL, 616 MG. SODIUM

LAMB CHOPS WITH HERBS

Adapted from *Beyond the Bay*
JUNIOR SERVICE LEAGUE OF PANAMA CITY

To lower the fat in this extra-special entrée, we browned the chops using no-stick spray instead of a mixture of butter and oil and substituted half-and-half for heavy cream.

8 lamb loin chops (about 3 ounces each), trimmed of all
  visible fat
1 cup half-and-half
1 teaspoon dried basil
½ teaspoon dried chives
½ teaspoon dried rosemary
¼ teaspoon ground black pepper

Coat a large skillet with no-stick spray. Place over medium heat. Add the lamb and cook for 12 minutes, or until the lamb is browned on both sides and has just a hint of pink in the center. Transfer the lamb to a platter; cover with foil and keep warm.

Stir the half-and-half, basil, chives, rosemary and pepper into the skillet. Bring just to a boil over medium heat. Reduce the heat to medium-low. Cook, stirring, for 4 minutes, or until slightly thickened. Serve with the lamb.

Makes 4 servings.

★ **PER SERVING:** 223 CALORIES, 11.8 G. TOTAL FAT, 5.1 G. SATURATED FAT, 91 MG. CHOLESTEROL, 83 MG. SODIUM

ROAST LEG OF LAMB WITH HERB CRUST

Adapted from *Hospitality*
SALEM HOSPITAL AID ASSOCIATION

A flavorful herb rub and a crusty bread-crumb topping give this leg of lamb a company-special touch. We found that lemon juice rubbed on the lamb is an excellent replacement for the olive oil generally called for in a recipe of this type.

3 cloves garlic, minced
1 teaspoon dried rosemary
1 teaspoon dried thyme
½ teaspoon ground black pepper
¼ teaspoon salt
2 teaspoons lemon juice
1 boneless leg of lamb (3 pounds), trimmed of all visible fat, rolled and tied
½ cup fine dry plain bread crumbs
¼ cup minced fresh parsley
⅓ cup water
1 tablespoon olive oil

In a small bowl, stir together the garlic, rosemary, thyme, pepper and salt. Rub the lemon juice into the lamb. Spread the garlic mixture over the lamb. Cover and refrigerate for 3 to 4 hours.

Preheat the oven to 300°. Coat a roasting rack with no-stick spray and place the rack in a roasting pan. Place the lamb on the rack and roast for 1 hour.

In a small bowl, stir together the bread crumbs and parsley. Stir in the water and oil to make a paste. Using the back of a large spoon, spread the paste over the lamb.

Bake for 55 to 70 minutes, or until a meat thermometer registers 145° (medium-rare) to 160° (medium).

Makes 8 servings.

★ PER SERVING: 202 CALORIES, 8.5 G. TOTAL FAT, 2.6 G. SATURATED FAT, 74 MG. CHOLESTEROL, 170 MG. SODIUM

POULTRY ON PARADE

CHICKEN SPOON BREAD

Adapted from *300 Years of Carolina Cooking*
JUNIOR LEAGUE OF GREENVILLE

This creative casserole has the fluffy texture and slightly crusty top that are characteristic of spoon bread.

1 can (10¾ ounces) low-fat, reduced-sodium condensed cream of chicken soup
1 cup chopped cooked chicken breast
¾ cup skim milk
½ cup yellow cornmeal
¼ teaspoon salt
¼ teaspoon ground black pepper
1 tablespoon tub-style reduced-calorie margarine
2 egg whites

Preheat the oven to 325°. Coat a 1½-quart casserole with no-stick spray; set aside.

In a medium saucepan, stir together the soup, chicken, milk, cornmeal, salt and pepper. Cook, stirring, over medium-high heat until bubbly. Stir in the margarine. Remove from the heat and let stand at room temperature for 15 minutes.

Place the egg whites in a small bowl. Using an electric mixer, beat the egg whites on high speed until soft peaks form. Fold into the soup mixture. Spoon into the prepared casserole.

Bake for 40 to 45 minutes, or until a knife inserted in the center comes out clean.

Makes 4 servings.

★ PER SERVING: 176 CALORIES, 4.3 G. TOTAL FAT, 0.6 G. SATURATED FAT, 25 MG. CHOLESTEROL, 562 MG. SODIUM

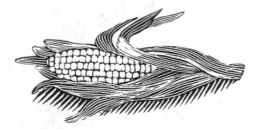

....

CHICKEN TORTILLA CASSEROLE

Adapted from *Holy Smoke*
PEACHTREE ROAD UNITED METHODIST CHURCH

To cut the fat, we used only half the cheese called for in the original recipe. You can trim the fat even further by substituting 2 cups of shredded reduced-fat mozzarella cheese for the Monterey Jack.

  1 can (10¾ ounces) low-fat, reduced-sodium condensed
    cream of chicken soup
  1 can (10¾ ounces) low-fat, reduced-sodium condensed
    cream of mushroom soup
1½ cups 2% low-fat milk
  1 can (7 ounces) green salsa
  1 small onion, finely chopped
  2 tablespoons defatted reduced-sodium chicken broth
  8 corn tortillas (6″ diameter)
  4 cups diced cooked chicken breast
  2 cups shredded Monterey Jack cheese

In a large bowl, stir together the cream of chicken soup, cream of mushroom soup, milk, salsa and onions.

Pour the broth into a 13″ × 9″ baking pan. Lay 4 of the tortillas in the dish. Spoon 2 cups of the chicken over the tortillas; top with half of the soup mixture. Repeat with the remaining tortillas, chicken and soup mixture. Cover and refrigerate for 4 to 24 hours.

Preheat the oven to 300°. Bake the casserole for 45 minutes, or until heated through. Sprinkle with the Monterey Jack; let stand for 5 minutes to melt the cheese.

TEST KITCHEN TIP: Vary the hotness in this spicy dish by choosing mild, medium or hot salsa to suit your taste.

Makes 6 servings.

★ PER SERVING: 452 CALORIES, 18.1 G. TOTAL FAT, 8.5 G. SATURATED FAT, 97 MG. CHOLESTEROL, 824 MG. SODIUM

COUNTRY CHICKEN PIE

Adapted from *Heart and Soul*
JUNIOR LEAGUE OF MEMPHIS

Nourish both heart and soul with this lightened version of chicken potpie. For a heart-healthy dish, we used margarine and canola oil in the crust rather than butter. And instead of heavy cream in the filling, we switched to skim milk enhanced with nonfat dry milk.

POTPIE FILLING

- 1 carrot, thinly cut on the diagonal
- 1 potato, peeled and cubed
- 1 onion, chopped
- ½ cup fresh or frozen peas
- 2 tablespoons cornstarch
- ¾ cup skim milk
- 1 can (10½ ounces) reduced-sodium chicken broth, defatted
- 2 tablespoons nonfat dry milk
- ½ teaspoon dried thyme
- ¼ teaspoon ground black pepper
- ¼ teaspoon salt
- ⅛ teaspoon ground sage or poultry seasoning
- 2 cups cubed cooked chicken breast

PASTRY

- 1 cup all-purpose flour
- 1 tablespoon stick margarine (not reduced-calorie)
- 2 tablespoons canola oil
- 4–6 teaspoons skim milk

TO MAKE THE POTPIE FILLING: Preheat the oven to 400°.

In a medium saucepan, combine the carrots, potatoes, onions, peas and a small amount of water. Cover and cook over medium heat for 10 minutes, or until crisp-tender. Drain and set aside.

In a medium saucepan, whisk together the cornstarch and ¼ cup of the skim milk until smooth. Then stir in the broth, dry milk, thyme, pepper, salt, sage or poultry seasoning and the remaining ½ cup skim milk. Cook, stirring, over medium heat until the mixture begins to thicken and just comes to a boil.

Add the chicken and reserved vegetables; heat through. Transfer the mixture to a shallow 1½-quart casserole or an 8″ × 8″ baking pan.

TO MAKE THE PASTRY: Place the flour in a small bowl. Using a pastry blender, cut in the margarine until the pieces are very fine.

In a custard cup, stir together the oil and 4 teaspoons of the milk. Drizzle the oil mixture over the flour mixture. Using a fork, toss and stir lightly until the dry ingredients are moistened. If necessary, add enough of the remaining 2 teaspoons milk to moisten. Then, using your hands, gently shape the mixture into a ball.

Place the ball of dough between two 12″-square pieces of wax paper. Gently roll out the dough to an 8″ circle or 9″ square to fit the size of the chosen baking pan. Remove the top piece of wax paper. Cut a few slits in the dough for the steam to escape. Carefully invert the dough on top of the filling. Remove the remaining piece of wax paper. Fold the edges of pastry under and flute them.

Bake for 25 to 30 minutes, or until the pastry is golden.

Makes 4 servings.

★ PER SERVING: 412 CALORIES, 12.2 G. TOTAL FAT, 1.8 G. SATURATED FAT, 49 MG. CHOLESTEROL, 410 MG. SODIUM

APPLE-GLAZED BARBECUED CHICKEN

Adapted from *From Generation to Generation*
SISTERHOOD OF TEMPLE EMANU-EL

Although all chicken is much leaner without the skin, skinless white meat has only about half the fat of skinless dark meat. That's why we chose chicken breast halves for this easy-to-prepare recipe.

  1 can (6 ounces) frozen apple juice concentrate, thawed
¼ cup reduced-sodium ketchup
  2 tablespoons packed brown sugar
  1 tablespoon cider vinegar
  1 teaspoon dried thyme
⅛ teaspoon hot-pepper sauce
  6 boneless, skinless chicken breast halves (4 ounces each)

In a small saucepan, combine the apple juice concentrate, ketchup, brown sugar, vinegar, thyme and hot-pepper sauce. Cook, stirring, over medium heat until the sugar completely dissolves. Remove from the heat and cool to room temperature.

Place the chicken in a single layer in a 13″ × 9″ baking pan. Pour about half of the cooled ketchup mixture over the chicken, turning once to coat both sides. Cover and refrigerate both the chicken and the remaining ketchup mixture for 4 to 24 hours.

Coat a grill rack with no-stick spray. Then light the grill according to the manufacturer's directions. Check the temperature for grilling; the temperature should be medium-hot (see the Test Kitchen Tip on the opposite page). Place the rack on the grill.

Remove the chicken from the ketchup mixture; discard whatever ketchup mixture remains in the baking pan. Coat the chicken pieces with no-stick spray and brush them with some of the remaining ketchup mixture.

Place the chicken on the rack and grill, uncovered, for 8 minutes. Turn the chicken over and brush with the remaining ketchup mixture. Grill for 7 to 10 minutes, or until the chicken is tender and cooked through. Discard any remaining ketchup mixture.

TEST KITCHEN TIP: When grilling, here's how to test the temperature of the coals: Place your hand 4″ above the heat source. Count the number of seconds that the palm of your hand can withstand the heat before you have to remove your hand. For a *hot* temperature, that should be 2 seconds. For a *medium-hot* temperature, it should be 3 seconds. *Medium* heat would be 4 seconds, and *low* would be 5 seconds.

To broil the chicken instead of grilling it, coat the rack of a broiling pan with no-stick spray. Remove the chicken from the ketchup mixture; discard whatever ketchup mixture remains in the baking pan. Coat the chicken pieces with no-stick spray and brush them with some of the remaining ketchup mixture.

Place the chicken on the rack. Broil 4″ from the heat for 5 minutes. Turn the chicken over and brush again with the remaining ketchup mixture. Broil for 4 to 6 minutes, or until the chicken is tender and cooked through. Discard any remaining ketchup mixture.

Makes 6 servings.

★ PER SERVING: 159 CALORIES, 2 G. TOTAL FAT, 0.6 G. SATURATED FAT, 46 MG. CHOLESTEROL, 122 MG. SODIUM

GRILLED LIME CHICKEN AND SALSA

Adapted from *Still Fiddling in the Kitchen*
NATIONAL COUNCIL OF JEWISH WOMEN

If you have salsa left over, use it as a dip for baked tortilla chips or as a topping for broiled fish.

    4 boneless, skinless chicken breast halves (4 ounces each)
    ¼ cup frozen apple juice concentrate, thawed
    ¼ cup + 1 teaspoon lime juice
    6 plum tomatoes, seeded and chopped
    ½ cup spicy vegetable juice
    ¼ cup chopped fresh cilantro
    4 scallions, finely chopped
    ¼ teaspoon salt
    ¼ teaspoon hot-pepper sauce

Place the chicken in a single layer in a shallow baking pan.

In a small bowl, stir together the apple juice concentrate and ¼ cup of the lime juice. Pour over the chicken. Cover and refrigerate for 4 to 24 hours.

In a medium bowl, stir together the tomatoes, vegetable juice, cilantro, scallions, salt, hot-pepper sauce and the remaining 1 teaspoon lime juice. Cover and refrigerate for at least 30 minutes.

Coat a grill rack with no-stick spray. Then light the grill according to the manufacturer's directions. Check the temperature for grilling; the temperature should be medium-hot (see the Test Kitchen Tip on page 111). Place the rack on the grill.

Remove the chicken from the marinade; discard the marinade. Place the chicken on the grill rack. Grill, uncovered, for 8 minutes. Turn the chicken over. Grill for 7 to 10 minutes, or until the chicken is tender and cooked through. Serve with the salsa.

TEST KITCHEN TIP: To broil the chicken instead of grilling it, coat the rack of a broiling pan with no-stick spray. Remove the chicken from the marinade and place on the rack. Broil 4″ from the heat for 5 minutes. Turn the chicken over. Broil for 4 to 6 minutes, or until the chicken is tender and cooked through.

Makes 4 servings.

★ PER SERVING: 139 CALORIES, 2.6 G. TOTAL FAT, 0.6 G. SATURATED FAT, 46 MG. CHOLESTEROL, 303 MG. SODIUM

Chicken Roll-Ups

Adapted from *Emory Seasons*
EMORY UNIVERSITY WOMAN'S CLUB

Emory Seasons notes that you can prepare the chicken rolls as much as 24 hours ahead and chill them in the refrigerator until cooking time.

> 4 boneless, skinless chicken breast halves (4 ounces each)
> 2 slices turkey bacon, halved crosswise
> ¼ cup pineapple juice
> 2 tablespoons Dijon mustard
> 1 tablespoon packed brown sugar

Starting at one of the narrow ends, roll up each chicken breast. Secure with a toothpick. Wrap a half-slice of bacon crosswise over the seam of each roll and secure the ends with a toothpick. Place the rolls in a pie plate.

In a small bowl, stir together the pineapple juice, mustard and brown sugar. Spoon over the chicken. Cover and refrigerate for 4 hours to blend the flavors.

Preheat the broiler. Coat the rack of a broiling pan with no-stick spray. Transfer the chicken to the rack, reserving the marinade. Broil 5″ from the heat for 8 minutes. Brush with the reserved marinade and broil for 5 to 7 minutes, or until the chicken is tender and cooked through. Discard any remaining marinade.

Makes 4 servings.

★ PER SERVING: 135 CALORIES, 3.7 G. TOTAL FAT, 0.9 G. SATURATED FAT, 50 MG. CHOLESTEROL, 144 MG. SODIUM

POLLO ARROLLADO

Adapted from *Sassafras! The Ozarks Cookbook*
JUNIOR LEAGUE OF SPRINGFIELD

The cook who contributed this recipe for chicken breasts stuffed with cheese and chili peppers described it as "chicken Kiev, Mexican-style." We cut the fat by using butter-flavored no-stick spray instead of melted butter to coat the chicken rolls.

¼ cup fine dry plain bread crumbs
2 tablespoons grated Parmesan cheese
1 tablespoon chili powder
¼ teaspoon garlic powder
¼ teaspoon ground cumin
¼ teaspoon ground black pepper
4 boneless, skinless chicken breast halves (4 ounces each)
1 can (4 ounces) whole green chili peppers, drained
2 ounces Monterey Jack cheese
½ cup taco sauce

In a shallow dish, combine the bread crumbs, Parmesan, chili powder, garlic powder, cumin and black pepper.

Place each chicken breast between 2 pieces of plastic wrap. Working from the center to the edges, lightly pound with the flat side of a meat mallet to ¼" thickness. Remove and discard the plastic wrap.

Cut the peppers into 4 equal pieces and remove the seeds. Cut the Monterey Jack into 4 sticks about 1½" × ½".

Place 1 pepper piece and 1 cheese stick on each breast. Roll up the chicken to enclose the filling. Coat the chicken with butter-flavored no-stick spray and roll in the bread-crumb mixture, coating evenly.

Place the chicken, seam side down, in an 8" × 8" baking pan. Coat the chicken again with no-stick spray. Cover and refrigerate for at least 4 hours or overnight.

Preheat the oven to 400°. Uncover the chicken and bake for 25 to 30 minutes, or until tender and cooked through. Serve with the taco sauce.

Junior League of Springfield

The Junior League of Springfield, Missouri, claims that the sassafras tree offers something for everyone, just like the Ozark Mountains where this native American tree flourishes. They might be right. Sassafras branches provide food for deer in spring, and the tree's ripe berries feed birds in autumn. Furniture crafters prize sassafras wood, and river rafters choose paddles hewn from sassafras. And what could be more bracing than a cup of sassafras tea?

As for the Ozark Mountains, they are a year-round natural wonder, with sparkling streams and lakes, lush forests, abundant wildlife and the famous morning mists.

If all this is true—as it no doubt is—then *Sassafras* is a perfect name for a book by the Junior League of Springfield. The League is as versatile as the Ozarks' sassafras—and so is its cookbook, *Sassafras! The Ozarks Cookbook*. The sixth edition of the book was printed on recycled paper, showing the League's commitment to preserving the beauty of its environment. Proceeds from the popular book support the many programs of the League.

TEST KITCHEN TIP: These crispy chicken rolls are equally tasty served with salsa or picante sauce instead of taco sauce. If sodium is a concern, opt for homemade sauce made with fresh tomatoes, hot chili peppers, lime juice and cilantro.

Makes 4 servings.

★ PER SERVING: 206 CALORIES, 8.5 G. TOTAL FAT, 3.9 G. SATURATED FAT, 61 MG. CHOLESTEROL, 700 MG. SODIUM

Oven Chicken Olé

Adapted from *Some Like It Hot*
JUNIOR LEAGUE OF MCALLEN

This chicken entrée satisfies both the eye and the palate. To make the serving size look more substantial, we folded the breasts in half to enclose the filling instead of rolling them up. Serve the chicken with a tossed salad or fat-free refried beans.

> 2 ounces light cream cheese, softened
> ⅓ cup thick mild picante sauce
> ½ cup sliced scallions
> 1 teaspoon ground cumin
> 4 boneless, skinless chicken breast halves (4 ounces each)
> ½ cup crushed no-oil, unsalted tortilla chips

Preheat the oven to 350°. Lightly coat an 8″ × 8″ baking pan with no-stick spray; set aside.

In a small bowl, stir together the cream cheese, picante sauce, scallions and cumin until well-combined.

Place each chicken breast between 2 pieces of plastic wrap. Working from the center to the edges, lightly pound with the flat side of a meat mallet to ¼″ thickness. Remove and discard the plastic wrap.

Place a heaping tablespoon of the sauce mixture in the center of each breast. Fold in half to enclose the sauce mixture. Secure with toothpicks.

Place the chicken in the prepared baking pan and top with the remaining sauce mixture. Bake for 30 minutes, or until the chicken is tender. Sprinkle with the chips before serving.

Makes 4 servings.

★ **PER SERVING:** 158 CALORIES, 5.4 G. TOTAL FAT, 2 G. SATURATED FAT, 51 MG. CHOLESTEROL, 289 MG. SODIUM

PARSLEY-PARMESAN CHICKEN

Adapted from *The Philadelphia Orchestra Cookbook*
WEST PHILADELPHIA COMMITTEE FOR THE PHILADELPHIA ORCHESTRA

Marinating the chicken in Italian salad dressing gives it a zippy herb flavor that complements the cheesy crumb coating. By using fat-free rather than regular salad dressing, we cut lots of fat but no flavor. For variety, use boneless, skinless chicken thighs and increase the baking time to 30 minutes.

6 boneless, skinless chicken breast halves (4 ounces each)
¼ cup fat-free Italian salad dressing
2 egg whites, lightly beaten
2 tablespoons water
½ cup fine dry plain bread crumbs
⅓ cup grated Parmesan cheese
2 tablespoons chopped fresh parsley
½ teaspoon paprika
½ teaspoon ground black pepper
¼ teaspoon salt

Place the chicken in a single layer in a 13" × 9" baking pan. Pour the dressing over the chicken. Cover and refrigerate for 1 hour, turning the pieces occasionally.

Preheat the oven to 400°. Line a jelly-roll pan with foil and coat with no-stick spray; set aside.

In a shallow dish, combine the egg whites and water.

In another shallow dish, combine the bread crumbs, Parmesan, parsley, paprika, pepper and salt.

Drain the chicken; discard the marinade. Dip the pieces first in the egg-white mixture, then in the bread-crumb mixture to coat well. Transfer to the prepared pan. Bake for 20 minutes, or until the chicken is tender and cooked through.

Makes 6 servings.

★ PER SERVING: 158 CALORIES, 4 G. TOTAL FAT, 1.7 G. SATURATED FAT, 50 MG. CHOLESTEROL, 333 MG. SODIUM

COUNTRY CAPTAIN CHICKEN

Adapted from *Savoring the Southwest*
ROSWELL SYMPHONY GUILD

To keep the fat and sodium low, cook the rice according to package directions but don't add any salt, butter, margarine or oil. Start with 1 cup uncooked long-grain white rice to get 3 cups cooked rice.

2½–3 pounds chicken pieces, skin removed
⅛ teaspoon ground black pepper
⅛ teaspoon + ¼ teaspoon salt
2 teaspoons olive oil
1 green pepper, chopped
1 onion, finely chopped
1 clove garlic, minced
¼ cup water
1 can (14½ ounces) no-salt-added tomatoes (with juice), cut up
1 tablespoon curry powder
1 teaspoon dried thyme
1 teaspoon dried parsley
¼ cup currants or raisins
1 tablespoon toasted and chopped blanched almonds
3 cups hot cooked rice

Preheat the oven to 350°. Coat a 13″ × 9″ baking pan with no-stick spray; set aside.

Lightly sprinkle the chicken with the black pepper and ⅛ teaspoon of the salt.

Place 1 teaspoon of the oil in a large no-stick skillet and warm over medium-high heat. Add half of the chicken pieces and cook for 2 to 3 minutes, or until lightly brown on all sides. Transfer to the prepared dish. Repeat with the remaining 1 teaspoon oil and the remaining chicken.

In a large saucepan, combine the green peppers, onions, garlic and water. Bring to a boil over high heat, then reduce the heat to low. Cover and simmer for 2 minutes. Remove from the heat. Stir in the tomatoes (with juice), curry powder, thyme, parsley and the remaining ¼ teaspoon salt. Spoon the tomato mixture over the chicken.

Cover and bake for 50 to 55 minutes, or until the chicken is tender and cooked through. Place the chicken and tomato mixture on a serving platter. Sprinkle with the currants or raisins and almonds. Serve with the rice.

Makes 4 servings.

★ PER SERVING: 504 CALORIES, 11.8 G. TOTAL FAT, 2.6 G. SATURATED FAT, 112 MG. CHOLESTEROL, 316 MG. SODIUM

JAN'S CHICKEN CASSEROLE

Adapted from *The Take Care Cookbook*
MID-FAIRFIELD HOSPICE

Look for individually wrapped slices of reduced-fat Swiss cheese alongside other sliced cheeses in the dairy case of your supermarket.

    8 boneless, skinless chicken breast halves (4 ounces each)
    4 slices (¾ ounce each) reduced-fat Swiss cheese, halved
    1 can (10¾ ounces) low-fat, reduced-sodium condensed
      cream of chicken soup
    ½ cup dry white wine or nonalcoholic white wine
    2 cups reduced-sodium stuffing mix
    ½ cup defatted reduced-sodium chicken broth

Preheat the oven to 350°.

Place the chicken in a single layer in a 13″ × 9″ baking pan. Top each breast with a slice of Swiss.

In a small bowl, stir together the soup and wine; pour over the chicken.

In a medium bowl, toss the stuffing mix with the broth until moistened. Spoon over the chicken. Bake for 40 minutes, or until the chicken is tender and cooked through.

TEST KITCHEN TIP: You may substitute ⅓ cup skim milk plus 2 tablespoons dry sherry for the white wine.

Makes 8 servings.

★ PER SERVING: 182 CALORIES, 4.7 G. TOTAL FAT, 1.7 G. SATURATED FAT, 53 MG. CHOLESTEROL, 353 MG. SODIUM

LEMON-GINGER CHICKEN

Adapted from *A Taste of New England*
JUNIOR LEAGUE OF WORCESTER

Lemon yogurt adds body and a touch of sweetness to the creamy sauce. This recipe uses bone-in chicken breasts. If desired, you could substitute boneless breasts and reduce the initial baking time by about 20 minutes.

  4 skinless bone-in chicken breast halves (6 ounces each)
 ⅛ teaspoon salt
 ⅛ teaspoon ground black pepper
  2 tablespoons lemon juice
  1 cup reduced-fat lemon yogurt
  2 teaspoons all-purpose flour
  1 clove garlic, minced
 ½ teaspoon ground ginger
 ¼ teaspoon finely shredded lemon rind

Preheat the oven to 350°.

Sprinkle the chicken with the salt and pepper. Place in a 13″ × 9″ baking pan. Sprinkle with the lemon juice. Cover and bake for 40 minutes, or until the chicken is tender and the juices run clear when you pierce the thickest part of the breast with a fork. Remove the chicken from the dish; discard the juices.

In a small bowl, stir together the yogurt, flour, garlic, ginger and lemon rind. Return the chicken to the baking pan. Spread the yogurt mixture over the chicken. Cover and bake for 10 minutes.

Makes 4 servings.

★ PER SERVING: 111 CALORIES, 1.6 G. TOTAL FAT, 0.7 G. SATURATED FAT, 25 MG. CHOLESTEROL, 120 MG. SODIUM

OUR CAUSE

Junior League of Worcester

Today's New Englanders owe a tremendous debt to the Native Americans who welcomed them to the shores of Massachusetts in the early part of the seventeenth century. For starters, those early colonists surely would have perished in that first harsh winter without the help of the Native Americans. But even today, the cuisine of New England harkens back to foods that the Native Americans taught the first settlers to catch or grow.

Over the generations, New England has become home to people from all over the world—people who braved long voyages and hardship to make America their home. And all of them have contributed to the character of the area's cuisine. *A Taste of New England* celebrates the diversity of that cuisine and includes recipes from local notables such as Barbara Bush and Michael Dukakis.

Proceeds from the book benefit the good work of the Junior League of Worcester, Massachusetts, especially Good Start, a training program for first-time parents, and the League's scholarship program for young women.

Oven-Barbecued Chicken

Adapted from *River Feast*
JUNIOR LEAGUE OF CINCINNATI

Reduced-sodium ketchup has only about half the sodium of regular ketchup. If you are really watching your sodium intake, use reduced-sodium Worcestershire sauce to cut an additional 50 milligrams of sodium per serving.

    4 boneless, skinless chicken breast halves (4 ounces each)
    ½ cup reduced-sodium ketchup
    ¼ cup water
    2 tablespoons Worcestershire sauce
    1 tablespoon red-wine vinegar
    1 tablespoon packed brown sugar
    ½ teaspoon dry mustard
    1 small onion, sliced crosswise and separated into rings
    1 lemon

Preheat the oven to 350°.

Place the chicken in a single layer in an 8″ × 8″ baking pan.

In a small bowl, combine the ketchup, water, Worcestershire sauce, vinegar, brown sugar and mustard. Pour over the chicken. Top with the onions.

Cut the lemon in half lengthwise and thinly slice one of the halves crosswise; reserve the remaining half for another use. Scatter the slices over the chicken.

Bake for 30 minutes, or until the chicken is tender and cooked through; baste the chicken several times as it bakes.

TEST KITCHEN TIP: Serve this saucy dish with hot cooked rice or no-yolk egg noodles.

Makes 4 servings.

★ PER SERVING: 130 CALORIES, 2 G. TOTAL FAT, 0.5 G. SATURATED FAT, 46 MG. CHOLESTEROL, 334 MG. SODIUM

Sweet-and-Spicy Stuffed Chicken

Adapted from *The Plaid Platter*
GREENWICH ACADEMY

Apples and apple jelly provide the "sweet," while hot-pepper sauce contributes the "spicy."

- 8 boneless, skinless chicken breast halves (4 ounces each)
- 2 cups reduced-sodium stuffing mix
- ½ cup chopped apples
- 2 tablespoons finely chopped toasted pecans
- ¼ teaspoon paprika
- ⅛ teaspoon salt
- ½ cup apple jelly
- 1 tablespoon Dijon mustard
- ¼ teaspoon hot-pepper sauce

Preheat the oven to 350°. Lightly coat a 13″ × 9″ baking pan with no-stick spray; set aside.

Place each chicken breast half between 2 pieces of plastic wrap. Working from the center to the edges, lightly pound with the flat side of a meat mallet to ¼″ thickness. Remove and discard the plastic wrap.

Prepare the stuffing mix according to package directions, but without adding any butter or margarine. Stir the apples, pecans, paprika and salt into the stuffing.

Spoon about ½ cup of the mixture onto each chicken breast; pat the stuffing evenly over the chicken. Roll the chicken around the stuffing and secure with a toothpick. Transfer to the prepared baking pan.

In a small bowl, stir together the jelly, mustard and hot-pepper sauce. Spoon over the chicken rolls. Cover and bake for 30 minutes, or until the chicken is tender and cooked through.

Makes 8 servings.

★ PER SERVING: 190 CALORIES, 3.5 G. TOTAL FAT, 0.6 G. SATURATED FAT, 46 MG. CHOLESTEROL, 201 MG. SODIUM

Grilled Cornish Hens with Strawberry Marinade

Adapted from *Celebrating California*
CHILDREN'S HOME SOCIETY OF CALIFORNIA

Sophisticated California cooks use fresh ingredients in imaginative ways. In this summer entrée, fresh ripe strawberries and strawberry vinegar create a distinctive marinade for grilled Cornish hens. If you don't have strawberry vinegar, substitute another mild fruit vinegar.

4 Cornish hens (1–1½ pounds each), split in half
1 cup strawberry vinegar
¾ cup pureed fresh or frozen strawberries
2 tablespoons minced fresh mint
1 tablespoon minced shallots or onions
   Grated rind of 1 lemon
⅛ teaspoon ground black pepper
2 tablespoons olive oil

Place the hens in a shallow glass or ceramic container large enough to hold them in a single layer.

In a small bowl, combine the vinegar, strawberries, mint, shallots or onions, lemon rind and pepper. Whisk in the oil. Pour over the hens. Loosen the skin slightly to place some marinade underneath. Cover and refrigerate for 4 hours.

Coat a grill rack with no-stick spray. Then light the grill according to the manufacturer's directions. Check the temperature for grilling; the temperature should be medium-hot (see the Test Kitchen Tip on page 111). Place the rack on the grill.

Remove the hens from the marinade; reserve the marinade. Place the hens, skin side down, on the rack. Cover the grill. Cook for 10 minutes. Turn the hens and cook, basting frequently with the reserved marinade, for 25 to 30 minutes, or until the juices at a leg joint run clear when pierced with a fork. Discard any remaining marinade.

Remove the hens from the grill and allow to stand for 10 minutes. Remove and discard the skin. Serve hot or at room temperature.

TEST KITCHEN TIP: If you have a bounty of ripe berries during strawberry season, you can make your own fruit-flavored vinegar. In a stainless-steel or no-stick saucepan, bring 1 quart white-wine vinegar and 2 cups cleaned, hulled strawberries to a simmer. Pour into a sterilized crock or jar. Cover and refrigerate for 2 weeks.

Strain the mixture through a cheesecloth-lined sieve into a sterilized bottle. Store in the refrigerator. Use in salads and marinades or sprinkle a few drops on grilled fish as an interesting change from lemon.

Makes 8 servings.

★ PER SERVING: 362 CALORIES, 16 G. TOTAL FAT, 3.9 G. SATURATED FAT, 154 MG. CHOLESTEROL, 149 MG. SODIUM

CORNISH HENS WITH PINEAPPLE-CORNBREAD STUFFING

Adapted from *Delicious Developments*
FRIENDS OF STRONG MEMORIAL HOSPITAL

By halving the hens before roasting, you can serve each of your guests a generous portion of hen and stuffing without fussing with carving at the table.

> 2 teaspoons butter or stick margarine (not reduced-calorie)
> ⅓ cup chopped celery
> ⅓ cup chopped scallions
> 1 can (8 ounces) crushed pineapple (packed in juice)
> ¼ cup chopped water chestnuts
> ¼ teaspoon dried thyme
> 1½ cups reduced-sodium cornbread stuffing mix
> 4 Cornish hens (1–1½ pounds each), split in half and skin removed

Preheat the oven to 350°.

In a medium no-stick skillet over medium heat, melt the butter or margarine. Add the celery and scallions; cook until crisp-tender. Stir in the pineapple (with juice), water chestnuts and thyme. Transfer the mixture to a large bowl, then add the stuffing mix and toss lightly to combine.

Spoon about ⅓ cup of the stuffing mixture into the cavity of each hen half.

Coat eight 9″ × 6″ pieces of foil with butter-flavored no-stick spray. Cover the stuffing in each hen half with a piece of foil, crimping the edges to secure.

Place the hens, breast side up, on a rack in a shallow roasting pan. Coat the hens with no-stick spray.

Roast for 65 to 75 minutes, or until the chicken is tender and the juices run clear when you pierce the thickest part of the breast with a fork. Carefully remove the foil before serving.

Makes 8 servings.

★ PER SERVING: 298 CALORIES, 13.8 G. TOTAL FAT, 4.1 G. SATURATED FAT, 96 MG. CHOLESTEROL, 165 MG. SODIUM

....

LOW-FAT MEXICAN CASSEROLE

Adapted from *The Authorized Texas Ranger Cookbook*
TEXAS RANGER MUSEUM AND HALL OF FAME

This can't-miss casserole tastes like tacos in a dish.

1 pound ground turkey breast
1 small onion, chopped
1 clove garlic, minced
1 can (15 ounces) no-salt-added red kidney beans, rinsed
   and drained
½ cup water
1 tablespoon vinegar
2 teaspoons chili powder
1½ teaspoons dried oregano
½ teaspoon ground cumin
⅛ teaspoon ground red pepper
1¾ cups picante sauce
6 corn tortillas (6" diameter), cut into 1"-wide strips
¾ cup shredded reduced-fat Cheddar cheese

Preheat the oven to 325°.

Coat a large skillet with no-stick spray. Add the turkey, onions and garlic. Cook over medium-high heat, stirring occasionally, for 10 minutes, or until the turkey is browned. Drain the turkey in a strainer or colander, then transfer it to a large plate lined with paper towels. Blot the top of the turkey with additional paper towels.

Wipe out the skillet with paper towels and return the turkey mixture to the skillet. Stir in the beans, water, vinegar, chili powder, oregano, cumin and red pepper. Bring to a boil over medium-high heat. Remove from the heat.

Spread about 2 tablespoons of the picante sauce over the bottom of a 13" × 9" baking pan.

Arrange half of the tortilla strips over the picante sauce. Top with about half of the turkey mixture. Spoon about half of the remaining picante sauce over the turkey.

Repeat the layers with the remaining tortilla strips, turkey mixture and picante sauce. Cover and bake for 25 minutes, or until bubbly around the edges. Uncover and sprinkle with the Cheddar. Bake for 5 minutes, or until the cheese is melted.

(continued)

TEST KITCHEN TIP: To make sure you're buying the leanest ground turkey available, check the label. Look for products made with only turkey breast meat. Many ground-turkey products contain the fattier dark meat as well as some skin.

Makes 6 servings.

★ PER SERVING: 292 CALORIES, 10.5 G. TOTAL FAT, 2.7 G. SATURATED FAT, 34 MG. CHOLESTEROL, 810 MG. SODIUM

GREAT TURKEY BURGERS

Adapted from *What's Cooking in Delaware*
AMERICAN RED CROSS IN DELAWARE

Just a few spoonfuls of applesauce keep these lean turkey burgers juicy. Serve on toasted whole-grain buns garnished with sliced tomatoes, crisp spinach leaves, sliced red onions or other fresh toppers. When mixing the meat for burgers, don't overhandle it or the burgers will be tough.

2 pounds ground turkey breast
½ cup minced onions
¼ cup unsweetened applesauce
3 tablespoons reduced-sodium ketchup
1 tablespoon reduced-sodium Worcestershire sauce
1 clove garlic, minced
1 teaspoon lemon pepper
½ teaspoon ground black pepper
½ teaspoon chili powder
8 whole-wheat buns, toasted (optional)

In a mixing bowl, mix the turkey, onions, applesauce, ketchup, Worcestershire sauce, garlic, lemon pepper, black pepper and chili powder. Shape into 8 patties. Broil for 5 minutes on each side, or until the burgers are no longer pink in the center. Serve in the buns (if using).

Makes 8 servings.

★ PER SERVING: 134 CALORIES, 0.7 G. FAT, 0.2 G. SATURATED FAT, 74 MG. CHOLESTEROL, 96 MG. SODIUM

ORANGE DUCK WITH WILD-RICE DRESSING

Adapted from *Florida Flavors*
ENVIRONMENTAL STUDIES COUNCIL

By using only lean duck breast instead of a well-padded whole duck, we were able to slash the fat content in half. The delicious result makes a stylish main course for a festive sit-down dinner.

WILD-RICE DRESSING

1 tablespoon tub-style reduced-calorie margarine
¼ cup chopped onions
¼ cup chopped celery
2½ cups cooked wild rice
1 cup fine dry plain bread crumbs
½ cup defatted reduced-sodium chicken broth
¼ cup chopped apples
1 teaspoon finely shredded orange rind
¼ teaspoon salt
¼ teaspoon poultry seasoning

DUCK

4 boneless, skinless duck breast halves (4 ounces each)

ORANGE SAUCE

2 tablespoons sugar
2 teaspoons cornstarch
¼ teaspoon finely shredded orange rind
⅔ cup orange juice
2 tablespoons port or nonalcoholic red wine

TO MAKE THE WILD-RICE DRESSING: Preheat the oven to 375°.
In a medium saucepan over medium heat, melt the margarine. Add the onions and celery; cook until crisp-tender. Add the wild rice, bread crumbs, broth, apples, orange rind, salt and poultry seasoning; toss to mix well and moisten the bread crumbs.

Transfer to an 18″ × 12″ piece of foil. Seal the foil tightly. Place on the lowest rack of the oven and bake for 45 minutes.

TO MAKE THE DUCK: Coat the rack of a broiling pan with butter-flavored no-stick spray. Coat the duck with no-stick spray; place on the rack. Broil 4″ from the heat for 10 minutes. Turn the duck over and broil for 6 to 8 minutes, or until the juices run clear when the duck is pierced with a fork.

(continued)

TO MAKE THE ORANGE SAUCE: In a small saucepan, stir together the sugar, cornstarch and orange rind. Whisk in the orange juice and port or wine. Cook over medium heat, whisking constantly, until the mixture comes to a boil. Cook, stirring, for 1 minute. Serve the orange sauce and wild-rice dressing with the duck.

TEST KITCHEN TIP: To get 2½ cups cooked wild rice, start with 1 cup uncooked wild rice and 2 cups water. Bring to a boil in a medium saucepan. Reduce the heat to low. Cover and simmer for 40 minutes, or until the wild rice is tender and the liquid is absorbed.

Makes 4 servings.

★ PER SERVING: 372 CALORIES, 8 G. TOTAL FAT, 2.4 G. SATURATED FAT, 39 MG. CHOLESTEROL, 448 MG. SODIUM

NET WORTH:
....
FISH AND SEAFOOD

FRIDAY-NIGHT FLOUNDER

Adapted from *Wild about Texas*
CYPRESS WOODLANDS JUNIOR FORUM

While the fish is baking, prepare some quick-cooking brown rice to soak up all the wonderful vegetable sauce.

      1 tablespoon canola oil
      8 ounces mushrooms, sliced
      2 onions, chopped
      2 cloves garlic, minced
      1 teaspoon dried basil
  1½ cups chopped tomatoes
      6 tablespoons lemon juice
      4 skinless flounder fillets (4 ounces each)
        Pinch of salt
        Pinch of ground black pepper
      1 pound fresh spinach

Preheat the oven to 350°.

In a large skillet over medium heat, warm the oil until hot. Add the mushrooms, onions, garlic and basil; sauté for 10 minutes, or until the onions are tender. Remove from the heat and add the tomatoes and lemon juice; set aside.

Lightly season the flounder with the salt and pepper. Coat a 2-quart baking dish with no-stick spray; place the flounder in the dish.

Cover with the vegetable mixture from the skillet. Bake for 20 to 25 minutes, or until the flounder is opaque in the center. Test by inserting a knife into the center of a fillet (see the Test Kitchen Tip on the opposite page).

Meanwhile, remove and discard any tough ribs and stems from the spinach. Chop the leaves coarsely and wash in a large amount of cold water. Drain and transfer to a large nonaluminum pot with only the water left clinging to the leaves.

Cover and cook over medium heat for 3 to 5 minutes, or until the spinach wilts. Drain and arrange on a large serving platter. Place the flounder and vegetables on the spinach.

Makes 4 servings.

TEST KITCHEN TIP: To check any fish for doneness, insert the tip of a table knife into the center of one fillet. When it looks opaque, not translucent like raw fish, it is ready to remove from the heat. Whether prepared in a conventional oven or a microwave, the fish will continue to cook after it is removed from the heat, so it's important not to overcook it.

★ PER SERVING: 225 CALORIES, 5.6 G. FAT, 0.7 G. SATURATED FAT, 60 MG. CHOLESTEROL, 192 MG. SODIUM

....

LEMONY ALMOND-TOPPED FILLETS

Adapted from *Tastes in Plaid*
ALAMANCE COUNTY HISTORICAL MUSEUM

This fish dish couldn't be simpler to make or more delicious. It's an excellent choice for a weeknight dinner.

> 1 pound skinless cod or orange roughy fillets (¾" thick)
> ½ cup fine dry plain bread crumbs
> 1 tablespoon stick margarine (not reduced-calorie) or butter, melted
> 1 teaspoon finely shredded lemon rind
> 3 tablespoons sliced almonds, toasted

Coat an 8" × 8" baking pan with no-stick spray. Place the fish in a single layer in the prepared dish.

In a small bowl, stir together bread crumbs, margarine and lemon rind. Sprinkle evenly over the fish, then top with the almonds.

Cover with microwave-safe plastic wrap. Microwave on high power for a total of 6 to 7 minutes, or until the flesh is opaque all the way through; stop and rotate the dish a half turn after 3 minutes. Test by inserting a knife into the center of a fillet.

TEST KITCHEN TIP: To bake the fish instead of using the microwave, preheat the oven to 450°. Ready the fish as directed above. Bake for 10 to 12 minutes.

Makes 4 servings.

★ PER SERVING: 192 CALORIES, 7 G. TOTAL FAT, 1 G. SATURATED FAT, 45 MG. CHOLESTEROL, 190 MG. SODIUM

Cajun Fish

Adapted from *Campsite to Kitchen*
OUTDOOR WRITERS ASSOCIATION OF AMERICA

The recipe in Campsite to Kitchen *recommends freshwater fish fillets. You might find that orange roughy, cod and haddock are more readily available. They're certainly equally delicious in this spicy dish.*

- ½ cup no-salt-added tomato sauce
- 1 envelope reduced-calorie Italian salad dressing mix
- 2 tablespoons chopped fresh parsley
- 1 pound skinless orange roughy, cod or haddock fillets (½″ thick)
- 1 tablespoon grated Parmesan cheese

Lightly coat a 13″ × 9″ baking pan with no-stick spray.

In a small bowl, combine the tomato sauce, salad dressing mix and parsley. Brush over the fish on all sides and place in the prepared baking pan. Cover with foil and refrigerate for 30 minutes.

Preheat the oven to 350°. Bake the fish, covered, for 30 minutes, or until the fish is opaque all the way through. Test by inserting a knife into the center of a fillet. Sprinkle with the Parmesan.

Makes 4 servings.

★ PER SERVING: 102 CALORIES, 1.3 G. TOTAL FAT, 2.3 G. SATURATED FAT, 25 MG. CHOLESTEROL, 284 MG. SODIUM

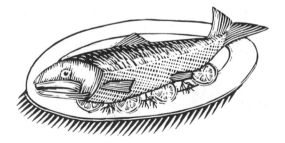

JIM'S FAVORITE BAKED WALLEYE

Adapted from *Nutbread and Nostalgia*
JUNIOR LEAGUE OF SOUTH BEND

Nonalcoholic white wine is a good substitute for dry sherry in the rich shrimp-and-cheese sauce that tops this fish. You can usually find the nonalcoholic wine in liquor stores or in the liquor department of your supermarket.

2 pounds skinless walleye or northern pike fillets (¾" thick)
⅛ teaspoon ground black pepper
  Pinch of salt
2 tablespoons all-purpose flour
¾ cup evaporated skim milk
¼ cup dry sherry or nonalcoholic white wine
2 slices (¾ ounce each) fat-free Swiss cheese, finely cut up
1 can (4½ ounces) tiny shrimp, drained

Preheat the oven to 425°.

Coat a 13" × 9" baking pan with no-stick spray. Place the fish in the prepared dish, folding under any thin edges. Sprinkle with the pepper and salt. Bake for 12 to 14 minutes, or until the fish is opaque all the way through. Test by inserting a knife into the center of a fillet.

Meanwhile, place the flour in a small saucepan. Whisk in the milk. Cook, stirring, over medium heat until the mixture begins to thicken and just comes to a boil. Then stir in the sherry or wine. Continue to cook, stirring, for 1 minute. Remove from the heat.

Add the Swiss and stir until melted. Stir in the shrimp. Spoon over the cooked fish. Bake for 5 minutes, or until the cheese mixture is lightly browned and bubbly.

Makes 6 servings.

★ PER SERVING: 217 CALORIES, 1.5 G. TOTAL FAT, 0.3 G. SATURATED FAT, 98 MG. CHOLESTEROL, 236 MG. SODIUM

HERB AND PARMESAN WALLEYE

Adapted from *Campsite to Kitchen*
OUTDOOR WRITERS ASSOCIATION OF AMERICA

*Take your choice of baking the Parmesan-coated fish in the
microwave or in a conventional oven (see the Test Kitchen Tip
below for oven directions). Either way, the dish is ready in only
minutes. When preparing this dish in the oven, you can easily
multiply the servings without increasing the baking time. If using
a microwave, do extra servings in separate batches.*

2 tablespoons grated Parmesan cheese
1 teaspoon dried parsley
½ teaspoon dried dill
½ teaspoon garlic powder
8 ounces skinless walleye fillets (½" thick)
3 scallions, chopped
2 lemon wedges

In a shallow dish, combine the Parmesan, parsley, dill and garlic powder.

Coat the fish with butter-flavored no-stick spray. Dip in the
Parmesan mixture, turning to coat the fillets evenly. Place the fish in
a microwave-safe 11″ × 7″ baking pan in a single layer, folding
under any thin edges. Sprinkle with the scallions.

Cover with microwave-safe plastic wrap. Microwave on high
power for a total of 4 to 5 minutes, or until the flesh is opaque all
the way through; stop and rotate the dish a half turn after 3 minutes.
Test by inserting a knife into the center of a fillet. Squeeze juice from
the lemon wedges over the fish and serve.

TEST KITCHEN TIP: To bake the fish instead of using the microwave, preheat the oven to 450°. Prepare the coated fish as above,
place in the baking pan and sprinkle with the scallions. Bake for 6
to 8 minutes.

Makes 2 servings.

★ PER SERVING: 137 CALORIES, 2.7 G. TOTAL FAT, 1.3 G. SATURATED FAT,
50 MG. CHOLESTEROL, 162 MG. SODIUM

Sautéed Halibut with Nectarine Salsa

Adapted from *Feast of Eden*
JUNIOR LEAGUE OF MONTEREY COUNTY

Cilantro gives a distinctive pungency to the fresh fruit salsa.
If you can't find fresh cilantro, use milder-flavored fresh parsley
and a bit of grated lime or lemon rind.

SALSA

> 2 nectarines, diced
> ½ cup finely chopped scallions
> ¼ sweet red pepper, chopped
> ¼ cup minced fresh chives
> 1½ teaspoons chopped fresh cilantro
> 3 tablespoons lime juice

HALIBUT

> 1 nectarine, chopped
> 4 halibut steaks (6 ounces each; 1″ thick)

TO MAKE THE SALSA: In a medium bowl, combine the nectarines, scallions, peppers, chives and cilantro. Stir in the lime juice. Cover and refrigerate for at least 1 hour to blend the flavors.

TO MAKE THE HALIBUT: Mash the nectarine and spread the pulp over the fish. Place the fish on a plate. Cover and marinate in the refrigerator for 1 hour.

Preheat the broiler. Coat the rack of a broiling pan with no-stick spray. Scrape the nectarine marinade from the fish and discard it. Coat the fish with no-stick spray and place on the rack. Broil 5″ to 6″ from the heat for 12 to 14 minutes, or until the fish is opaque all the way through. Test by inserting a knife into the center of a steak. Serve with the salsa.

TEST KITCHEN TIP: If the salsa seems too tangy, stir in 1 or 2 teaspoons sugar.

Makes 4 servings.

★ PER SERVING: 243 CALORIES, 4.4 G. TOTAL FAT, 0.6 G. SATURATED FAT, 55 MG. CHOLESTEROL, 93 MG. SODIUM

BAKED RED SNAPPER

Adapted from *Foods à la Louisiane*
LOUISIANA FARM BUREAU FEDERATION

This is an interesting way to prepare a whole fish for a festive occasion.

STUFFING

> 6 scallions, chopped
> 2 stalks celery, chopped
> 2 tablespoons chopped fresh parsley
> 1 tablespoon butter or stick margarine (not reduced-calorie)
> 1 cup toasted bread crumbs
> ½ teaspoon dried thyme
> ½ teaspoon dried basil
> Pinch of salt
> Pinch of ground black pepper
> 1 cup lump crabmeat, picked over and flaked
> ¼ cup white wine or nonalcoholic white wine

RED SNAPPER

> 1 whole red snapper (6 pounds), cleaned, head on
> ¼ cup chopped onions
> ¼ cup water

SAUCE

> 1 egg, beaten
> 1 tablespoon melted butter or stick margarine (not reduced-calorie), cooled
> 1 teaspoon lemon juice
> 1 teaspoon all-purpose flour
> ½ teaspoon dried basil
> ½ teaspoon sugar
> 1 bay leaf
> Pinch of salt
> Pinch of ground black pepper

TO MAKE THE STUFFING: In a medium saucepan over low heat, sauté the scallions, celery and parsley in the butter or margarine for 5 minutes, or until tender. Remove from the heat.

Moisten the bread crumbs with a little water. Add the bread crumbs, thyme, basil, salt and pepper to the saucepan. Mix in the crabmeat and wine.

TO MAKE THE RED SNAPPER: Preheat the oven to 350°.

Lightly coat a baking pan large enough to hold the fish with no-stick spray. Place the fish in the dish and coat lightly with no-stick spray. Spoon the stuffing into the fish cavity. Fasten the cavity closed with a skewer. Scatter the onions around the fish. Add the water to the dish.

Bake for 30 minutes, basting occasionally and adding additional water if necessary. Remove from the oven. Using two large spatulas, remove the fish to a platter.

Pour the cooking juices from the baking pan into a small bowl. Return the fish to the baking pan.

TO MAKE THE SAUCE: Reduce the oven temperature to 275°.

To the juices in the bowl, add the egg, butter or margarine, lemon juice, flour, basil, sugar, bay leaf, salt and pepper. Whisk until smooth. Add water if necessary to make a saucelike consistency.

Pour the sauce over the fish and bake for 30 minutes, or until the flesh is opaque. Test by inserting a knife into the center of the fish.

Remove and discard the bay leaf. Fillet the fish; discard the skin and bones. Serve with the stuffing and sauce.

Makes 8 servings.

★ PER SERVING: 294 CALORIES, 6.9 G. PROTEIN, 2.7 G. FAT, 128 MG. CHOLESTEROL, 210 MG. SODIUM

Honey-Dijon Salmon

Adapted from *Presentations*
FRIENDS OF LIED CENTER FOR PERFORMING ARTS

In this recipe, a blend of honey and Dijon mustard is accented by rum extract to create a perfect complement for the salmon.

4 teaspoons Dijon mustard
1 tablespoon honey
1 tablespoon lemon juice
¼ teaspoon ground black pepper
¼ teaspoon rum extract
4 salmon steaks (5 ounces each; 1″ thick)

In small bowl, whisk together the mustard, honey, lemon juice, pepper and rum extract.

Place the salmon on a plate. Spread the mustard mixture over it, using the back of the spoon to evenly cover the surface. Cover and refrigerate for 1 hour.

Preheat the broiler. Coat the rack of a broiling pan with no-stick spray. Place the salmon on the rack. Broil 4″ from the heat for 8 to 10 minutes, or until the fish is opaque all the way through. Test by inserting a knife into the center of a steak.

Makes 4 servings.

★ PER SERVING: 153 CALORIES, 5.1 G. TOTAL FAT, 1 G. SATURATED FAT, 25 MG. CHOLESTEROL, 934 MG. SODIUM

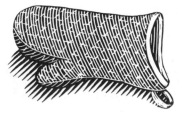

SWEET-AND-SPICY GRILLED SALMON

Adapted from *Settings*
JUNIOR LEAGUE OF PHILADELPHIA

The sweet-spicy sauce that tops these salmon fillets would also enhance swordfish, catfish or orange roughy.

SAUCE

1 shallot, finely chopped
2 tablespoons red-wine vinegar
2 tablespoons lime juice
2 tablespoons reduced-sodium soy sauce
1 tablespoon very finely chopped fresh parsley
1½ teaspoons honey
1 teaspoon grated fresh ginger
Pinch of ground red pepper

SALMON

1 pound skinless salmon fillets (about ½" thick)

Coat a grill rack with no-stick spray. Then light the grill according to the manufacturer's directions. Check the temperature for grilling; the temperature should be medium-hot (see the Test Kitchen Tip on page 111). Place the rack on the grill.

TO MAKE THE SAUCE: Lightly coat a small saucepan with no-stick spray. Add the shallots. Cook, stirring, over medium heat for 3 minutes, or until the shallots are tender.

Stir in the vinegar, lime juice, soy sauce, parsley, honey, ginger and pepper until well-combined. Remove from the heat and set aside.

TO MAKE THE SALMON: Coat a grill basket or a piece of heavy foil with no-stick spray. Place the salmon in the basket or on the foil. Brush both sides of the fillets with the sauce. Grill, uncovered, over the coals for 5 minutes, brushing often with the sauce. Turn the fish over and grill, brushing often with the sauce, for 5 minutes, or until the salmon is opaque all the way through. Test by inserting a knife into the center of a fillet.

Makes 4 servings.

★ PER SERVING: 174 CALORIES, 7.2 G. TOTAL FAT, 1.1 G. SATURATED FAT, 63 MG. CHOLESTEROL, 361 MG. SODIUM

CREOLE SAUCE FOR FISH

Adapted from *Cotton Country Cooking*
JUNIOR LEAGUE OF MORGAN COUNTY

Serve this vegetable-laden sauce warm or chilled over any type of broiled or grilled fish.

1 cup chopped celery
1 onion, finely chopped
1 green pepper, finely chopped
1 can (14½ ounces) no-salt-added tomatoes (with juice), cut up
1 tablespoon Worcestershire sauce
1 tablespoon lemon juice
1 bay leaf
⅛ teaspoon ground black pepper
Dash of hot-pepper sauce
Pinch of salt

Coat a medium skillet with no-stick spray. Add the celery, onions and green peppers. Cook, stirring, over medium heat for 8 minutes, or until the celery is tender. Stir in the tomatoes (with juice), Worcestershire sauce, lemon juice, bay leaf, black pepper, hot-pepper sauce and salt.

Bring to a boil, then reduce the heat to low. Cook for 5 minutes, or until the liquid is slightly thickened. Remove and discard the bay leaf before serving.

Makes 3 cups; 6 servings.

★ PER ½ CUP: 31 CALORIES, 0.3 G. TOTAL FAT, 0 G. SATURATED FAT, 0 MG. CHOLESTEROL, 52 MG. SODIUM

Savory Crab on Rice

Adapted from *Plain and Elegant*
WEST GEORGIA MEDICAL CENTER AUXILIARY

Originally, this recipe was baked before serving, but we streamlined the process by completely heating the crab mixture in a saucepan. If sodium intake is a concern for you, be aware that most of the sodium in this dish comes from the crab. You could reduce the amount by substituting cooked and flaked white fish fillets for all or part of the crab.

1 tablespoon butter or stick margarine (not reduced-calorie)
¼ cup finely chopped onions
¼ cup chopped green peppers
2 tablespoons all-purpose flour
1¼ cups skim milk
12 ounces lump crabmeat, picked over and flaked
1 teaspoon Worcestershire sauce
⅛ teaspoon ground black pepper
Pinch of salt
1 hard-cooked egg, chopped
3 cups hot cooked rice

In a small saucepan, melt the butter or margarine over medium heat. Add the onions and green peppers; cook for 5 minutes, or until tender.

Place the flour in a small bowl. Whisk in the milk. Stir the milk mixture into the vegetables in the saucepan. Cook, stirring, over medium heat until the mixture begins to thicken and just comes to a boil. Continue to cook, stirring, for 1 minute.

Stir in the crabmeat, Worcestershire sauce, black pepper and salt; heat through. Gently stir in the hard-cooked egg. Serve over the rice.

Makes 4 servings.

TEST KITCHEN TIP: If fresh crab is not available, substitute 2 cans (6 ounces each) of crab, drained and flaked.

★ PER SERVING: 371 CALORIES, 6 G. TOTAL FAT, 2.5 G. SATURATED FAT, 107 MG. CHOLESTEROL, 1,012 MG. SODIUM

LIGHT CRAB QUICHE

Adapted from *Beyond the Bay*
JUNIOR SERVICE LEAGUE OF PANAMA CITY

We used reduced-fat and fat-free versions of certain products to make this brunch dish more healthful. And to further lighten it, we substituted evaporated skim milk for light cream. If fresh crab is too expensive, you can substitute surimi, the imitation crab.

PASTRY

    1⅓ cups all-purpose flour
    Pinch of salt
    ¼ cup canola oil
    3 tablespoons skim milk

FILLING

    ¾ cup reduced-fat sour cream
    ¼ cup reduced-fat mayonnaise
    1 tablespoon all-purpose flour
    2 eggs, lightly beaten
    2 egg whites, lightly beaten
    ⅔ cup evaporated skim milk
    1 jar (2½ ounces) sliced mushrooms, drained
    6 ounces lump crabmeat, picked over and flaked
    8 slices (¾ ounce each) fat-free Swiss cheese, finely cut up

TO MAKE THE PASTRY: Preheat the oven to 450°.

In a medium bowl, stir together the flour and salt. Add the oil and milk all at once. Using a fork, toss and stir lightly until the flour is moistened. Then, using your hands, gently shape the mixture into a ball.

Place the ball of dough between two 12″ × 12″ pieces of wax paper. Gently roll out the dough into a 12″ circle. Remove the top piece of wax paper. Then invert the dough onto a 9″ pie plate.

Remove the remaining piece of wax paper and gently fit the dough into the pan. Fold the edges of the pastry under and flute them. Do not prick the pastry.

Line the pastry with a double thickness of heavy foil. Bake for 7 minutes. Remove from the oven, then remove the foil. Reduce the oven temperature to 350°.

Junior Service League of Panama City

Panama City, Florida, looks like the quintessential sleepy ocean-side community. But beyond the glittering waters of the Gulf of Mexico, away from the sugar-white sand and the moss-laden trees that edge St. Andrews Bay, there are people in Panama City who need help, just as in any community. Luckily, the word *sleepy* doesn't apply to the city's Junior Service League.

The League, now in its 44th year, raises some $70,000 a year to help young, old and those in between. One favorite activity of the group is an annual shopping spree for schoolchildren. Each fall, 300 children are taken to a local department store. There, with the help of League members, each child picks out a new school wardrobe, from shoes to jeans to jackets.

Equally special is "Calls from the Heart," a year-round program that enables residents of nursing homes in the area to make free long-distance calls to friends and family.

Proceeds from the League's two books, *Bay Leaves* and *Beyond the Bay*, go toward these and many other worthwhile projects. *Bay Leaves* is now in its tenth printing and already topping the $100,000 mark in earnings.

TO MAKE THE FILLING: Meanwhile, in a small bowl, stir together the sour cream, mayonnaise and flour. Stir in the eggs, egg whites and milk.

Sprinkle the mushrooms in the hot pastry shell. Sprinkle the crabmeat, then the Swiss, over the mushrooms. Pour the sour-cream mixture into the pastry shell.

Bake for 35 to 40 minutes, or until a knife inserted in the center comes out clean. Remove from the oven and let stand for 5 minutes before serving.

Makes 6 servings.

★ PER SERVING: 375 CALORIES, 15.7 G. TOTAL FAT, 2.3 G. SATURATED FAT, 103 MG. CHOLESTEROL, 653 MG. SODIUM

SHRIMP-AND-CRAB CAKES

Adapted from *Campsite to Kitchen*
OUTDOOR WRITERS ASSOCIATION OF AMERICA

*We found that coating the skillet with no-stick spray allowed us
to use only 1 tablespoon of oil to fry these savory seafood cakes.
A no-stick skillet provides even more insurance against sticking.*

12	ounces medium shrimp, peeled and deveined
2	egg whites
3	tablespoons skim milk
¼	teaspoon ground black pepper
⅛	teaspoon salt
8	ounces lump crabmeat, picked over and flaked
½	cup fine dry plain bread crumbs
2	tablespoons thinly sliced scallions
2	teaspoons prepared mustard
1	tablespoon oil

In a blender or food processor, blend the shrimp, egg whites,
milk, pepper and salt until smooth. Transfer to a medium bowl. Stir
in the crabmeat, bread crumbs, scallions and mustard until well-
mixed. Shape into 8 patties, using about ¼ cup of the mixture for
each patty.

Preheat the oven to 300°.

Coat a large skillet with no-stick spray. Add the oil, then place
over medium heat until hot. Add half of the patties and cook until
browned on both sides, turning once. (If the patties are browning
too fast, lower the heat to medium-low.) Transfer the patties to a
serving plate, then cover with foil. Place in the oven to keep warm.
Add the remaining patties to the skillet and cook until browned on
both sides.

TEST KITCHEN TIP: The crab mixture is quite soft, so flour
your hands before shaping it into patties. Alternatively, refrigerate
the mixture for at least an hour to firm it up.

Makes 8 patties; 4 servings.

★ PER SERVING: 216 CALORIES, 5.7 G. TOTAL FAT, 0.8 G. SATURATED FAT,
161 MG. CHOLESTEROL, 982 MG. SODIUM

GARLIC-SCENTED BROILED SHRIMP

Adapted from *Campsite to Kitchen*
OUTDOOR WRITERS ASSOCIATION OF AMERICA

To make it easier to turn the shrimp, thread them onto skewers before broiling. If you're using wooden skewers, soak them in warm water for 10 minutes before threading on the shrimp to reduce the likelihood of burning the wood. Be sure to leave a little space between the shrimp so they cook evenly.

¾ cup cider or apple juice
4 teaspoons Worcestershire sauce
2 tablespoons chopped fresh parsley
1 clove garlic, minced
¼ teaspoon ground black pepper
2 pounds large shrimp, peeled and deveined

In a large bowl, stir together the cider or apple juice, Worcestershire sauce, parsley, garlic and pepper. Stir in the shrimp. Cover and marinate in the refrigerator for at least 2 hours.

Preheat the broiler. Drain the shrimp, reserving the marinade.

Coat the rack of a broiling pan with no-stick spray. Place the shrimp on the prepared rack. Broil 4″ to 5″ from the heat for 3 minutes. Turn the shrimp, then brush with the marinade. Broil for 2 minutes, or until the shrimp turn pink.

TEST KITCHEN TIP: If you purchase the shrimp already peeled and deveined rather than in the shell, you'll need to buy only 1½ pounds. For variety, you could replace the cider or apple juice with nonalcoholic beer.

Makes 6 servings.

★ PER SERVING: 130 CALORIES, 1.3 G. TOTAL FAT, 0.3 G. SATURATED FAT, 232 MG. CHOLESTEROL, 300 MG. SODIUM

SHRIMP STROGANOFF

Adapted from *Critics' Choice*
GUILD OF CORINTH THEATRE ARTS

We used reduced-fat sour cream, which has less than half the fat of regular sour cream, to lend creamy richness to this lean sauce.

- 1 tablespoon butter or stick margarine (not reduced-calorie)
- 8 ounces mushrooms, sliced
- ½ cup sliced scallions
- 1½ pounds medium shrimp, peeled and deveined
- ½ teaspoon salt
- ¼ teaspoon ground black pepper
- 4 ounces vermicelli
- 1 cup reduced-fat sour cream
- 2 tablespoons all-purpose flour
- ¼ cup dry sherry or nonalcoholic white wine

Coat a large skillet with no-stick spray. Add the butter or margarine and place over medium heat until melted. Add the mushrooms and scallions. Cook, stirring, until tender. Add the shrimp and cook, stirring, for 4 minutes, or until the shrimp turn pink. Stir in the salt and pepper.

Meanwhile, cook the vermicelli according to the package directions, but without adding salt or fat. Drain, rinse with cold water and drain again.

In a small bowl, stir together the sour cream and flour. Stir the sour-cream mixture and sherry or wine into the shrimp mixture. Cook, stirring, over medium heat just until the mixture is thickened. Toss with the cooked vermicelli.

TEST KITCHEN TIP: You may substitute 4 ounces of thin spaghetti for the vermicelli.

Makes 4 servings.

★ PER SERVING: 377 CALORIES, 8.2 G. TOTAL FAT, 4.3 G. SATURATED FAT, 293 MG. CHOLESTEROL, 670 MG. SODIUM

STEAMED MUSSELS BISTRO-STYLE

Adapted from *Cooking in the Litchfield Hills*
PRATT NATURE CENTER

Tailor this dish to your taste by adding capers or using different fresh herbs, such as tarragon or thyme. No matter how you flavor them, serve the mussels with French bread to soak up the savory broth.

1	tablespoon olive oil
¼	cup leeks, cut into julienne strips
1	tablespoon minced garlic
2	teaspoons chopped shallots or onions
1	cup chopped tomatoes
1	tablespoon finely chopped fresh basil
1	teaspoon finely chopped fresh rosemary
¾	cup dry white wine or nonalcoholic white wine
½	cup bottled clam juice
	Pinch of salt
	Pinch of ground black pepper
36	small mussels in the shell (1″–2″ in diameter), scrubbed and beards removed
1	teaspoon butter or stick margarine (not reduced-calorie)

Coat a Dutch oven with no-stick spray. Add the oil and place over high heat until hot. Add the leeks, garlic and shallots or onions; cook, stirring, for 1 minute. Stir in the tomatoes, basil and rosemary. Cook, stirring, for 30 seconds.

Add the wine, clam juice, salt and pepper. Add the mussels. Bring to a boil, then reduce the heat to low. Cover and simmer for 3 minutes, or until the mussels have opened. Simmer 5 minutes more. Add the butter or margarine and swirl until incorporated.

Makes 4 servings.

TEST KITCHEN TIP: Some mussels have dark threads protruding from between the shells, known as beards. Remove them by pulling gently or snipping with scissors. Do this just before cooking.

★ PER SERVING: 147 CALORIES, 5.9 G. TOTAL FAT, 1.1 G. SATURATED FAT, 38 MG. CHOLESTEROL, 237 MG. SODIUM

QUICK SHRIMP SKILLET

Adapted from *Tastes in Plaid*
ALAMANCE COUNTY HISTORICAL MUSEUM

Diagonally slicing the celery, carrots and scallions speeds cooking time and makes a prettier presentation.

2 cups sliced celery
1 cup sliced mushrooms
1 cup thinly sliced carrots
½ cup sliced scallions
2 cloves garlic, minced
12 ounces peeled and deveined medium shrimp
2 tablespoons water
2 teaspoons reduced-sodium soy sauce
½ teaspoon ground ginger
⅛ teaspoon ground black pepper
3 cups hot cooked rice

Lightly coat a large skillet with no-stick spray. Place over medium-high heat. Add the celery, mushrooms, carrots, scallions and garlic. Stir-fry for 5 minutes, or until the vegetables are almost crisp-tender. Add the shrimp, water, soy sauce, ginger and pepper. Stir-fry for 3 minutes, or until the shrimp turn pink. Serve over the rice.

Makes 4 servings.

★ PER SERVING: 297 CALORIES, 1.4 G. TOTAL FAT, 0.4 G. SATURATED FAT, 131 MG. CHOLESTEROL, 304 MG. SODIUM

OUR CAUSE

Alamance County Historical Museum

The folks in Alamance County, North Carolina, are mad for plaid. It put their Piedmont area on the map back in 1853, when Edwin Michael Holt's textile mill produced the first commercially woven cotton plaid fabric in the South.

The house where Holt was born, now on the National Register of Historic Places, is the home of the Alamance County Historical Museum and stands as testimony to the importance of the southern textile industry to the economic prosperity of the country.

Built in 1790 as a modest two-room structure, the house was overbuilt in 1800 to create a two-story home typical of the area's nineteenth-century farmhouses. In 1875 Holt's sixth son and his wife expanded and remodeled the house in Italianate Revival style. The Holts had a sizable plantation on the site, with a blacksmith shop, a distillery, a woodworking shop and a gristmill in addition to farming and factory operations.

Tastes in Plaid, the museum's cookbook, celebrates the South's legendary hospitality as well as the important role of E. M. Holt in bringing prosperity to the region.

SHRIMP-STUFFED PEPPERS

Adapted from *Beyond the Bay*
JUNIOR SERVICE LEAGUE OF PANAMA CITY

This beautifully seasoned shrimp mixture also makes a great stuffing for fish or baked mushroom appetizers.

4 green peppers
1 small onion, finely chopped
1 stalk celery, finely chopped
2 cloves garlic, minced
1 pound small shrimp, peeled, deveined and chopped
½ cup fine dry seasoned bread crumbs
¼ cup grated Parmesan cheese
2 tablespoons chopped fresh parsley
2 tablespoons reduced-sodium ketchup
⅛ teaspoon hot-pepper sauce

Preheat the oven to 350°.

Fill a Dutch oven halfway with water and bring to a boil.

Cut the peppers in half lengthwise; remove the seeds and stems. Place the peppers in the boiling water and cook for 3 minutes. Drain and set aside.

Coat a large skillet with no-stick spray. Add the onions, celery and garlic. Cook, stirring, over medium-high heat for 5 minutes, or until tender. Add the shrimp and cook, stirring, for 2 minutes, or until the shrimp turn pink.

Remove from the heat. Stir in the bread crumbs, Parmesan, parsley, ketchup and hot-pepper sauce. Spoon the mixture into the pepper halves, using ¼ to ⅓ cup for each half.

Place in a 13″ × 9″ baking pan. Cover and bake for 25 to 30 minutes, or until heated through.

Makes 4 servings.

★ PER SERVING: 201 CALORIES, 3.7 G. TOTAL FAT, 1.6 G. SATURATED FAT, 179 MG. CHOLESTEROL, 465 MG. SODIUM

Seafood Casseroles

Adapted from *The Gulf Gourmet*
WESTMINSTER ACADEMY PTA

Knowing that these superb single-serving casseroles are very low in fat can be your little secret. Just let your guests enjoy. If you'd prefer to make a single casserole, use a 1-quart dish and bake for about 25 minutes.

⅓ cup chopped onions
3 tablespoons all-purpose flour
¼ cup skim milk
¾ cup defatted reduced-sodium chicken broth
2 tablespoons dry sherry or ½ teaspoon sherry extract
1 tablespoon lemon juice
1 tablespoon nonfat dry milk
8 ounces peeled and cooked medium shrimp
8 ounces king crab or lump crabmeat, picked over and flaked
1 can (4 ounces) sliced mushrooms, drained
1 cup fresh bread crumbs
4 teaspoons grated Parmesan cheese (optional)

Preheat the oven to 400°. Lightly coat four 10-ounce casserole dishes with no-stick spray; set aside.

Lightly coat a medium saucepan with no-stick spray. Add the onions. Cook, stirring, over medium heat for 3 minutes, or until the onions are tender.

Place the flour in a small bowl. Whisk in the skim milk. Then stir the mixture into the onions. Add the broth, sherry or sherry extract, lemon juice and dry milk. Cook, stirring, until the mixture begins to thicken and just comes to a boil. Remove from the heat.

Gently stir in the shrimp, crab and mushrooms. Spoon the mixture into the prepared casseroles. Top with the bread crumbs and Parmesan (if using).

Bake for 10 minutes, or until heated through. Let stand for 5 minutes before serving.

TEST KITCHEN TIPS: If you prefer to use fresh mushrooms, use 1 cup sliced mushrooms and cook them with the onions. If nec-

(continued)

essary, drain off their juices before stirring in the flour-and-milk mixture.

To make 1 cup of fresh bread crumbs, tear 1 or 2 slices of bread into pieces and pulverize in a blender or food processor.

Makes 4 servings.

★PER SERVING: 200 CALORIES, 2.2 G. TOTAL FAT, 0.4 G. SATURATED FAT, 168 MG. CHOLESTEROL, 566 MG. SODIUM

THE WELL-STOCKED
PANTRY

FRUITED CURRY RICE

Adapted from *Peachtree Bouquet*
JUNIOR LEAGUE OF DEKALB COUNTY

For a nice homemade gift, make up a package of the dry ingredients for this pretty rice mix. (Be sure to include a small card containing the cooking instructions with the gift.) The mix itself keeps well and makes a less-expensive, lower-sodium alternative to commercial flavored rice. Dried fruits add color and flavor to the dish without added fat.

½ cup long-grain white rice
¼ cup chopped mixed dried fruit
2 tablespoons golden raisins
1½ teaspoons dried minced onions
½–1 teaspoon curry powder
1 teaspoon reduced-sodium chicken or beef bouillon granules
1¼ cups water

In a small bowl, mix the rice, fruit, raisins, onions, curry powder and bouillon.

In a small saucepan over high heat, bring the water to a boil. Add the rice mixture. Reduce the heat, cover and simmer for 20 minutes, or until the rice is tender and the liquid is absorbed. Fluff with a fork before serving.

Makes 4 servings.

★ PER SERVING: 126 CALORIES, 0.4 G. TOTAL FAT, 0.1 G. SATURATED FAT, 0 MG. CHOLESTEROL, 142 MG. SODIUM

....

CHEESY CARROT-RICE RING

Adapted from *Smoky Mountain Magic*
JUNIOR LEAGUE OF JOHNSON CITY

This colorful rice mold is pretty baked in a ring, but it's every bit as delicious served in a casserole. It's a great side dish that could double as a main course for two. An attractive way to serve the rice mold is with cooked peas in the center.

> 1½ cups shredded carrots
> 1 cup hot cooked rice
> ¾ cup shredded reduced-fat Cheddar cheese
> 1 egg, lightly beaten
> 1 tablespoon chopped onions
> Pinch of salt
> Pinch of ground black pepper
> Pinch of ground nutmeg

Preheat the oven to 350°.

Fill a 2-quart saucepan half full of water; cover and bring to a boil over medium heat. Add the carrots. Boil for 5 minutes, then drain and place in a medium bowl.

Stir in the rice, Cheddar, egg, onions, salt, pepper and nutmeg into the bowl.

Coat a 2-cup ovenproof ring mold with no-stick spray. Spoon in the rice mixture. Bake for 25 minutes, or until the rice in the center of the ring is hot. Unmold the rice on a serving dish.

Makes 4 servings.

★ PER SERVING: 157 CALORIES, 4.5 G. FAT, 2.2 G. SATURATED FAT, 62 MG. CHOLESTEROL, 334 MG. SODIUM

FRIED RICE

Adapted from *Changing Thymes*
AUSTIN JUNIOR FORUM

You'll never crave Chinese carry-out again after you taste how fresh and light fried rice can be. Keep this main-dish recipe in mind as a convenient family meal when you have leftover cooked rice on hand.

1 slice turkey bacon, diced
4 ounces peeled and chopped shrimp
1 cup bean sprouts
½ cup chopped onions
4 cups cold cooked rice
1 cup shredded cooked chicken
½ cup fat-free egg substitute
1 tablespoon reduced-sodium soy sauce
2 scallions, chopped

In a large no-stick skillet over medium heat, fry the bacon until crisp. Add the shrimp, sprouts and onions. Cook over medium heat for 3 minutes, or until the onions are translucent.

Add the rice and chicken. Toss over medium heat until heated through. With a spatula, push the rice mixture to one side of the skillet, leaving space for the egg. Add the egg substitute and cook for 3 minutes, or until set. Toss with the rice mixture. Add the soy sauce and toss again. Sprinkle with the scallions.

Makes 4 servings.

★ PER SERVING: 379 CALORIES, 2.6 G. FAT, 0.7 G. SATURATED FAT, 82 MG. CHOLESTEROL, 264 MG. SODIUM

OUR CAUSE

Austin Junior Forum

Texas is a Caddo Indian word for friendship, and the Austin Junior Forum takes that term seriously, working to enrich the community in a wide variety of ways. Children are a favorite focus of the Forum, and a pet project is the annual Teddy Bear Picnic, an affair that raises money to buy stuffed animals that the fire and police departments then give to children in distress situations.

Lone Star Legacy began as a fund-raiser to help the Forum renovate its headquarters, the historic Daniel H. Caswell House. Built in 1899, it was scheduled for demolition, but the Forum was determined to save it. The first edition of the cookbook was released in 1981 and sold so well that the group paid the bills for the renovation much more quickly than it had imagined. The Caswell House is on the National Register of Historic Places and has been named a Texas Historic Landmark.

Meanwhile, the book is in its eighth printing and has sold 180,000 copies. The continued popularity of *Lone Star Legacy* enables the Forum to provide grants to many of Austin's charitable organizations, particularly those that help children in need.

The Forum has two other books that help provide money for its good works: *Changing Thymes* and *Lone Star Legacy II*.

Spanish Rice

Adapted from *Smoky Mountain Magic*
JUNIOR LEAGUE OF JOHNSON CITY

*This savory rice mixture is a fine companion to roast chicken,
pork tenderloin or grilled fish.*

1 tablespoon butter or stick margarine (not reduced-calorie)
1 cup chopped onions
½ cup diced celery
½ cup diced green peppers
½ cup long-grain white rice
1 cup chopped tomatoes
1 tablespoon sliced green olives
1 teaspoon ground black pepper
½ teaspoon salt
1¼ cups boiling water

Preheat the oven to 350°.

In a large skillet over medium heat, melt the butter or margarine. Add the onions, celery and green peppers. Sauté for 10 minutes, or until the vegetables are almost tender. Add the rice and cook, stirring frequently, for 2 minutes.

Remove the skillet from the heat. Stir in the tomatoes, olives, black pepper and salt. Add the water.

Coat a 1½-quart ovenproof casserole with no-stick spray. Add the rice mixture. Bake for 1 hour, or until the rice is tender and the liquid is absorbed.

Makes 6 servings.

★ PER SERVING: 96 CALORIES, 2.3 G. FAT, 0.4 G. SATURATED FAT, 0 MG. CHOLESTEROL, 302 MG. SODIUM

....

ORZO AND PINE-NUT PILAF

Adapted from *Family Creations*
GLADNEY FUND VOLUNTEER AUXILIARIES

Orzo is semolina pasta shaped like extra-plump grains of rice. Look for imported Italian brands, available in some supermarkets and Italian food shops—they tend to hold their shape better during cooking. For variety, add some finely diced tomatoes, carrots or red peppers to the recipe along with the onions and celery.

1 tablespoon olive oil
1 small onion, chopped
1 stalk celery, chopped
1 cup orzo
2 cups defatted reduced-sodium chicken broth
1 tablespoon pine nuts, toasted
1 tablespoon minced parsley
¼ teaspoon ground black pepper
  Grated Parmesan cheese

In a medium saucepan over medium heat, warm the oil. Add the onions and celery; cook, stirring, for 8 minutes, or until tender and golden.

Stir in the orzo and mix well. Add the broth. Bring to a boil. Reduce the heat, cover and simmer for 15 minutes, or until the orzo is cooked.

Stir in the pine nuts, parsley and pepper. Sprinkle with the Parmesan.

TEST KITCHEN TIP: To toast pine nuts, place the nuts in a small heavy skillet. Cook over medium-high heat, stirring frequently, for 4 to 5 minutes, or until the nuts are golden. Pour the nuts onto a plate in a single layer to cool. If desired, you may toast the pine nuts in larger quantities and freeze them for convenience. To thaw the nuts, microwave them on high power for 1 minute. The smoky flavored nuts make a wonderful garnish for meatless pasta, salad and vegetable dishes.

Makes 6 servings.

★ PER SERVING: 169 CALORIES, 4.1 G. FAT, 0.5 G. SATURATED FAT, 33 MG. CHOLESTEROL, 170 MG. SODIUM

PASTA WITH TOMATOES AND HERBS

Adapted from *Cajun Men Cook*
BEAVER CLUB OF LAFAYETTE

Cajun Men Cook *stresses that ripe homegrown tomatoes are the best choice for this pasta side dish and also points out that it is the reaction of cold with hot that releases the unique fresh flavors.*

> 2 large tomatoes, coarsely chopped
> 4 cloves garlic, minced
> 20 large fresh basil leaves, torn into small pieces
> 3 tablespoons olive oil
> ⅛ teaspoon ground black pepper
>   Pinch of salt
> 6 ounces tiny shell pasta

In a medium bowl, stir together the tomatoes, garlic, basil, oil, pepper and salt. Cover and refrigerate for at least 2 hours to blend the flavors.

Cook the shells according to the package directions, but without adding salt or fat. Drain, rinse with hot water and drain again. Quickly transfer the hot pasta to a serving bowl. Add the chilled tomato mixture and toss to mix well. Serve immediately.

Makes 3 servings.

★ **PER SERVING:** 338 CALORIES, 15.4 G. TOTAL FAT, 2 G. SATURATED FAT, 48 MG. CHOLESTEROL, 18 MG. SODIUM

Beaver Club of Lafayette

Plenty of men are terrific cooks. But it's a safe bet that there's no place in the country where they cook with as much joie de vivre as in southern Louisiana's Acadiana region.

In Acadiana, cooking is pure art. This rich cultural gumbo started simmering 200 years ago with the Native Americans who originally populated the lush bayous. Ingredients from Spanish, African, French and English settlers soon were stirred into the pot.

Cajun Men Cook is delicious proof of the artistry of the region's cuisine. This collection of recipes and anecdotes is as exuberant as the Beaver Club itself.

The organization started as a Lion's Club chapter in 1939 and became an independent civic group in 1959. Sales of *Cajun Men Cook* help the devoted members continue their civic successes. Their first big project, the 1960 creation of a sprawling city park along the Vermilion River, set the standard to which they aspire.

Pasta with Tender Kale

Adapted from *Cooking in the Litchfield Hills*
PRATT NATURE CENTER

Kale makes this low-fat fettuccine and vegetable combo high in beta-carotene and calcium. Cooking in the Litchfield Hills suggests planting the Dwarf Blue Curled variety of kale as a border in your garden, so you'll have tender, sweet leaves all summer long.

- ⅓ cup boiling water
- 6 sun-dried tomato halves, snipped
- 1 large onion, chopped
- 8 ounces mushrooms, sliced
- 2–3 cloves garlic, minced
- 8 cups fresh kale, torn from ribs
- 1 cup chopped fresh sorrel or spinach
- 4 ounces yolk-free fettuccine
- ½ cup fat-free plain yogurt
- 2 tablespoons grated Parmesan cheese

In a small bowl, combine the water and tomatoes. Let stand for 15 minutes, or until the tomatoes are softened.

Coat a large skillet with olive oil no-stick spray. Add the onions. Cook, stirring, over medium heat for 3 minutes, or until the onions are tender. Add the mushrooms and garlic. Cook, stirring, for 5 minutes. Stir in the tomatoes, kale and sorrel or spinach. Cover and cook for 8 minutes, or until the greens are softened.

Cook the fettuccine according to the package directions, but without adding salt or fat. Drain, rinse with hot water and drain again. Toss the hot pasta with the kale mixture, yogurt and Parmesan.

Makes 2 servings.

★ PER SERVING: 454 CALORIES, 4.2 G. TOTAL FAT, 1.6 G. SATURATED FAT, 6 MG. CHOLESTEROL, 250 MG. SODIUM

....

RED PEPPER AND RICOTTA PUREE WITH LINGUINE

Adapted from *Virginia Fare*
JUNIOR LEAGUE OF RICHMOND

Because this healthful dish is served at room temperature, it's ideal to make ahead for casual entertaining.

    1 pound linguine
    1 container (15 ounces) reduced-fat ricotta cheese
    1 jar (7 ounces) roasted sweet red peppers, drained
    ⅓ cup grated Parmesan cheese
    ¼ cup defatted reduced-sodium chicken broth
  1–2 tablespoons lemon juice
    1 clove garlic, minced
      Pinch of ground black pepper
      Minced fresh parsley

Cook the linguine according to the package directions, but without adding salt or fat. Drain, rinse with cold water and drain again. Place in a large bowl and set aside.

In a food processor, puree the ricotta, red peppers, Parmesan, broth, lemon juice, garlic and black pepper. Pour over the pasta; toss to combine. Sprinkle with the parsley.

Serve at room temperature.

TEST KITCHEN TIP: Using a fresh sweet red pepper in this recipe will increase the flavor and reduce the sodium. To roast the pepper, broil it or place it directly over a gas flame or hot coals. Turn it frequently until completely charred. Place the pepper in a plastic bag. Seal tightly and set aside for 10 minutes. Working over a fine sieve set over a measuring cup or bowl, remove the core, seeds and charred skin. Cut the pepper flesh into strips. Any juice gotten from the pepper can be added to the pureed ricotta mixture.

Makes 6 servings.

★ PER SERVING: 359 CALORIES, 6 G. FAT, 1.4 G. SATURATED FAT, 80 MG. CHOLESTEROL, 136 MG. SODIUM

LIGHT FETTUCCINE

Adapted from *Some Like It Hot*
JUNIOR LEAGUE OF MCALLEN

This lightened version of fettuccine Alfredo is a favorite of the Junior League of McAllen, Texas. You can easily double the recipe to turn it into a main course.

- 6 ounces yolk-free fettuccine
- ¼ cup tub-style reduced-calorie margarine
- ½ cup reduced-fat sour cream
- ⅓ cup 1% low-fat milk
- 1 tablespoon grated Parmesan cheese
- ½ teaspoon dried parsley
- ⅛ teaspoon paprika
- ⅛ teaspoon salt-free garlic-and-herb seasoning or poultry seasoning
- ⅛ teaspoon ground black pepper

Cook the fettuccine according to the package directions, but without adding salt or fat. Drain, rinse with hot water and drain again.

In a large saucepan over medium heat, melt the margarine. Stir in the sour cream, milk, Parmesan, parsley, paprika, salt-free seasoning or poultry seasoning and pepper. Cook, stirring, over low heat until heated.

Add the fettuccine and toss until coated.

Makes 3 servings.

★PER SERVING: 384 CALORIES, 16.8 G. TOTAL FAT, 3.4 G. SATURATED FAT, 2 MG. CHOLESTEROL, 268 MG. SODIUM

MUSHROOM-SAUCED NOODLES

Adapted from *Nutbread and Nostalgia*
JUNIOR LEAGUE OF SOUTH BEND

*We combined half-and-half with fat-free sour cream to keep the
rich, creamy flavor of the original recipe while trimming fat.*

1½ cups half-and-half
⅔ cup fat-free sour cream
½ cup fat-free egg substitute
¼ cup all-purpose flour
⅔ cup finely chopped onions
16 ounces mushrooms, sliced
½ cup dry white wine or nonalcoholic white wine
½ teaspoon salt
½ teaspoon ground black pepper
8 ounces yolk-free egg noodles
¼ cup grated Parmesan cheese

In a medium bowl, whisk together the half-and-half, sour cream,
egg substitute and flour. Set aside.

Coat a large saucepan with no-stick spray. Add the onions.
Cook, stirring, over medium heat for 3 minutes, or until the onions
are tender. Add the mushrooms, wine, salt and pepper. Cover and
cook for 5 minutes.

Cook the noodles according to the package directions, but without adding salt or fat. Drain, rinse with hot water and drain again.
Set aside.

Slowly stir the half-and-half mixture into the mushroom mixture. Cook, stirring, over medium heat until the mixture just begins
to thicken. Gently stir in the noodles and Parmesan.

Makes 4 servings.

★ PER SERVING: 241 CALORIES, 6.8 G. TOTAL FAT, 3.9 G. SATURATED FAT,
19 MG. CHOLESTEROL, 266 MG. SODIUM

SPINACH LASAGNA

Adapted from *Florida Flavors*
ENVIRONMENTAL STUDIES COUNCIL

Using uncooked lasagna noodles makes this inviting Italian-style entrée extra easy.

> 1 container (15 ounces) fat-free ricotta cheese
> 1 package (10 ounces) frozen chopped spinach, thawed and well-drained
> 2 egg whites
> 1 teaspoon dried oregano
> ¼ teaspoon salt
>   Pinch of ground black pepper
> 2 cups shredded reduced-fat mozzarella cheese
> 3 cups fat-free spaghetti sauce
> 9 lasagna noodles
> 1 cup water

Preheat the oven to 350°. Coat a 13″ × 9″ baking pan with no-stick spray; set aside.

In a large bowl, stir together the ricotta, spinach, egg whites, oregano, salt, pepper and 1 cup of the mozzarella.

Spread 1 cup of the spaghetti sauce in the prepared baking pan; top with 3 of the lasagna noodles and half of the ricotta mixture. Repeat with 1 cup sauce, 3 lasagna noodles and the remaining ricotta mixture. Top with the remaining 3 noodles and the remaining 1 cup sauce. Sprinkle with the remaining 1 cup mozzarella.

Pour the water around the edges of the baking pan. Cover tightly with foil and bake for 1¼ hours, or until the noodles are tender. Let stand for 15 minutes before cutting.

TEST KITCHEN TIP: To make this casserole even lower in fat, use fat-free mozzarella cheese. Since fat-free cheese may get rubbery when cooked, sprinkle the remaining 1 cup of cheese over the casserole just before serving rather than putting it on top before baking.

Makes 6 servings.

★ PER SERVING: 373 CALORIES, 5.5 G. TOTAL FAT, 0 G. SATURATED FAT, 21 MG. CHOLESTEROL, 713 MG. SODIUM

OUR CAUSE

Environmental Studies Council

In a 1930s Spanish-style building on the banks of the Indian River in Jensen Beach, Florida, elementary students in the Martin County school system have learned two important things since 1972.

First, they have learned much about the complex, fascinating and beautiful world that exists apart from (or maybe in spite of) humans—the world of the fish, birds, insects, soil, plants and water that make up our natural environment. Perhaps just as important, they've also learned that school can be fun, at least at the Environmental Studies Center.

The Environmental Studies Center was the brainchild of two Martin County Middle School science teachers. With encouragement from the superintendent of schools and the school board, the pair secured a federal grant to provide a model program of hands-on environmental education. The pilot program opened its doors to students in 1972. When the grant ended, the Martin County school system assumed funding of the program, which serves students in kindergarten through seventh grade. The materials and programs developed at the Center have become models for similar programs in other parts of the country.

Profits from *Florida Flavors* go into the Council's trust fund, which supplements budget shortfalls and funds enhancement projects.

LAZY LASAGNA

Adapted from *Cooking with Class*
PARENTS' COUNCIL OF CHARLOTTE LATIN SCHOOL

With yolk-free egg noodles, reduced-fat ricotta, part-skim mozzarella and fat-free spaghetti sauce, this luscious version of lasagna is as low in fat as it is delicious. You can easily double the recipe.

8 ounces yolk-free egg noodles
1½ cups reduced-fat ricotta cheese
⅔ cup shredded reduced-fat mozzarella cheese
⅓ cup skim milk
¼ cup grated Parmesan cheese
2½ cups fat-free spaghetti sauce

Preheat the oven to 375°.

Cook the noodles according to the package directions, but without adding salt or fat. Drain, rinse with cold water and drain again.

In a large bowl, stir together the ricotta, mozzarella, milk and Parmesan. Add the noodles and mix well.

Spoon enough of the spaghetti sauce into an 8″ × 8″ baking pan to cover the bottom of the dish.

Spoon half of the noodle mixture into the dish. Top with half of the remaining spaghetti sauce. Repeat to use the remaining noodle mixture and spaghetti sauce.

Bake for 25 to 30 minutes, or until heated through.

Makes 4 servings.

★ **PER SERVING:** 430 CALORIES, 8.4 G. TOTAL FAT, 3.2 G. SATURATED FAT, 28 MG. CHOLESTEROL, 626 MG. SODIUM

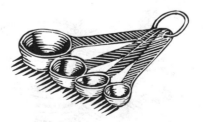

Pasta with Carrots and Ham

Adapted from *The Texas Experience*
RICHARDSON WOMAN'S CLUB

This pasta dish is quick, different and delicious. It makes a pleasant change when you want to break out of the pasta-with-red-sauce rut.

    4 carrots, sliced
    1 pound tagliatelle or spaghetti
    1 tablespoon butter or stick margarine (not reduced-calorie)
    1 cup finely diced lean ham
    3 tablespoons chopped fresh parsley
       Pinch of ground black pepper
    2 tablespoons grated Parmesan cheese

Bring a large pot of water to a boil over high heat. Add the carrots and cook for 8 to 10 minutes, or until tender but still firm. With a slotted spoon, remove the carrots and set aside.

Return the water to a boil; add the pasta. Cook, stirring frequently, for 7 to 8 minutes, or until tender but still firm. Reserve ½ cup of the cooking water, then drain the pasta.

Return the pot to medium heat. Add the butter or margarine and melt. Add the ham and cook for 2 minutes. Add the pasta, carrots, parsley, pepper and enough of the reserved cooking water to moisten the pasta. Heat thoroughly, tossing occasionally.

Serve sprinkled with the Parmesan.

Makes 6 servings.

★PER SERVING: 338 CALORIES, 5.9 G. FAT, 2.2 G. SATURATED FAT, 79 MG. CHOLESTEROL, 352 MG. SODIUM

LENTIL-BARLEY BAKE

Adapted from *Country Treasures*
VIRGINIA FARM BUREAU

Country Treasures *says that you can substitute an equal amount of honey or brown sugar for the molasses in this side-dish recipe.*

3½ cups water
1 cup green lentils, sorted and rinsed
1 medium onion, chopped
2 carrots, diced
6 tablespoons pearl barley
1 bay leaf
½ teaspoon salt
3 tablespoons molasses
2 tablespoons cider vinegar
1 clove garlic, minced
1 teaspoon dry mustard

Preheat the oven to 350°.

In a large saucepan, combine the water, lentils, onions, carrots, barley, bay leaf and ¼ teaspoon of the salt. Bring to a boil over high heat. Reduce the heat to medium-low, cover and simmer for 45 minutes, or until the lentils and barley are tender. Remove and discard the bay leaf. Transfer to a 2-quart casserole.

In a small bowl, stir together the molasses, vinegar, garlic, mustard and the remaining ¼ teaspoon salt. Add to the barley mixture in the casserole. Bake for 20 minutes, or until heated through.

Makes 4 servings.

★ PER SERVING: 180 CALORIES, 0.6 G. TOTAL FAT, 0.1 G. SATURATED FAT, 0 MG. CHOLESTEROL, 167 MG. SODIUM

....

JOHN'S FAMOUS BEANS

Adapted from *Coastal Cuisine, Texas Style*
JUNIOR SERVICE LEAGUE OF BRAZOSPORT

John likes to add ground beef and cheese to his beans. We followed the recommendation in Coastal Cuisine *to omit the meat and cheese for a low-fat, heart-healthy side dish.*

2½ cups dried pinto beans, soaked overnight and drained
10 cups water
1 can (14½ ounces) stewed tomatoes (with juice), cut up
1 large onion, chopped
4 cloves garlic, minced
3 tablespoons reduced-sodium Worcestershire sauce
2 tablespoons picante sauce
1½ teaspoons chili powder
1 teaspoon ground cumin
1 teaspoon dried cilantro

In a Dutch oven, combine the beans and water. Bring to a boil over high heat. Reduce the heat to medium, cover and simmer for 1 hour, or until the beans are almost tender. Drain, reserving 1 cup of the liquid.

Add the liquid back to the beans. Stir in the tomatoes (with juice), onions, garlic, Worcestershire sauce, picante sauce, chili powder, cumin and cilantro. Bring to a boil over high heat. Reduce the heat to medium, cover and simmer for 45 to 60 minutes, or until the beans are tender and the mixture is of the desired consistency.

TEST KITCHEN TIP: If you don't want to soak the beans overnight, use this quicker method. In a Dutch oven, combine the pinto beans and 10 cups cold water. Bring to a boil and boil for 2 minutes. Remove from the heat and let stand for 1 hour. Drain and rinse the beans. Continue as above.

Makes 8 servings.

★ PER SERVING: 213 CALORIES, 1 G. TOTAL FAT, 0.2 G. SATURATED FAT, 0 MG. CHOLESTEROL, 206 MG. SODIUM

TRIPLE-BEAN BAKE

Adapted from *Delicious Developments*
FRIENDS OF STRONG MEMORIAL HOSPITAL

This tempting bean-and-tomato medley gets its irresistible flavor from ketchup, molasses and brown sugar.

1 cup dried black beans, soaked overnight and drained
1 cup dried Great Northern beans, soaked overnight and drained
1 cup dried red kidney beans, soaked overnight and drained
3 bay leaves
8 cups water
1 can (14½ ounces) no-salt-added tomatoes (with juice), cut up
1 medium onion, chopped
1 green pepper, chopped
1 cup brewed coffee or water
⅔ cup reduced-sodium ketchup
½ cup dark molasses
⅓ cup packed brown sugar
1 tablespoon Worcestershire sauce
2 teaspoons mustard seeds
½ teaspoon salt

In a Dutch oven, combine the black beans, Great Northern beans, kidney beans, bay leaves and water. Bring to a boil over high heat. Reduce the heat to medium, cover and simmer for 1 hour, or until the beans are almost tender. Drain and return the beans to the pan.

Preheat the oven to 350°.

Stir the tomatoes (with juice), onions, peppers, coffee or water, ketchup, molasses, brown sugar, Worcestershire sauce, mustard seeds and salt into the drained beans. Bake, stirring occasionally, for 2 hours, or until the beans are tender and the mixture thickens. Remove and discard the bay leaves.

Makes 12 servings.

★PER SERVING: 187 CALORIES, 0.8 G. TOTAL FAT, 0.1 G. SATURATED FAT, 0 MG. CHOLESTEROL, 221 MG. SODIUM

OUR CAUSE

Friends of Strong Memorial Hospital

Strong Memorial Hospital, located in upstate New York, is a dynamic institution. A nationally recognized provider of outstanding health care services, it also serves as the principal teaching hospital of the University of Rochester.

Equally vibrant is the 1,100-member Friends of Strong, a volunteer group that provides support to the hospital's mission of excellence in patient care, education and research.

Friends of Strong brings a high degree of professionalism to volunteerism. Friends' leaders work directly with the hospital administrators to deliver vital services in 120 job categories.

Through sales of *Delicious Developments*, the Friends of Strong donates funds to the hospital's Trauma Center. This state-designated regional facility serves the nine-county Finger Lakes Region, providing lifesaving comprehensive emergency and critical-care services.

RED BEANS AND RICE

Adapted from *Rave Reviews*
JUNIOR LEAGUE OF NORTH LITTLE ROCK

*Salt pork and smoked sausages are often a staple of this saucy
New Orleans classic. A lighter, healthier approach uses turkey
bacon, turkey sausages and a few drops of liquid smoke. At only
6.2 grams of fat per serving, you won't miss the excess baggage.*

- 8 ounces dried red beans, soaked overnight and drained
- 5 cups water
- 1 small onion, chopped
- 3 slices turkey bacon, finely cut up
- 1 tablespoon dried parsley
- 1½ teaspoons Worcestershire sauce
- 1 clove garlic, minced
- ½ teaspoon ground black pepper
- ½ teaspoon salt
- ¼ teaspoon dried basil
- 2 dashes hot-pepper sauce
- 6 ounces fully cooked smoked turkey sausage, halved lengthwise and sliced ½″ thick
- 1–3 drops liquid smoke
- 4 cups hot cooked rice

In a large saucepan, combine the beans and water. Bring to a
boil over high heat. Reduce the heat to medium, cover and simmer
for 45 minutes.

Add the onions, bacon, parsley, Worcestershire sauce, garlic,
black pepper, salt, basil and hot-pepper sauce. Cover and cook over
low heat, stirring occasionally, for 30 minutes.

Add the sausage and liquid smoke. Cover and cook for 45 minutes, stirring occasionally. Uncover and gently simmer for 20 minutes, or until the mixture reaches the desired consistency. Serve over
the rice.

Makes 4 servings.

★PER SERVING: 536 CALORIES, 6.2 G. TOTAL FAT, 1.6 G. SATURATED FAT,
34 MG. CHOLESTEROL, 652 MG. SODIUM

QUICK BREAKFAST PIZZA

Adapted from *Cafe Oklahoma*
JUNIOR SERVICE LEAGUE OF MIDWEST CITY

For a jazzy brunch variation, use frozen hash-brown potatoes with onions and peppers. If you prefer, you can use a 13" × 9" baking pan instead of a pizza pan.

> 1 pound pork loin, trimmed of all visible fat and ground
> ½ teaspoon dried sage
> ¾ teaspoon ground black pepper
> 1 can (8 rolls) refrigerated crescent rolls
> 1 cup frozen hash-brown potatoes, thawed
> 1 cup shredded reduced-fat Cheddar cheese
> 4 egg whites
> 3 eggs
> ¼ cup skim milk
> ¼ teaspoon salt

Preheat the oven to 375°.

Coat a large skillet with no-stick spray; add the pork, sage and ¼ teaspoon of the pepper. Cook, stirring, until the pork is no longer pink. Drain off the fat.

Coat a 12" pizza pan (with sides) with no-stick spray. Separate the crescent-roll dough into 8 triangles and place on the prepared pan. Press the dough into the pan and up the sides to form a crust. Seal the perforations.

Spoon the pork mixture evenly over the crust. Spread the potatoes and Cheddar evenly over the pork.

In a medium bowl, beat together the egg whites, eggs, milk, salt and the remaining ½ teaspoon pepper. Pour the egg mixture over the dough.

Bake for 25 minutes, or until the crust is cooked through and the egg mixture is set.

TEST KITCHEN TIP: To make this dish lower in fat, use fat-free Cheddar cheese.

Makes 8 servings.

★ PER SERVING: 286 CALORIES, 15.9 G. TOTAL FAT, 4.9 G. SATURATED FAT, 112 MG. CHOLESTEROL, 580 MG. SODIUM

Fancy Egg Scrambles

Adapted from *Critics' Choice*
GUILD OF CORINTH THEATRE ARTS

We kept the rich taste of this tantalizing brunch dish but shortchanged the fat by replacing some of the whole eggs with egg whites, using evaporated skim milk and using reduced-fat Cheddar cheese.

EGGS

4 eggs
4 egg whites
1 tablespoon tub-style reduced-calorie margarine
½ cup diced Canadian bacon
1 jar (2½ ounces) sliced mushrooms, drained
2 tablespoons chopped scallions

CHEESE SAUCE

2 tablespoons all-purpose flour
1 can (12 ounces) evaporated skim milk
⅛ teaspoon ground black pepper
½ cup shredded reduced-fat Cheddar cheese

CRUMBS

1 cup fresh bread crumbs
1 tablespoon tub-style reduced-calorie margarine, melted
⅛ teaspoon paprika

TO MAKE THE EGGS: In a medium bowl, whisk together the eggs and egg whites.

Coat a large skillet with no-stick spray. Add the margarine and melt over medium heat. Add the bacon, mushrooms and scallions. Cook, stirring, for 2 to 3 minutes, or until the scallions are tender.

Pour the eggs into the skillet. Cook for 2 to 3 minutes, or until the eggs begin to set. Using a large spoon, lift and turn the egg mixture so it cooks evenly. Continue cooking until the egg mixture is thoroughly cooked but still glossy and moist on top. Remove the skillet from the heat.

Transfer the mixture to an 11″ × 7″ baking pan. Preheat the oven to 325°.

TO MAKE THE CHEESE SAUCE: Place the flour in a medium saucepan. Whisk in the milk and pepper. Cook, stirring, over medium heat until the mixture begins to thicken and just comes to a boil. Cook, stirring, 1 minute more. Remove from the heat, then stir in the Cheddar until melted. Spoon over the egg mixture in the baking pan.

TO MAKE THE CRUMBS: In a small bowl, toss together the bread crumbs, margarine and paprika until well-mixed. Sprinkle over the cheese sauce in the baking pan. Bake for 20 minutes, or until heated through.

Makes 4 servings.

★ PER SERVING: 299 CALORIES, 12 G. TOTAL FAT, 3.7 G. SATURATED FAT, 231 MG. CHOLESTEROL, 867 MG. SODIUM

Quick Swiss Soufflé

Adapted from *Cooking with Class*
PARENTS' COUNCIL OF CHARLOTTE LATIN SCHOOL

Although it's called a quick soufflé, this cheese-and-bacon dish is more like a strata because of the bread cubes. Use cubed whole-wheat bread for additional flavor and fiber. This makes a fine breakfast, brunch or light lunch entrée.

4 cups cubed white bread (no crusts)
8 ounces sliced reduced-fat Swiss cheese, finely cut up
2 tablespoons bacon bits
4 egg whites
2 eggs
1 teaspoon dry mustard
2¾ cups skim milk
1 can (10¾ ounces) low-fat, reduced-sodium condensed cream of mushroom soup

Coat a 13″ × 9″ baking pan with no-stick spray.

In a medium bowl, toss together the bread and Swiss. Transfer to the prepared dish. Sprinkle with the bacon bits.

In a medium bowl, whisk together the egg whites, eggs, mustard and 2¼ cups of the milk. Pour evenly over the bread mixture. Cover and refrigerate for 8 hours or overnight.

Preheat the oven to 300°.

In a small bowl, stir together the soup and the remaining ½ cup milk. Pour over the mixture in the baking pan. Bake for 1 hour, or until a knife inserted in the center comes out clean.

TEST KITCHEN TIP: Look for already cooked real bacon bits in the salad-dressing section of your supermarket.

Makes 8 servings.

★PER SERVING: 233 CALORIES, 8.3 G. TOTAL FAT, 3.6 G. SATURATED FAT, 73 MG. CHOLESTEROL, 464 MG. SODIUM

CALLING ALL SALADS

APRICOT SALAD

Adapted from *Plain and Elegant*
WEST GEORGIA MEDICAL CENTER AUXILIARY

*The comfort appeal of a classic American gelatin salad is
considerable. This version wisely retains the creamy appeal
but relies on sugar-free and nonfat ingredients to heighten
the natural fruit and nut flavors.*

1 can (8 ounces) crushed pineapple (packed in juice),
   undrained
1 package (4-serving-size) sugar-free apricot-flavored
   gelatin
1 cup nonfat buttermilk
½ cup toasted and chopped pecans
1 container (8 ounces) reduced-fat frozen whipped topping,
   thawed

In a small saucepan, combine the pineapple (with juice) and
gelatin. Place over low heat and stir just until the gelatin is dissolved.

Transfer the gelatin mixture to a medium bowl. Stir in the buttermilk. Refrigerate for 1 hour, or until partially set (the consistency
of unbeaten egg whites).

Gently fold in the pecans, then fold in the whipped topping. Refrigerate for 2 to 3 hours, or until firm.

TEST KITCHEN TIP: If you can't find apricot gelatin, you can
substitute pineapple for equally delicious results.

Makes 10 servings.

★ PER SERVING: 112 CALORIES, 9.3 G. TOTAL FAT, 0.3 G. SATURATED FAT,
   1 MG. CHOLESTEROL, 63 MG. SODIUM

OUR CAUSE

West Georgia Medical Center Auxiliary

The west Georgia city of LaGrange has a history of hospitality dating back to the Civil War. In April 1865, when a Union brigade marched into LaGrange, the local women discovered that some of their husbands were among the Confederate prisoners with the brigade. The Union colonel in command offered the prisoners a night's parole to spend with their families. To repay his kindness, one LaGrange woman invited him to dinner, where her Southern hospitality and cooking so impressed the colonel that he spared LaGrange from the fiery destruction he had planned.

LaGrange is now a thriving center of industry, but the hospitality that impressed the colonel is still very much alive. And thankfully, the many beautiful antebellum homes that were spared by the colonel's mercy still grace the town.

Also special to LaGrange is the West Georgia Medical Center, which serves the entire state of Georgia with its state-of-the-art equipment and technology and its genuinely caring attitude toward patients. Money raised by *Plain and Elegant* benefits the center's outreach programs to help the region's elderly.

STRAWBERRY-NUT SALAD

Adapted from *Foods à la Louisiane*
LOUISIANA FARM BUREAU FEDERATION

This gelatin salad is a fruit fiesta of strawberries, bananas and pineapple with a surprise stripe of sour cream in the center. It can double as a lovely light dessert. If you don't have fresh strawberries, you can substitute 2½ cups frozen unsweetened berries. Partially thaw and slice them before adding to the gelatin mixture.

1 package (8-serving-size) sugar-free strawberry-flavored gelatin
1 cup boiling water
3 bananas, mashed
2 cups sliced fresh strawberries
⅔ cup toasted and finely chopped walnuts
⅔ cup undrained crushed pineapple (packed in juice)
1 container (16 ounces) fat-free sour cream

Lightly coat an 11″ × 7″ baking pan with no-stick spray; set aside.

In a medium bowl, combine the gelatin and water, stirring until the gelatin is completely dissolved. Stir in the bananas until combined. Stir in the strawberries, walnuts and pineapple (with juice).

Spoon half of the gelatin mixture into the prepared dish. Refrigerate for 30 to 60 minutes, or until set. Let the remaining gelatin mixture stand at room temperature during this time.

Spread the sour cream on top of the set gelatin mixture. Carefully spoon the reserved gelatin mixture on top of the sour cream. Refrigerate for 2 to 3 hours, or until set.

TEST KITCHEN TIP: This salad is perfect for a large crowd or as a potluck dish. But if you're serving just a few, you can easily cut the recipe in half. Start with a 4-serving-size package of gelatin and halve the remaining ingredients. Spoon the mixture into an 8″ × 8″ baking pan.

Makes 12 servings.

★ PER SERVING: 126 CALORIES, 4.2 G. TOTAL FAT, 0.3 G. SATURATED FAT, 0 MG. CHOLESTEROL, 91 MG. SODIUM

MINTED FRUIT SALAD

Adapted from *Celebrations on the Bayou*
JUNIOR LEAGUE OF MONROE

For a fancy presentation, garnish this refreshing salad with fresh mint sprigs or edible flowers such as nasturtiums or violets. Be sure to select blooms that have not been sprayed with pesticides.

½ cup orange juice
¼ cup lemon juice
2 tablespoons sugar
3 teaspoons chopped fresh mint
1 pint strawberries
3 kiwifruit, thinly sliced
1 medium cantaloupe, cut into cubes or balls
1 medium honeydew melon, cut into cubes or balls

In a large glass or ceramic bowl, mix the orange juice, lemon juice, sugar and mint. Add the strawberries, kiwifruit, cantaloupe and honeydew. Toss gently; cover and refrigerate for 2 to 3 hours. Toss gently before serving.

Makes 20 servings.

★ PER SERVING: 31 CALORIES, 0.2 G. TOTAL FAT, 0 G. SATURATED FAT,
0 MG. CHOLESTEROL, 4 MG. SODIUM

TAPIOCA FRUIT SALAD

Adapted from *Florida's Finest*
JUNIOR LEAGUE OF SOUTH BREVARD COUNTY

Tapioca mimics the luscious mouthfeel of whipped cream–based fruit salads but without the dairy fat. To make this recipe even healthier, we decreased the sugar and used pineapple packed in juice instead of sugar syrup. It makes a lovely, light dessert.

       1 can (8 ounces) pineapple chunks (packed in juice), undrained
    1½ cups water
       ⅓ cup sugar
       3 tablespoons quick-cooking tapioca
       1 can (10½ ounces) mandarin orange sections (packed in water), drained
       1 cup halved red or green grapes
       1 banana, sliced
       ⅓ cup frozen orange juice concentrate, thawed

Drain the juice from the pineapple and place the juice in a small saucepan; set the pineapple aside.

Stir the water, sugar and tapioca into the pineapple juice. Let stand for 5 minutes. Then cook, stirring, over medium-high heat until the mixture comes to a full boil. (The mixture will thicken during cooling.) Remove from the heat and cool for 10 minutes, stirring occasionally.

Meanwhile, in a medium bowl, combine the reserved pineapple, oranges, grapes and bananas.

Stir the orange juice concentrate into the tapioca mixture. Then pour over the fruit. Gently toss until the fruit is evenly coated. Cover and refrigerate for 3 hours before serving.

Makes 8 servings.

TEST KITCHEN TIP: Here's a salad you can change to suit your fruit fancy. Apples, apricots, blueberries, mangoes, pears and dates are good selections.

★ PER SERVING: 115 CALORIES, 0.2 G. TOTAL FAT, 0 G. SATURATED FAT, 0 MG. CHOLESTEROL, 3 MG. SODIUM

Pomegranate Fruit Salad

Adapted from *Holy Cow, Chicago's Cooking!*
WOMEN OF THE CHURCH OF THE HOLY COMFORTER

Pomegranate seeds add a spark of color with a burst of sweet juice to almost any salad. Try them as a high-fiber, low-fat substitute for nuts.

DRESSING

6	ounces light cream cheese, softened
¼	cup fat-free mayonnaise
¼	cup pineapple juice
1½–2	tablespoons honey
½	teaspoon celery seeds

FRUIT SALAD

8–16	whole lettuce leaves
2	grapefruit or 3 oranges, peeled and sectioned
1	large apple or pear, cut into thin wedges
¼	cup pomegranate seeds

TO MAKE THE DRESSING: In a small bowl, stir together the cream cheese and mayonnaise until well-combined. Then stir in the pineapple juice, honey and celery seeds. If desired, cover and refrigerate until serving time. Stir before serving.

TO MAKE THE FRUIT SALAD: Line a serving platter or individual plates with the lettuce. On the lettuce, arrange the grapefruit or oranges and apples or pears. Then drizzle the dressing over the fruit and sprinkle with the pomegranate seeds.

Makes 8 servings.

★ PER SERVING: 103 CALORIES, 4 G. TOTAL FAT, 2.3 G. SATURATED FAT,
   7 MG. CHOLESTEROL, 219 MG. SODIUM

Pear and Celery Salad

Adapted from *Dinner Chimes*
FIRST PRESBYTERIAN CHURCH

You're sure to fall for this salad. Make it as part of an autumn dinner when pears are newly harvested. Choose Roquefort, Gorgonzola, Stilton or your favorite blue-veined cheese as a piquant contrast to the ripe, sweet fruit.

1½ cups chopped celery
½ cup golden raisins
⅓ cup reduced-fat mayonnaise
1 tablespoon honey
2 tablespoons lemon juice
   Lettuce leaves
2 large ripe but firm pears
2 tablespoons crumbled blue cheese

In a small bowl, combine the celery, raisins, mayonnaise, honey and 1 tablespoon of the lemon juice. Cover and refrigerate for several hours.

Arrange the lettuce on 4 salad plates. Cut each pear into 10 slices; brush with the remaining 1 tablespoon lemon juice. Arrange 5 pear slices on each lettuce-lined plate. Spoon about ½ cup of the celery mixture on each salad, then sprinkle with the blue cheese.

Makes 4 servings.

★ PER SERVING: 202 CALORIES, 6.8 G. TOTAL FAT, 0.7 G. SATURATED FAT, 9 MG. CHOLESTEROL, 91 MG. SODIUM

Pineapple Coleslaw

Adapted from *Plain and Elegant*
WEST GEORGIA MEDICAL CENTER AUXILIARY

*Sweet, juicy pineapple plays perfect counterpoint to the slightly
sharp taste of cabbage in this distinctive salad. Be sure to
choose fruit packed in its own juice instead of heavy syrup.
You'll eliminate lots of unnecessary sugar calories.*

> 2 cups shredded cabbage
> ½ cup pineapple tidbits or crushed pineapple
> (packed in juice), drained
> ¼ cup chopped celery
> ⅓ cup nonfat ranch-style or honey-Dijon salad dressing

In a medium bowl, stir together the cabbage, pineapple and celery. Add the salad dressing and gently toss until the cabbage mixture
is evenly coated. Cover and refrigerate for up to 8 hours before serving.

Makes 4 servings.

★ **PER SERVING:** 36 CALORIES, 0.1 G. TOTAL FAT, 0 G. SATURATED FAT,
0 MG. CHOLESTEROL, 143 MG. SODIUM

BASIL-BALSAMIC POTATO SALAD

Adapted from *Nothin' Finer*
CHAPEL HILL SERVICE LEAGUE

Well-aged Italian balsamic vinegar is so mellow that you need only a small amount of olive oil to round out the dressing for this potato salad.

1 pound tiny red potatoes
¼ cup balsamic vinegar
1½ teaspoons Dijon mustard
2 tablespoons chopped fresh basil
1 tablespoon olive oil
Pinch of salt
Pinch of ground black pepper
1 small scallion, chopped
1 tablespoon chopped fresh parsley

Place the potatoes in a large saucepan and cover with cold water. Cover and cook over medium heat for 15 to 20 minutes, or just until tender. Drain and cool slightly. Using a sharp knife, slice the potatoes ¼" thick and transfer them to a large bowl.

In a small bowl, whisk together the vinegar, mustard, basil, oil, salt and pepper. Pour over the potatoes. Gently toss until the potatoes are evenly coated. Add the scallions and parsley; toss gently. Cover and let stand at room temperature or in the refrigerator for at least 4 hours to blend the flavors.

Makes 6 servings.

★ PER SERVING: 96 CALORIES, 2.4 G. TOTAL FAT, 0.3 G. SATURATED FAT, 0 MG. CHOLESTEROL, 23 MG. SODIUM

Chapel Hill Service League

Cookbooks are nothing new for the busy Chapel Hill Service League. *Nothin' Finer* is the league's sixth cookbook, and each has been a resounding success. Maybe that's because the recipes are always as appealing as North Carolina itself. Since the first English settlers arrived in 1597, North Carolina's temperate climate, stunning topography and rich natural resources have made it an obvious choice for commerce, industry and academics.

The Chapel Hill Service League formed in 1939 and published its first cookbook in 1953. *Nothin' Finer* continues the group's custom of saluting the warm and wonderful down-home cooking of the Tarheel State. Recipes that have become enduring classics from past League cookbooks are featured throughout the latest volume.

The League will use the proceeds from sales of this newest book to fund the many community projects it sponsors, especially those that entail outreach to children and families.

Tortellini with Tomatoes and Herb Dressing

Adapted from *Albuquerque Academy à la Carte*
ALBUQUERQUE ACADEMY PARENTS' ASSOCIATION

Make an impression at the next potluck. Instead of boring macaroni salad, bring a vibrant tortellini salad seasoned with fresh tomatoes and herbs in Italian dressing.

1 package (9 ounces) fresh cheese-filled tortellini
1 teaspoon olive oil
¼ cup loosely packed fresh basil, torn
¼ cup loosely packed fresh parsley
3 tablespoons reduced-fat Italian salad dressing
1 small clove garlic, minced
Pinch of ground black pepper
2 small tomatoes, seeded and chopped
2 tablespoons finely chopped onions

Cook the tortellini according to the package directions, but without adding salt. Drain, rinse with hot water and drain again. Transfer the tortellini to a medium bowl. Drizzle with the oil, then toss until evenly coated. Cool to room temperature.

In a blender or small food processor, blend the basil, parsley, salad dressing, garlic and pepper until the herbs are very finely chopped and the mixture is well-combined. (If necessary, stop and scrape down the sides of the container.)

Add the tomatoes and onions to the tortellini. Gently toss until combined. Then add the basil mixture and toss until the tortellini mixture is evenly coated. Serve at room temperature.

Makes 6 servings.

★ PER SERVING: 149 CALORIES, 4.3 G. TOTAL FAT, 1.6 G. SATURATED FAT, 22 MG. CHOLESTEROL, 257 MG. SODIUM

MARINATED VEGETABLE SALAD

Adapted from *Lone Star Legacy*
AUSTIN JUNIOR FORUM

Most commercial salad dressings come in fat-free and reduced-fat versions, which make easy, fast marinades for vegetables and meats. This recipe calls for Italian dressing, but you could use almost any low-fat herb-flavored vinaigrette.

1½ cups fat-free or reduced-fat Italian salad dressing
¼ cup chopped fresh parsley
1 package (10 ounces) frozen brussels sprouts, thawed and halved
1 package (9 ounces) frozen artichoke hearts, thawed and quartered
2 carrots, thinly sliced on the diagonal
1 cucumber, sliced
1 green or sweet yellow pepper, chopped
1 cup small cauliflower florets
1 cup small broccoli florets
2 cups sliced mushrooms

In a large bowl, stir together the salad dressing and parsley. Add the brussels sprouts, artichokes, carrots, cucumbers, peppers, cauliflower and broccoli. Stir until coated. Cover and refrigerate for at least 2 hours, stirring occasionally.

Just before serving, add the mushrooms and gently stir until coated.

Makes 20 servings.

★ PER SERVING: 78 CALORIES, 0.1 G. TOTAL FAT, 0 G. SATURATED FAT, 0 MG. CHOLESTEROL, 318 MG. SODIUM

BLACK-BEAN AND CORN SALAD

Adapted from *Virginia Fare*
JUNIOR LEAGUE OF RICHMOND

This nutritious high-fiber salad was made even more healthful by replacing most of the oil in the dressing with broth.

DRESSING

⅓ cup lemon juice
3 tablespoons reduced-sodium vegetable or defatted chicken broth
2 tablespoons olive oil
Pinch of salt

SALAD

1 can (15 ounces) black beans, rinsed and drained
1 cup frozen baby corn or white whole-kernel corn, thawed
1 can (4 ounces) diced green chili peppers, drained
1 tomato, chopped
½ cup thinly sliced scallions
½ cup finely chopped fresh parsley
¼–½ cup chopped fresh cilantro

TO MAKE THE DRESSING: In a medium bowl, whisk together the lemon juice, broth, oil and salt.

TO MAKE THE SALAD: To the dressing, add the beans, corn, peppers, tomatoes, scallions, parsley and cilantro. Gently toss until the bean mixture is evenly coated with the dressing.

Cover and let stand at room temperature for at least 2 hours to blend the flavors. Refrigerate for longer storage.

TEST KITCHEN TIP: If you have more time, you can reduce the sodium a bit further by using cooked dried black beans instead of canned beans.

For 1 cup of cooked beans, begin with ¾ cup dried black beans. Sort and rinse the beans, then soak them overnight in plenty of cold water. Drain and place in a saucepan with enough fresh cold water to cover them by 2″. Cook 1 to 1½ hours, or until tender but firm. Drain the beans before using.

Makes 8 servings.

★ PER SERVING: 102 CALORIES, 3.9 G. TOTAL FAT, 0.5 G. SATURATED FAT, 0 MG. CHOLESTEROL, 346 MG. SODIUM

....

CUCUMBER AND TOMATO SALAD WITH SOUR-CREAM DRESSING

Adapted from *Georgia on My Menu*
JUNIOR LEAGUE OF COBB-MARIETTA COUNTY

Cucumbers in sour-cream dressing is an old-fashioned American favorite. Add ripe tomatoes, and you have a salad made for summer.

    2 cucumbers, peeled and very thinly sliced
    ½ cup reduced-fat sour cream
    2 tablespoons lemon juice
      Pinch of salt
      Pinch of sugar
      Dash of ground red pepper
    3 ripe tomatoes, sliced

In a small bowl, combine the cucumbers, sour cream, lemon juice, salt, sugar and pepper. Cover and refrigerate for several hours. To serve, spoon the cucumber mixture over the tomatoes.

Makes 6 servings.

★ PER SERVING: 51 CALORIES, 1.3 G. TOTAL FAT, 0.7 G. SATURATED FAT, 0 MG. CHOLESTEROL, 30 MG. SODIUM

CREAMY CAESAR SALAD

Adapted from *West of the Rockies*
JUNIOR SERVICE LEAGUE OF GRAND JUNCTION

This recipe is featured in the "Light and Healthy" chapter of
West of the Rockies. *If you want to top it with croutons that are
low in fat, toast some whole-grain bread, then cut it into cubes.
Or simply crumble purchased melba toast over the salad.*

7   cups torn romaine lettuce
¼   cup fat-free mayonnaise
2   tablespoons finely shredded Parmesan cheese
1   tablespoon lemon juice
1   tablespoon water
½   teaspoon white-wine Worcestershire sauce
½   teaspoon Dijon mustard
1   clove garlic, minced
¼   teaspoon ground black pepper
¼   teaspoon anchovy paste

Place the lettuce in a large bowl and set aside.

In a small bowl, whisk together the mayonnaise, Parmesan, lemon juice, water, Worcestershire sauce, mustard, garlic, pepper and anchovy paste. Pour over the lettuce and gently toss until the lettuce is evenly coated.

TEST KITCHEN TIP: If you don't have white-wine Worcestershire sauce on hand, you can use the regular variety. However, expect the dressing to be a bit darker in color and to have a slightly stronger Worcestershire flavor.

Makes 6 servings.

★ PER SERVING: 31 CALORIES, 0.8 G. TOTAL FAT, 0.4 G. SATURATED FAT, 2 MG. CHOLESTEROL, 191 MG. SODIUM

CRANBERRY-ORANGE SALAD

Adapted from *Treasures of the Smokies*
JUNIOR LEAGUE OF JOHNSON CITY

Make this salad for a knockout side dish next Thanksgiving.

SALAD

> 7 cups torn Boston or Bibb lettuce
> 1 can (8 ounces) mandarin orange sections
>   (packed in water), drained
> 1 small red onion, sliced and separated into rings
> ½ cup fresh or dried cranberries

DRESSING

> ½ cup fat-free raspberry yogurt
> 1 tablespoon vinegar
> 1½ teaspoons maple syrup

TO MAKE THE SALAD: In a large bowl, combine the lettuce, oranges, onions and cranberries.

TO MAKE THE DRESSING: In a small bowl, stir together the yogurt, vinegar and maple syrup. Pour over the lettuce mixture. Gently toss until the lettuce mixture is evenly coated.

Makes 6 servings.

★ PER SERVING: 52 CALORIES, 0.3 G. TOTAL FAT, 0 G. SATURATED FAT,
0 MG. CHOLESTEROL, 17 MG. SODIUM

STEAK SALAD

Adapted from *Of Tide and Thyme*
JUNIOR LEAGUE OF ANNAPOLIS

*Even hearty appetites will be well-satisfied with this robustly
flavored, yet surprisingly light, main-course salad. It's a natural
for a casual summer buffet or potluck.*

STEAK SALAD

1½ pounds beef top sirloin or top round steak,
   grilled and cubed
8 ounces mushrooms, sliced
1 jar (13 ounces) artichoke hearts, drained and quartered
1 bunch scallions, thinly sliced
2 tablespoons minced fresh parsley
2 tomatoes, cut into wedges
   Pinch of salt
   Pinch of ground black pepper
1 medium head romaine lettuce

DRESSING

2 tablespoons tarragon or other herb vinegar
1½ teaspoons lemon juice
½ teaspoon salt
¼ cup fat-free egg substitute
1 teaspoon Dijon mustard
1 teaspoon honey
2 tablespoons olive oil

TO MAKE THE STEAK SALAD: In a salad bowl, combine the beef,
mushrooms, artichokes, scallions, parsley, tomatoes, salt and pepper. Toss gently to combine.

TO MAKE THE DRESSING: In a blender, combine the vinegar,
lemon juice, salt, egg substitute, mustard and honey. With the ma-
chine running, add the oil in a steady stream.

To serve, arrange the lettuce on dinner plates, top with the salad
mixture and drizzle with the dressing.

Makes 6 servings.

★ PER SERVING: 282 CALORIES, 10.4 G. TOTAL FAT, 2.5 G. SATURATED FAT,
72 MG. CHOLESTEROL, 325 MG. SODIUM

Junior League of Annapolis

Annapolis is a jewel of a city, with many sparkling facets.

For history buffs it's a vibrant slice of colonial America. Many buildings, still in use today, date back to the early eighteenth century. To stand under the 400-year-old Liberty Tree on the grounds of St. John's College is to feel a vital connection to the colonial Sons of Liberty who argued for freedom in that same spot.

For graduates of the United States Naval Academy, Annapolis has been a spiritual home since 1845.

For professional and amateur sailors, the city is a hub of keen sailing competitions, including the Annapolis-to-Bermuda and Annapolis-to-Newport biennial races.

For the Junior League of Annapolis, the city is a gem, which they constantly strive to polish. Started as a committee of the Junior League of Baltimore, the Annapolis League is now a thriving organization with 275 members committed to improving life for all in Anne Arundel County. Proceeds from *Of Tide and Thyme* support the Back-to-School Book project, the Emergency Baby Pantry, Food Link, Kiva Club (a shelter for abused teens) and more.

....

ORANGE SALAD WITH HONEY VINAIGRETTE

Adapted from *A Shining Feast*
FIRST BAPTIST CHURCH OF SHREVEPORT

This sunny salad, with its helping of vitamin C, is especially welcome in the winter when garden-ripe tomatoes aren't available.

DRESSING

    1½ tablespoons white-wine vinegar
    1 tablespoon water
    1 tablespoon orange juice
    1 tablespoon honey
    2 teaspoons canola oil

SALAD

    2 cups torn red-leaf lettuce
    2 cups torn romaine lettuce
    2 navel oranges, peeled and cut into crosswise slices
    1 small red onion, thinly sliced and separated into rings

TO MAKE THE DRESSING: In a small bowl, whisk together the vinegar, water, orange juice, honey and oil.

TO MAKE THE SALAD: In a medium bowl, toss together the red-leaf lettuce and romaine lettuce. Transfer to salad plates. Arrange the oranges and onions on top. Drizzle with the dressing.

Makes 4 servings.

★ PER SERVING: 98 CALORIES, 2.6 G. TOTAL FAT, 0.2 G. SATURATED FAT, 0 MG. CHOLESTEROL, 6 MG. SODIUM

....

Beef Club Salad

Adapted from *Presentations*
FRIENDS OF LIED CENTER FOR PERFORMING ARTS

This delightful main-course salad needed only a bit of nutritional fine-tuning. We decreased the meat and increased the quotient of vitamin- and fiber-rich broccoli and cauliflower. By substituting reduced-fat mayonnaise for oil and using frozen artichoke hearts instead of canned ones, we reduced the fat and sodium.

DRESSING

⅓ cup reduced-fat mayonnaise
3 tablespoons red-wine vinegar
1 teaspoon finely chopped fresh basil
1 teaspoon finely chopped fresh oregano
½ teaspoon sugar
1 clove garlic, minced
Pinch of ground black pepper

SALAD

1½ cups small cauliflower florets
1½ cups small broccoli florets
12 ounces cooked beef sirloin or tenderloin steak, thinly sliced and cut into bite-size strips
1 package (9 ounces) frozen artichoke hearts, thawed and quartered
1 small sweet red pepper, thinly sliced
¼ cup sliced scallions
Large red or green lettuce leaves

TO MAKE THE DRESSING: In a small bowl, whisk together the mayonnaise, vinegar, basil, oregano, sugar, garlic and pepper. Cover and refrigerate for at least 2 hours to blend the flavors.

TO MAKE THE SALAD: In a large saucepan with a tight-fitting lid, bring 1″ of water to a boil. Place the cauliflower and broccoli in a steamer basket and set the basket in the saucepan, making sure the basket sits above the water.

Cover and steam for 3 to 4 minutes, or just until the vegetables are slightly tender but still very crisp. Chill the vegetables before serving.

In a large bowl, combine the cauliflower, broccoli, beef, arti-

(continued)

chokes, peppers and scallions. Add the dressing, then gently toss until the vegetable mixture is evenly coated.

Serve on plates lined with the lettuce.

Makes 4 servings.

★ PER SERVING: 291 CALORIES, 13.2 G. TOTAL FAT, 3.1 G. SATURATED FAT, 82 MG. CHOLESTEROL, 132 MG. SODIUM

···

CURRIED PORK-AND-APPLE SALAD

Adapted from *The Take Care Cookbook*
MID-FAIRFIELD HOSPICE

This recipe is a delicious way to use up cooked lean pork, beef, poultry or firm white fish. Simply start with about 2 cups cooked protein and proceed from the second step in the recipe.

SALAD

  1 pork tenderloin (¾–1 pound), trimmed of all visible fat
  5 apples, diced
1¼ cups sliced celery
 ½ cup raisins
 ⅓ cup sliced scallions
 ¼ cup slivered almonds, toasted
 ¼ cup sliced ripe olives
  6 lettuce leaf cups

DRESSING

 ½ cup reduced-fat mayonnaise
 2 tablespoons skim milk
 2 teaspoons lemon juice
 1 teaspoon curry powder
   Pinch of ground black pepper

TO MAKE THE SALAD: Preheat the oven to 425°.

If necessary, to make the tenderloin a uniform size, fold the narrow ends under and tie with kitchen string. Place the tenderloin on a rack in a shallow roasting pan. Insert a meat thermometer near the center of the roast. Roast for 30 minutes, or until the thermometer registers 160°. Cover and refrigerate overnight.

Mid-Fairfield Hospice

There is something special about individuals who devote their days to caring for the terminally ill. But the volunteers at Mid-Fairfield Hospice would argue that it is their patients, not themselves, who are truly special.

Since 1982 the devoted doctors, nurses, social workers and volunteers of the nonprofit agency have worked to achieve a fundamental right for their patients. They believe everyone has the right to spend his last days on earth in comfort and dignity, surrounded by loved ones.

The Take Care Cookbook is a collection of recipes from staff, volunteers and supporters of the agency as well as from the many fine restaurants in Fairfield County, Connecticut. The hospice agency believes that terminally ill patients deserve to die in dignity, free from fear and pain, in their own homes, whether or not they are capable of paying for in-home hospice care. Proceeds from *The Take Care Cookbook* provide this humane service to patients who otherwise couldn't afford it.

Cut the tenderloin into ½″ cubes. Place in a large bowl and add the apples, celery, raisins, scallions, almonds and olives. Toss to mix well.

TO MAKE THE DRESSING: In a small bowl, whisk together the mayonnaise, milk, lemon juice, curry powder and pepper. Pour over the pork mixture. Gently toss to coat evenly.

Spoon into the lettuce cups to serve.

TEST KITCHEN TIP: Choose either sweet or slightly tart apples for this salad. Sweet apples include Red Delicious, Fuji and Gala; slightly tart ones include Jonathan, Rome Beauty and Winesap.

Makes 6 servings.

★ PER SERVING: 268 CALORIES, 11.1 G. TOTAL FAT, 1.1 G. SATURATED FAT, 47 MG. CHOLESTEROL, 77 MG. SODIUM

....

BARBECUE PIG IN THE GREENS

Adapted from *Cafe Oklahoma*
JUNIOR SERVICE LEAGUE OF MIDWEST CITY

Welcome to the New South. This savory barbecue salad is lightened up with lean pork loin and a roster of reduced-fat condiments.

DRESSING

¼ cup reduced-fat mayonnaise
¼ cup barbecue sauce
2 tablespoons fat-free sour cream
2 tablespoons nonfat buttermilk or skim milk
1 tablespoon finely chopped onions
1 tablespoon lemon juice
¼ teaspoon sugar
¼ teaspoon ground black pepper

SALAD

6 cups torn mixed salad greens
½ cup quartered cherry tomatoes
⅓ cup chopped green or sweet red peppers
¼ cup sliced celery
¼ cup thinly sliced carrots
¼ cup shredded reduced-fat Cheddar cheese
¼ cup shredded reduced-fat Monterey Jack cheese
1½ cups shredded cooked pork loin

TO MAKE THE DRESSING: In a small bowl, whisk together the mayonnaise, barbecue sauce, sour cream, milk, onions, lemon juice, sugar and pepper. If desired, cover and refrigerate until serving time.

TO MAKE THE SALAD: In a large bowl, combine the salad greens, tomatoes, peppers, celery, carrots and Cheddar and Monterey Jack. Gently toss until combined.

To serve, transfer the lettuce mixture to large salad plates. Top with the pork and drizzle with the dressing.

TEST KITCHEN TIP: You may substitute shredded cooked lean beef, chicken breast or turkey breast for the pork.

Makes 4 servings.

★ PER SERVING: 239 CALORIES, 13.6 G. TOTAL FAT, 4.2 G. SATURATED FAT, 56 MG. CHOLESTEROL, 286 MG. SODIUM

....

South-of-the-Border Chicken

Adapted from *Nothin' Finer*
CHAPEL HILL SERVICE LEAGUE

Make this salad and your meal is complete. It's a boldly flavored bowlful, featuring a whole grain, a complex carbohydrate, a vegetable and a lean protein.

SALAD

2 cups cooked brown rice
2 cups frozen whole-kernel corn, thawed
1 can (15 ounces) black beans, rinsed and drained
1½ cups cubed cooked chicken breast
2 cups no-oil, unsalted tortilla chips

DRESSING

¼ cup orange juice
2 tablespoons canola oil
2 tablespoons finely chopped fresh cilantro
½ jalapeño pepper, seeded and finely chopped
(wear plastic gloves when handling)
2 teaspoons chili powder
Pinch of salt

TO MAKE THE SALAD: In a large bowl, stir together the rice, corn, beans and chicken.

TO MAKE THE DRESSING: In a small bowl, whisk together the orange juice, oil, cilantro, peppers, chili powder and salt. Pour over the salad mixture. Gently toss until the rice mixture is evenly coated. Cover and refrigerate for 3 hours before serving.

Serve garnished with the tortilla chips.

Makes 4 servings.

★ PER SERVING: 458 CALORIES, 11.1 G. TOTAL FAT, 1.1 G. SATURATED FAT, 36 MG. CHOLESTEROL, 385 MG. SODIUM

Paella Salad

Adapted from *Holy Smoke*
PEACHTREE ROAD UNITED METHODIST CHURCH

Paella pleases, whether in the form of the traditional Spanish hot-rice casserole or in this contemporary salad.

SALAD

1⅓ cups water
⅔ cup long-grain white rice
⅛ teaspoon ground saffron or turmeric
8 ounces small shrimp, peeled and deveined
1½ cups chopped cooked chicken breast
1 tomato, chopped
½ cup frozen peas, thawed
⅓ cup thinly sliced celery
¼ cup finely chopped onions
1 jar (2 ounces) pimentos, drained and chopped

DRESSING

¼ cup tarragon vinegar
1 tablespoon olive oil
1 tablespoon defatted reduced-sodium chicken broth
¼ teaspoon curry powder
⅛ teaspoon dry mustard
⅛ teaspoon ground white pepper

TO MAKE THE SALAD: Place the water in a medium saucepan. Add the rice and saffron or turmeric. Bring to a boil, then reduce the heat. Cover and simmer for 20 minutes, or until the rice is tender.

Meanwhile, place the shrimp in a medium skillet. Add cold water to cover. Bring to a boil, then reduce the heat to low. Gently simmer for 1 to 3 minutes, or until the shrimp turn pink. Drain and place in a large bowl. Add the rice, chicken, tomatoes, peas, celery, onions and pimentos; toss to mix well.

TO MAKE THE DRESSING: In a bowl, whisk together the vinegar, oil, broth, curry powder, mustard and pepper. Pour over the rice mixture and toss. Cover and refrigerate for at least 4 hours.

Makes 4 servings.

★ PER SERVING: 291 CALORIES, 5.9 G. TOTAL FAT, 1.1 G. SATURATED FAT, 123 MG. CHOLESTEROL, 169 MG. SODIUM

WHITE-BEAN AND TUNA SALAD

Adapted from *Presentations*
FRIENDS OF LIED CENTER FOR PERFORMING ARTS

In the northern Italian city of Florence, bean and tuna crostini (toast rounds with assorted savory toppings) are a popular street-side snack. With this main-dish version, you can serve Italian bread on the side.

DRESSING

> 2 tablespoons defatted reduced-sodium chicken broth
> 1 tablespoon olive oil
> 1 tablespoon lemon juice
> 2 teaspoons Dijon mustard
> Pinch of ground black pepper
> 2 tablespoons chopped fresh basil

SALAD

> 1 can (15½ ounces) Great Northern beans or cannellini beans, rinsed and drained
> ½ cup chopped tomatoes
> ⅓ cup finely chopped onions
> 2 cans (6 ounces each) reduced-sodium water-packed albacore tuna, drained and broken into small chunks
> Lettuce leaves

TO MAKE THE DRESSING: In a medium bowl, whisk together the broth, oil, lemon juice, mustard and pepper. Stir in the basil.

TO MAKE THE SALAD: Add the beans, tomatoes and onions to the dressing. Gently toss until the bean mixture is evenly coated. Add the tuna and toss again. Serve on the lettuce.

TEST KITCHEN TIP: For variety, the Friends of Lied suggest substituting 2 cups chopped cooked chicken breast for the tuna.

Makes 3 servings.

★ PER SERVING: 304 CALORIES, 8 G. TOTAL FAT, 1 G. SATURATED FAT, 40 MG. CHOLESTEROL, 401 MG. SODIUM

Dijon-Honey Dressing

Adapted from *Simple Elegance*
OUR LADY OF PERPETUAL HELP WOMEN'S GUILD

For a creamy homemade honey-mustard salad dressing, try this recipe. We used reduced-fat mayonnaise and skim milk to keep it low in fat. Serve the dressing over spinach or Bibb or Boston lettuce.

½ cup reduced-fat mayonnaise
2 tablespoons Dijon mustard
2 tablespoons honey
1 tablespoon skim milk
¼–½ teaspoon cider vinegar
Pinch of ground red pepper

In a small bowl, whisk together the mayonnaise, mustard, honey, milk, vinegar and pepper.

Makes ¾ cup; 6 servings.

★ PER 2 TABLESPOONS: 81 CALORIES, 5.7 G. TOTAL FAT, 1.3 G. SATURATED FAT, 0 MG. CHOLESTEROL, 216 MG. SODIUM

Ranch Pepper Dressing

Adapted from *What's Cooking in Delaware*
AMERICAN RED CROSS IN DELAWARE

*While bottled salad dressings are convenient, nothing beats the
flavor of homemade—especially when you control the fat and
calories as is done here.*

½ cup fat-free mayonnaise
¼ cup reduced-fat sour cream
¼ cup skim milk or nonfat buttermilk
1 tablespoon finely chopped fresh parsley
½ teaspoon cracked black pepper
½ teaspoon onion powder
1 clove garlic, minced

In a small bowl, whisk together the mayonnaise, sour cream,
milk, parsley, pepper, onion powder and garlic. Cover and refrigerate for at least 3 hours to blend the flavors.

Makes ¾ cup; 6 servings.

★ PER 2 TABLESPOONS: 33 CALORIES, 0.5 G. TOTAL FAT, 0.3 G. SATURATED
FAT, 0 MG. CHOLESTEROL, 270 MG. SODIUM

WATERCRESS SALAD DRESSING

Adapted from *The Maine Collection*
PORTLAND MUSEUM OF ART GUILD

The Portland Museum of Art Guild used buttermilk to reduce the fat in this creamy dressing. Serve it over a tossed salad of mixed greens, tomatoes and cucumbers.

½	cup nonfat buttermilk
1½	cups loosely packed watercress with stems removed
1	small scallion, minced
½	cup reduced-fat mayonnaise
	Pinch of salt
	Pinch of ground black pepper
1–2	tablespoons skim milk (optional)

In a blender or a small food processor, blend the buttermilk, watercress and scallions until pureed.

Transfer the mixture to a small bowl. Stir in the mayonnaise, salt and pepper. If desired, stir in enough of the milk to make a thinner consistency.

Makes 1 cup; 8 servings.

★ PER 2 TABLESPOONS: 46 CALORIES, 4 G. TOTAL FAT, 1 G. SATURATED FAT, 0 MG. CHOLESTEROL, 129 MG. SODIUM

Portland Museum of Art Guild

Perhaps because so much of Maine has stayed unspoiled and undeveloped, the state has relatively few buildings that are federally designated National Historic Landmarks. One of the 34 such-named houses, though, is the McLellan-Sweat House of the Portland Museum of Art, and it is a beauty.

This grand three-story brick house was built in 1800 at the height of the Federal Period in architecture and design. Sadly, the house has been closed to the public for the past ten years. *The Maine Collection* cookbook, by the Portland Museum of Art Guild, should change all that. Earnings from this compilation of Down East recipes go toward refurbishing and reopening the house.

The McLellan-Sweat House, named for its first and last owners, was the original home of the museum. Houses built in the Federal style seem to proclaim the eighteenth- and nineteenth-century belief in Manifest Destiny for America. The house, with its vast but graceful proportions and its carefully wrought staircases, moldings and other details, fairly shouts this confident philosophy.

NEW ORLEANS SALAD DRESSING

Adapted from *RSVP*
JUNIOR LEAGUE OF PORTLAND

This vinaigrette uses white grape juice thickened with a little cornstarch to cut back on fat.

⅔ cup white grape juice
¼ cup white-wine vinegar or cider vinegar
3 tablespoons canola oil
1 teaspoon cornstarch
½ teaspoon salt
½ teaspoon dry mustard
½ teaspoon paprika
½ teaspoon Worcestershire sauce
¼ teaspoon ground black pepper

In a small saucepan, whisk together the grape juice, vinegar, oil and cornstarch until well-combined. Cook, stirring, over medium heat until the mixture begins to thicken and just comes to a boil. Cook, stirring, for 1 minute more. Remove from the heat and cool to room temperature.

Stir in the salt, mustard, paprika, Worcestershire sauce and pepper.

Makes 1 cup; 8 servings.

★ PER 2 TABLESPOONS: 65 CALORIES, 5.2 G. TOTAL FAT, 0.4 G. SATURATED FAT, 0 MG. CHOLESTEROL, 137 MG. SODIUM

FROM THE GARDEN

FRESH ARTICHOKES WITH MUSTARD SAUCE

Adapted from *Prairie Potpourri*
IMMANUEL MEDICAL CENTER AUXILIARY

*This mustard sauce made with fat-free mayonnaise is a tangy,
low-fat alternative to the melted butter or hollandaise sauce
routinely served with artichokes.*

ARTICHOKES

  4 large artichokes
  1 tablespoon lemon juice
  1 clove garlic
  ¼ teaspoon salt

SAUCE

  ½ cup fat-free mayonnaise
  2 teaspoons lemon juice
  1 teaspoon prepared mustard

TO MAKE THE ARTICHOKES: Trim the stems from the artichokes.
Remove and discard the tough outer leaves. Cut a 1″ slice crosswise
from the top of each artichoke and discard. Wash the artichokes well
and drain.

In a large saucepan, place the artichokes in 1″ of water. Add the
lemon juice, garlic and salt. Bring to a boil. Reduce the heat to low.
Cover and simmer for 25 minutes, or until a leaf may be pulled out
easily. Drain on paper towels.

TO MAKE THE SAUCE: In a small bowl, stir together the mayonnaise, lemon juice and mustard. Serve the sauce with the artichokes.

Makes 4 servings.

★ PER SERVING: 86 CALORIES, 0.2 G. TOTAL FAT, 0 G. SATURATED FAT,
 0 MG. CHOLESTEROL, 524 MG. SODIUM

Immanuel Medical Center Auxiliary

In 1895 a group of Omaha women formed a sewing circle to raise money for the Immanuel Hospital. In the century since, the Immanuel Auxiliary has given more than $1 million to the Immanuel Medical Center, a comprehensive medical facility that provides long-term and acute care, geriatric services, mental health services, rehabilitation, senior citizen programs and more. The auxiliary has also awarded more than $100,000 in scholarships to Immanuel employees who want to continue their education.

The 600 men and women volunteers of the auxiliary devote thousands of hours annually to sponsoring fund-raising activities and providing an endless variety of services for the hospital and its patients. The money raised from *Prairie Potpourri* goes toward an endowment for the Immanuel Auxiliary Hospitality House, a 22-room facility where families of patients may stay for a nominal cost. This endowment enables families that could not otherwise afford it to stay in the Hospitality House.

....

Thai Asparagus

Adapted from *Feast of Eden*
JUNIOR LEAGUE OF MONTEREY COUNTY

Look for Chinese black mushrooms and oyster sauce in Asian specialty markets and some large supermarkets. The mushrooms sometimes are labeled "black fungus"—but don't worry, they taste better than they sound.

1 pound fresh asparagus
1 ounce dried black mushrooms
1 tablespoon canola oil
2 cloves garlic, minced
3 tablespoons oyster sauce
1 small red chili pepper, seeded and sliced
   (wear plastic gloves when handling)

Snap off the woody ends of the asparagus where they naturally break. (Or, if you want to use more of the stalk, use a vegetable peeler to remove the tough skin.) Cut the asparagus into 1″ pieces.

Soak the mushrooms in warm water for 15 minutes. Drain; remove and discard the stems. Slice the mushrooms into 1″ strips.

Coat a large skillet with no-stick spray. Add the oil and swirl to coat the bottom of the skillet. Add the mushrooms and garlic. Stir-fry for 1 minute. Add the asparagus, oyster sauce and chili peppers. Stir-fry for 3 to 5 minutes, or until the asparagus is crisp-tender.

TEST KITCHEN TIP: Handle chili peppers carefully to avoid burning your skin or eyes. Cover your hands with plastic or disposable gloves or small plastic bags when chopping or otherwise handling the peppers.

Makes 4 servings.

★ PER SERVING: 92 CALORIES, 3.8 G. TOTAL FAT, 0.3 G. SATURATED FAT, 0 MG. CHOLESTEROL, 122 MG. SODIUM

Green Beans and Tomatoes

Adapted from *Lone Star Legacy II*
AUSTIN JUNIOR FORUM

This is a perfect dish to make when garden-fresh beans and tomatoes are in season. If you don't have the time to julienne the beans, simply leave them whole or cut them into 1" lengths.

2 teaspoons canola oil
2 tablespoons chopped onions
1 clove garlic, minced
4 tomatoes, chopped.
Pinch of salt
1½ pounds green beans, cooked and julienned
2 tablespoons chopped fresh parsley

In a medium no-stick skillet over medium heat, warm the oil. Add the onions and garlic; sauté for 5 minutes, or until tender. Add the tomatoes and salt. Cover and simmer for 10 minutes, or until the tomatoes are softened. Add the beans; heat through. Sprinkle with the parsley.

Makes 6 servings.

★ PER SERVING: 72 CALORIES, 2 G. TOTAL FAT, 0.2 G. SATURATED FAT,
0 MG. CHOLESTEROL, 11 MG. SODIUM

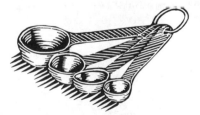

CREOLE LIMA BEANS

Adapted from *A Shining Feast*
FIRST BAPTIST CHURCH OF SHREVEPORT

You'll find already cooked, finely crumbled real bacon bits in the salad-dressing section of your supermarket. They're a good way to get bacon flavor without buying a whole pound of bacon strips.

2 packages (10 ounces each) frozen lima beans
1 medium onion, chopped
¼ cup chopped green peppers
1 can (14½ ounces) no-salt-added tomatoes (with juice), cut up
1 teaspoon sugar
⅛ teaspoon salt
⅛ teaspoon ground black pepper
1 tablespoon bacon bits

Cook the lima beans according to the package directions, but without adding salt or fat.

Lightly coat a medium saucepan with no-stick spray. Add the onions and green peppers. Cook, stirring, over medium heat for 4 minutes, or until the vegetables are tender. Add the tomatoes (with juice), sugar, salt and black pepper. Cook for 15 minutes, stirring occasionally.

Add the lima beans. Cook for 5 minutes more. Transfer to a serving bowl and sprinkle with the bacon bits.

Makes 6 servings.

★ PER SERVING: 124 CALORIES, 0.8 G. TOTAL FAT, 0.1 G. SATURATED FAT, 0 MG. CHOLESTEROL, 132 MG. SODIUM

Ginger Beets

Adapted from *Nothin' Finer*
CHAPEL HILL SERVICE LEAGUE

It was easy to lower the fat in this tasty vegetable dish. We just used butter-flavored sprinkles instead of butter.

6 medium beets
1 small onion
1 tablespoon sugar
1 tablespoon grated fresh ginger
2 teaspoons butter-flavored sprinkles
   Pinch of salt
   Pinch of ground black pepper
2 tablespoons water

Preheat the oven to 400°. Lightly coat a 1½-quart casserole with no-stick spray; set aside.

Peel and slice the beets. Cut the onion into thin crosswise slices. Separate the slices into rings. Layer the beets and onions in the prepared casserole. Sprinkle with the sugar and ginger.

In a small cup, stir together the butter-flavored sprinkles, salt and pepper. Add the water. Spoon over the beets and onions.

Cover and bake for 45 minutes, or until the beets are tender; stir twice during this time and add more water if necessary.

Makes 4 servings.

★ PER SERVING: 44 CALORIES, 0 G. TOTAL FAT, 0 G. SATURATED FAT, 0 MG. CHOLESTEROL, 38 MG. SODIUM

ORANGE-WALNUT BROCCOLI

Adapted from *Desert Treasures*
JUNIOR LEAGUE OF PHOENIX

For best quality, choose broccoli with firm stalks and heads that are deep green or green with a touch of purple.

1½ pounds broccoli, cut into serving-size spears
1 package (8 ounces) light cream cheese
⅓ cup skim milk
¼ cup orange juice
½ teaspoon salt
½ teaspoon finely shredded orange rind
¼ teaspoon dried thyme
1 tablespoon toasted and chopped walnuts

In a large saucepan with a tight-fitting lid, bring 1″ of water to a boil. Place the broccoli in a steamer basket and set the basket in the saucepan, making sure the basket sits above the water. Cover and steam for 8 to 12 minutes, or until the broccoli is crisp-tender.

In a small saucepan, whisk together the cream cheese, milk, orange juice, salt, orange rind and thyme. Cook over medium heat, whisking constantly, until smooth and heated through.

Transfer the broccoli to a serving dish and top with the cream-cheese mixture. Sprinkle with the walnuts.

Makes 6 servings.

★ PER SERVING: 130 CALORIES, 7.9 G. TOTAL FAT, 4.2 G. SATURATED FAT, 14 MG. CHOLESTEROL, 430 MG. SODIUM

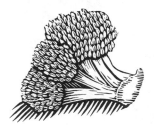

Broccoli Buffet Casserole

Adapted from *Pass the Plate*
EPISCOPAL CHURCH WOMEN OF CHRIST CHURCH

If you like, substitute fresh bread crumbs for the herb-seasoned stuffing mix. One slice of bread will give you ½ cup of crumbs.

- 2 packages (10 ounces each) frozen broccoli spears
- 1 can (10¾ ounces) low-fat, reduced-sodium condensed cream of chicken soup
- 2 teaspoons lemon juice
- 1 tablespoon tub-style reduced-calorie margarine
- ½ cup reduced-sodium herb-seasoned stuffing mix, crushed
- ¼ cup shredded reduced-fat Cheddar cheese

Preheat the oven to 350°.

Cook the broccoli according to the package directions, but without adding salt or fat. Drain well and cut into bite-size pieces. Arrange evenly in an 8″ × 8″ baking pan.

In a medium bowl, whisk together the soup and lemon juice. Pour over the broccoli.

Melt the margarine in a small saucepan. Add the stuffing mix and toss to coat with the margarine. Sprinkle on top of the broccoli and soup.

Bake for 20 to 30 minutes, or until heated through. Sprinkle with the Cheddar.

PER SERVING: 89 CALORIES, 2.8 G. TOTAL FAT, 0.6 G. SATURATED FAT, 4 MG. CHOLESTEROL, 415 MG. SODIUM

BROCCOLI-CAULIFLOWER CASSEROLE

Adapted from *Foods à la Louisiane*
LOUISIANA FARM BUREAU FEDERATION

What could be more traditional than a canned-soup vegetable casserole? What could be smarter than reducing the fat and sodium while keeping in all the comfort?

2 cups chopped broccoli
2 cups chopped cauliflower
1 tablespoon butter or stick margarine (not reduced-calorie)
1 large onion, chopped
1 can (5 ounces) evaporated skim milk
1 can (10¾ ounces) low-fat, reduced-sodium condensed cream of chicken soup
¼ cup grated Parmesan cheese
½ teaspoon ground black pepper
½ cup soft bread crumbs

Preheat the oven to 350°.

In a large pot of boiling water, cook the broccoli and cauliflower for 5 minutes, or until tender but still crisp. Drain and set aside.

In a medium saucepan over medium heat, melt the butter or margarine. Add the onions and sauté for 5 minutes, or until tender. Remove from the heat; add the milk, soup, Parmesan and pepper, stirring well.

Coat a 2-quart ovenproof casserole with no-stick spray. Layer the broccoli and cauliflower in the casserole. Pour the soup mixture over the vegetables. Top with the bread crumbs. Coat lightly with no-stick spray. Bake for 25 minutes, or until the mixture is bubbly.

Makes 8 servings.

TEST KITCHEN TIP: If desired, substitute frozen broccoli and cauliflower for the fresh. In each case, 2 of the 10-ounce packages will be sufficient. Thaw them before using.

★ PER SERVING: 100 CALORIES, 3.3 G. TOTAL FAT, 1.6 G. SATURATED FAT, 7 MG. CHOLESTEROL, 266 MG. SODIUM

CREOLE CABBAGE

Adapted from *Welcome Home*
THOMASVILLE CIVIC CENTER FOUNDATION

Good-quality canned tomatoes are almost always a better choice than fresh tomatoes during the winter months. In this dish, canned tomatoes, combined with green peppers and onions, enliven a dish of braised cabbage wedges topped with reduced-fat Cheddar.

½ medium head green cabbage, cored
    and cut into 6 wedges
1 tablespoon butter or stick margarine (not reduced-
    calorie)
1 onion, thinly sliced and separated into rings
1 green pepper, thinly sliced into rings
1 can (28 ounces) plum tomatoes, drained and quartered
½ teaspoon salt
¼ teaspoon ground black pepper
1 teaspoon sugar
½ cup shredded reduced-fat Cheddar cheese

Preheat the oven to 350°.

In a large pot, bring 2″ of water to a boil. Place the cabbage in the pot, cover and cook for 10 minutes, or until softened. Drain well.

Coat a 2-quart shallow baking dish with no-stick spray; place the cabbage in the dish. Set aside.

In a large skillet over medium heat, melt the butter or margarine. Add the onions and green peppers; sauté for 5 minutes, or until tender. Add the tomatoes, salt, black pepper and sugar. Simmer for 3 minutes. Pour over the cabbage.

Bake for 20 minutes. Sprinkle with the Cheddar and bake for 2 minutes to melt the Cheddar.

Makes 6 servings.

★ PER SERVING: 96 CALORIES, 3.8 G. TOTAL FAT, 1.2 G. SATURATED FAT,
    4 MG. CHOLESTEROL, 564 MG. SODIUM

Grilled Eggplant with Marinara Sauce

Adapted from *Feast of Eden*
JUNIOR LEAGUE OF MONTEREY COUNTY

For a hint of fresh-from-the-garden goodness, garnish this exceptional eggplant dish with sprigs of fresh basil.

⅓ cup chopped mushrooms
¼ cup chopped celery
¼ cup chopped green peppers
1 tablespoon finely chopped onions
1 can (8 ounces) no-salt-added tomato sauce
1 clove garlic, minced
½ teaspoon dried oregano
½ teaspoon dried basil
¼ teaspoon salt
   Pinch of ground black pepper
1 medium eggplant (about 1 pound)
   Garlic powder
2 tablespoons grated Parmesan cheese

Lightly coat a medium saucepan with olive oil no-stick spray. Add the mushrooms, celery, green peppers and onions. Cook, stirring, over medium heat until the vegetables are tender.

Add the tomato sauce, garlic, oregano, basil, salt and black pepper. Bring to a boil, then reduce the heat. Simmer for 10 minutes, stirring occasionally.

Coat a grill rack with no-stick spray. Then light the grill according to the manufacturer's directions. Check the temperature for grilling; the temperature should be medium-hot (see the Test Kitchen Tip on page 111). Place the rack on the grill.

Meanwhile, cut the eggplant into ½"-thick slices. Coat with olive oil no-stick spray and sprinkle with the garlic powder. Place the slices on the rack over the coals. Grill for 4 to 6 minutes, or until crisp-tender, turning once.

Transfer the eggplant to a serving platter. Top with the mushroom mixture. Sprinkle with the Parmesan.

TEST KITCHEN TIP: You may broil the eggplant instead of grilling it. Preheat the broiler and coat the rack of a broiling pan with olive oil no-stick spray. Place the eggplant slices on the rack.

OUR CAUSE

Junior League of Monterey County

Feast of Eden is subtitled *Recipes from California's Garden Paradise*. It would be hard to find more appropriate words to describe picturesque Monterey County. From dramatic rocky cliffs rising above the Big Sur coast to stately ancient redwoods and to the lush, loamy inland fields of Salinas, it's easy to imagine that Paradise might be a lot like this northern California place. From the sea to the farms to the vineyards, there is enticing fresh bounty year-round to please the most discriminating food lovers.

This area is rich in resources, indeed, and the Junior League of Monterey County is one more asset to the community. Some 500 women from all over the county are joined in dedication to the belief that caring individuals can improve the quality of life in their community. The recipes and menus in *Feast of Eden* embody the relaxed and elegant style so typical of California. Proceeds from the book go to the Monterey County Children's Museum.

Broil 4″ from the heat for 4 to 6 minutes, or until crisp-tender, turning once.

Makes 4 servings.

★ PER SERVING: 70 CALORIES, 1.2 G. TOTAL FAT, 0.6 G. SATURATED FAT, 2 MG. CHOLESTEROL, 218 MG. SODIUM

Apricot-Glazed Carrots

Adapted from *Cooking in the Litchfield Hills*
PRATT NATURE CENTER

Cooking in the Litchfield Hills boasts that even carrot-haters will like this sassy side dish. It's especially good with poultry or pork.

    8 carrots, cut diagonally into ½"-thick slices
    ⅓ cup water
      Pinch of salt
    ¼ cup apricot preserves
    1 tablespoon tub-style reduced-calorie margarine
    2 teaspoons lemon juice
    1 teaspoon finely shredded orange rind
    ¼ teaspoon ground nutmeg

In a medium saucepan, combine the carrots, water and salt. Bring to a boil over high heat. Reduce the heat to medium, cover and simmer for 5 to 8 minutes, or until the carrots are crisp-tender. Drain. Return the carrots to the saucepan.

Cut up any large pieces of apricot in the preserves.

In a small saucepan, melt the margarine over medium heat. Stir in the preserves, lemon juice, orange rind and nutmeg. Heat until the preserves are melted. Pour over the carrots and toss until well-coated.

TEST KITCHEN TIP: You can use 2½ cups baby carrots instead of the sliced carrots. Cook the baby carrots as directed above, allowing 8 to 10 minutes for them to reach the crisp-tender stage.

Makes 4 servings.

★ PER SERVING: 131 CALORIES, 1.7 G. TOTAL FAT, 0.3 G. SATURATED FAT, 0 MG. CHOLESTEROL, 85 MG. SODIUM

....

CORN-CASSEROLE SOUFFLÉ

Adapted from *The Authorized Texas Ranger Cookbook*
TEXAS RANGER MUSEUM AND HALL OF FAME

This savory side dish reminds us of a Tex-Mex version of spoon bread.

½ cup finely chopped onions
1 can (16½ ounces) reduced-sodium cream-style corn
½ cup skim milk
2 egg whites, lightly beaten
1 can (4 ounces) diced green chili peppers, drained
½ cup yellow cornmeal
½ teaspoon garlic powder
¼ teaspoon baking soda

Preheat the oven to 350°. Coat an 8″ × 8″ baking pan with no-stick spray; set aside.

Coat a small skillet with no-stick spray and place over medium-high heat. Add the onions and cook, stirring, until tender.

Transfer to a large bowl. Add the corn, milk, egg whites and chili peppers.

In a small bowl, stir together the cornmeal, garlic powder and baking soda. Add to the corn mixture and combine well. Spoon into the prepared baking pan.

Bake for 35 minutes, or until a knife inserted in the center comes out clean. Let stand for 5 minutes before serving.

Makes 4 servings.

★ PER SERVING: 175 CALORIES, 1.6 G. TOTAL FAT, 0.2 G. SATURATED FAT,
   1 MG. CHOLESTEROL, 406 MG. SODIUM

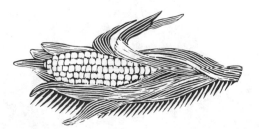

CORN PUDDING

Adapted from *Country Treasures*
VIRGINIA FARM BUREAU

Here's a down-home corn pudding that's lower in sugar than most. Country Treasures *recommends using shoe peg corn.*

2 egg whites
1 egg
1 cup skim milk
2 tablespoons sugar
2 tablespoons all-purpose flour
2 tablespoons tub-style reduced-calorie margarine, melted
¼ teaspoon salt
2 cups fresh or thawed frozen whole-kernel corn

Preheat the oven to 325°. Coat a 1½-quart casserole with no-stick spray.

In a medium bowl, whisk together the egg whites and egg. Add the milk, sugar, flour, margarine and salt. Stir in the corn and mix well. Spoon into the prepared casserole. Bake for 40 to 45 minutes, or until a knife inserted in the center comes out clean.

Makes 4 servings.

★ PER SERVING: 177 CALORIES, 4.3 G. TOTAL FAT, 1 G. SATURATED FAT, 54 MG. CHOLESTEROL, 277 MG. SODIUM

MINTED PEAS

Adapted from *Pass the Plate*
EPISCOPAL CHURCH WOMEN OF CHRIST CHURCH

*Mint really perks up the flavor of frozen peas. Try this side dish
with an entrée of roasted or grilled poultry, seafood, beef or lamb.*

    ½ cup water
    1 teaspoon dried mint
    ⅛ teaspoon salt
    ⅛ teaspoon ground black pepper
       Pinch of sugar
    1 package (10 ounces) frozen tiny peas
    1 teaspoon tub-style reduced-calorie margarine

In a small saucepan, combine the water, mint, salt, pepper and
sugar. Bring to a boil. Add the peas and cook for 2 to 3 minutes, or
until tender. Drain. Add the margarine and toss until melted.

Makes 3 servings.

★ PER SERVING: 79 CALORIES, 0.9 G. TOTAL FAT, 0.1 G. SATURATED FAT,
  0 MG. CHOLESTEROL, 105 MG. SODIUM

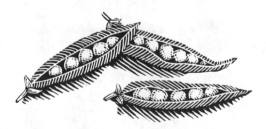

PEPPERONATA

Adapted from *M. D. Anderson Volunteers Cooking for Fun*
M. D. ANDERSON CANCER CENTER VOLUNTEERS

This versatile vegetable combination is high in vitamin C and low in fat. Play with the herbs if you like. Rosemary or the bottled herbes de provence would both be tasty alternatives to oregano.

> 1 onion, sliced
> 1 clove garlic, minced
> 1 large potato, peeled and cut into ½" cubes
> ¼ cup water
> 2 large green, yellow or sweet red peppers, cut into strips
> 1 large tomato, peeled and cut into large chunks
> ½ teaspoon dried oregano
> ¼ teaspoon salt
> ¼ teaspoon dried thyme

Coat a large no-stick skillet with olive oil no-stick spray. Add the onions and garlic. Cook, stirring, over medium heat for 5 minutes, or until the onions are crisp-tender.

Stir in the potatoes and water; cover and cook over low heat for 10 minutes, stirring occasionally. Stir in the peppers, tomatoes, oregano, salt and thyme. Cover and cook for 10 minutes, or until the potatoes and peppers are crisp-tender.

TEST KITCHEN TIP: To easily peel a tomato, place it in enough boiling water to cover. Carefully remove the tomato with a slotted spoon after 30 seconds and place under cold running water. When cool enough to handle, use a sharp paring knife to peel off the skin.

Makes 6 servings.

★ PER SERVING: 39 CALORIES, 0.2 G. TOTAL FAT, 0 G. SATURATED FAT, 0 MG. CHOLESTEROL, 93 MG. SODIUM

M. D. Anderson Cancer Center Volunteers

At Houston's M. D. Anderson Cancer Center, volunteers are as numerous, and as life-affirming, as Texas bluebonnets in spring. The facility has 2,000 volunteers—more than any other health care institution in the Lone Star state.

These volunteers are a dedicated group. Many have lost loved ones to cancer, and many are cancer survivors themselves. Their range of services is extraordinary. They ring up sales in the gift shop, sit quietly with patients who need a dose of companionship and also tend the center's rose gardens. Some even assist with scientific research.

Some of the center's most successful programs are inspired and implemented by volunteers. The Anderson Network, for example, matches new patients with buddies who are also cancer patients. The Adopt-a-Friend program provides companions to patients from outside Houston.

Their most stellar success is the Children's Art project. Since 1974, the center has raised more than $5 million through sales of more than 25 million holiday cards designed by young patients at the facility.

Money raised from the sales of *M. D. Anderson Volunteers Cooking for Fun* funds a number of volunteer projects, including new art and music therapy programs.

SEASONED RED POTATOES

Adapted from *Coastal Cuisine, Texas Style*
JUNIOR SERVICE LEAGUE OF BRAZOSPORT

It's hard to believe a recipe this easy tastes so good.

>   4 medium red potatoes
>   1 red onion
>   1 green pepper
>   1 sweet red pepper
>   ½ cup fat-free Italian salad dressing

Preheat the oven to 400°. Cut the potatoes into eighths. Cut the onion, green pepper and red pepper into bite-size chunks.

Arrange the vegetables in a single layer in a jelly-roll pan. Drizzle with the dressing; toss to coat evenly. Bake for 45 minutes, or until the potatoes are tender; stir after 30 minutes to brown the vegetables evenly.

Makes 4 servings.

★ **PER SERVING:** 146 CALORIES, 0.2 G. TOTAL FAT, 0 G. SATURATED FAT, 0 MG. CHOLESTEROL, 73 MG. SODIUM

BAKED SWEET POTATOES AND APPLES

Adapted from *Country Treasures*
VIRGINIA FARM BUREAU

At holiday time, use this tasty side dish as a low-fat, higher-fiber alternative to candied sweet potatoes.

>   4 medium sweet potatoes, peeled and cut into ½″ slices
>   ½ cup + ⅓ cup water
>   1 apple, thinly sliced
>   ⅓ cup packed brown sugar
>   ¾ teaspoon ground cinnamon
>   1 tablespoon tub-style reduced-calorie margarine

In a large saucepan, combine the sweet potatoes and ½ cup of the water. Bring to a boil over high heat. Reduce the heat to medium, cover and simmer for 30 minutes, or until tender.

Preheat the oven to 350°.

Arrange the sweet potatoes in a 13″ × 9″ baking pan. Top with the apples.

In a small bowl, stir together the brown sugar and cinnamon. Sprinkle over the apples. Dot with the margarine. Pour on the remaining ⅓ cup water.

Cover and bake for 40 minutes, or until the apples are tender. Uncover and bake for 5 minutes.

TEST KITCHEN TIP: If fresh sweet potatoes are unavailable, you can use 4 cups vacuum-packed canned sweet potatoes instead.

Makes 4 servings.

★ PER SERVING: 219 CALORIES, 1.7 G. TOTAL FAT, 0.3 G. SATURATED FAT, 0 MG. CHOLESTEROL, 50 MG. SODIUM

AUTUMN STIR-FRY

Adapted from *Pass It On*
DELTA DELTA DELTA NATIONAL FRATERNITY

This nutritious vegetable medley can also be served as a main course. Extend it with hot cooked rice.

 2 teaspoons canola oil
 2 cloves garlic, minced
 1 teaspoon minced fresh ginger
 2 cups broccoli florets
 1 sweet red or yellow pepper, cut into 1″ pieces
 1 sweet potato, peeled and shredded
 2 cups shredded cabbage
 1 tablespoon chopped roasted peanuts

Warm the oil in a wok or large skillet over medium-high heat. Add the garlic and ginger. Cook, stirring constantly, for 2 minutes. Add the broccoli and stir-fry for 3 minutes.

Add the peppers, sweet potatoes and cabbage. Stir-fry for 3 to 4 minutes, or until the vegetables are crisp-tender. Sprinkle with the peanuts.

Makes 6 servings.

★ PER SERVING: 67 CALORIES, 2.5 G. TOTAL FAT, 0.2 G. SATURATED FAT, 0 MG. CHOLESTEROL, 27 MG. SODIUM

Oven-Baked Cottage Fries

Adapted from *A Place Called Hope*
JUNIOR AUXILIARY OF HOPE

Potatoes should be a part of every healthy diet. They're a satisfying complex carbohydrate that boosts the daily nutritional scores of potassium, vitamin C and B vitamins.

½ cup water
2 large baking potatoes, scrubbed and cut into ¼" slices
1 tablespoon tub-style reduced-calorie margarine
½ teaspoon garlic powder
2 tablespoons grated Parmesan cheese
¼ teaspoon paprika
⅛ teaspoon ground black pepper

Preheat the oven to 425°.

Pour the water into a no-stick jelly-roll pan. Arrange the potatoes in a single layer in the pan.

In a small saucepan over low heat, melt the margarine. Stir in the garlic powder. Drizzle over the potatoes. Bake for 20 minutes, or until the potatoes are tender when pierced with a sharp knife.

In a small bowl, combine the Parmesan, paprika and pepper. Sprinkle over the potatoes. Broil for 2 to 3 minutes, or until golden.

TEST KITCHEN TIP: For a fresher taste, you can use 1 clove of minced garlic instead of the garlic powder. Adding 1 teaspoon crushed dried rosemary or oregano leaves when you add the garlic would also make a flavorful variation.

Makes 6 servings.

★ PER SERVING: 67 CALORIES, 1.6 G. TOTAL FAT, 0.6 G. SATURATED FAT, 2 MG. CHOLESTEROL, 63 MG. SODIUM

SWEETS AND TREATS

Vanilla Cheesecake

Adapted from *California Kosher*
WOMEN'S LEAGUE OF ADAT ARI EL SYNAGOGUE

Sliced fresh strawberries or reduced-calorie cherry pie filling
makes a refreshing topping for this rich-tasting cheesecake.

CRUST

1½ cups low-fat graham crackers crushed to fine crumbs
¼ cup sugar
1 egg white, lightly beaten
3 tablespoons tub-style reduced-calorie margarine,
melted and cooled

FILLING

1 package (8 ounces) light cream cheese, softened
1 cup 1% low-fat cottage cheese
¾ cup sugar
½ cup skim milk
2 tablespoons all-purpose flour
1 teaspoon vanilla
Pinch of salt
4 egg whites

TO MAKE THE CRUST: Preheat the oven to 350°.

In a small bowl, stir together the cracker crumbs and sugar.

In a cup, stir together the egg white and margarine. Add to the
crumb mixture and stir until well-mixed.

Lightly coat a 9″ springform pan with no-stick spray. Pat the
crumb mixture into the bottom and 2″ up the side of the pan. Bake
for 15 minutes. Cool on a wire rack.

TO MAKE THE FILLING: Meanwhile, in a large bowl, use an electric mixer to beat together the cream cheese and cottage cheese. Stir
in the sugar, milk, flour, vanilla and salt.

Wash and dry the beaters. In a medium bowl, beat the egg whites
with the electric mixer on high speed until soft peaks form. Fold into
the cream-cheese mixture. Pour into the cooled crust.

Bake for 1 hour, or until set in the center. Cool the cheesecake in
the pan on a wire rack for 30 minutes. Loosen the sides of the pan
and cool completely.

Cover and refrigerate until serving time. Store any remaining
cheesecake in the refrigerator.

OUR CAUSE

Women's League of Adat Ari El Synagogue

The rest of the country hardly thinks of California as a bastion of tradition. The Women's League of North Hollywood's Adat Ari El Synagogue is just that, though: a bulwark of Jewish tradition and a guardian of the community. The Conservative Jewish Congregation of Adat Ari El was founded in 1939 and is the oldest in the San Fernando Valley. The Women's League, which formed the following year, is a large and busy group, with a membership of 400 from the congregation's 1,000 families.

It's not surprising that a group that so cherishes the culinary traditions of its faith is also a co-sponsor of the North Hollywood Food Pantry. Other projects dear to the League are programs to help battered women, the homeless and new immigrants. The group also runs an adult education program that's been open to the public for three decades.

California Kosher, the League's fourth cookbook, merges the best of Jewish culinary tradition with the innovation that has made California cuisine a trendsetter worldwide.

TEST KITCHEN TIP: If low-fat kosher graham crackers are unavailable, substitute regular kosher graham crackers. Just be aware that the fat content will increase. Some supermarkets carry kosher ready-made reduced-fat graham cracker crusts.

Makes 12 servings.

★ PER SERVING: 166 CALORIES, 5 G. TOTAL FAT, 2.4 G. SATURATED FAT, 8 MG. CHOLESTEROL, 252 MG. SODIUM

Italian Cake

Adapted from *M. D. Anderson Volunteers Cooking for Fun*
M. D. ANDERSON CANCER CENTER VOLUNTEERS

For a dramatic presentation, spoon a little of the raspberry sauce on a dessert plate, lay a slice of the ricotta-filled cake on top and drizzle with a little more of the sauce.

RASPBERRY SAUCE

2 cups fresh or thawed frozen red raspberries
1 cup water
¼ cup sugar
2 tablespoons cornstarch

RICOTTA FILLING

1 container (15 ounces) reduced-fat ricotta cheese
1 package (8 ounces) light cream cheese, softened
⅓ cup sugar
1 teaspoon vanilla
Grated rind of 1 lemon
Grated rind of 1 orange

CAKE

1 purchased or homemade 10″ angel-food cake

TO MAKE THE RASPBERRY SAUCE: In a blender or food processor, blend the raspberries, water, sugar and cornstarch until smooth. Transfer to a small saucepan.

Cook, stirring, over medium heat until the sauce begins to thicken and just comes to a boil. Strain through a sieve; discard the raspberry seeds. Cover and refrigerate for at least 1 hour.

TO MAKE THE RICOTTA FILLING: In a large bowl, use an electric mixer to beat the ricotta, cream cheese, sugar, vanilla, lemon rind and orange rind until well-mixed.

TO MAKE THE CAKE: Use a long-bladed serrated knife to slice the cake horizontally into 3 layers. Spread half of the ricotta filling between the layers. Frost the cake with the remaining filling. Cover and refrigerate until serving time.

Stir the raspberry sauce. Slice the cake and serve with the sauce.

Makes 16 servings.

★ PER SERVING: 204 CALORIES, 3.4 G. TOTAL FAT, 1.5 G. SATURATED FAT, 9 MG. CHOLESTEROL, 306 MG. SODIUM

LOW-FAT TREATS

Sure, some desserts take hours to execute. But lots of others don't. Tempting lower-fat treats are minutes away.

Shortcut Shortcake. In a bowl, toss cut-up ripe fruit or berries with honey or sugar (2 teaspoons per cup of fruit) and lemon juice (1 teaspoon per cup of fruit). Set aside for 15 minutes. Stir, then spoon over slices of angel food cake. Garnish with reduced-fat whipped topping.

Dried-Fruit Bonbons. In a food processor, chop dried fruit—such as pitted dates, apricots, raisins, apples, cherries or a mixture of several kinds—with reduced-fat graham cracker crumbs (8 ounces fruit to 2 tablespoons crumbs) until the mixture sticks together when pressed. Shape into tiny balls or logs and roll in powdered sugar. Store in a cookie tin.

Fruit Kabobs. Thread chunks of ripe but firm fruit on wooden skewers. Brush with apple jelly thinned with a little water. Broil for 4 to 5 minutes, turning once, until the fruit is warm. Serve with low-fat vanilla yogurt for dipping.

Mini Grape Sorbets. Place washed and dried seedless grapes (green, red or some of each) on a tray. Place in the freezer for several hours, until firm. Serve at the close of a summer party.

Bananarama. Cut 2 ripe but firm bananas in half crosswise, then into quarters lengthwise. Coat a no-stick skillet with no-stick spray. Melt 2 teaspoons butter in the skillet. Sauté the bananas for 2 minutes on each side, until golden. Sprinkle lightly with sugar and cinnamon. Place on dessert dishes and drizzle lightly with chocolate syrup.

....

SPICED ZUCCHINI CAKE

Adapted from *Between Greene Leaves*
GREENE COUNTY HOMEMAKERS EXTENSION ASSOCIATION

Using a combination of buttermilk and applesauce results in a rich, moist cake that's low in fat. To make the cake virtually fat-free, you can leave out the walnuts and sprinkle the top with powdered sugar instead of using frosting.

CAKE

1 tablespoon + 3 cups all-purpose flour
2 teaspoons baking powder
1½ teaspoons ground cinnamon
1 teaspoon baking soda
½ teaspoon salt
8 egg whites
2 cups sugar
1 cup unsweetened applesauce
½ cup nonfat buttermilk
1 tablespoon vanilla
1 teaspoon finely shredded orange rind
3 cups shredded zucchini
⅔ cup toasted and chopped walnuts

CREAM-CHEESE FROSTING

4 ounces light cream cheese, softened
2 tablespoons tub-style reduced-calorie margarine
1 teaspoon finely shredded orange rind
2 teaspoons orange juice
2–2¼ cups powdered sugar

TO MAKE THE CAKE: Preheat the oven to 300°. Lightly coat a 13″ × 9″ baking pan with no-stick spray; sprinkle with 1 tablespoon of the flour. Shake the pan, tilting it back and forth, until it is coated with a light dusting of the flour. Remove and discard the excess flour. Set the pan aside.

Place the remaining 3 cups flour in a large bowl. Stir in the baking powder, cinnamon, baking soda and salt.

In another large bowl, use an electric mixer to beat the egg whites on high speed until soft peaks form. Slowly beat in the sugar. Then slowly beat in the applesauce, buttermilk, vanilla and orange rind.

OUR CAUSE

Greene County
Homemakers Extension Association

Since 1935, the Greene County Homemakers Extension Association has been a vital part of the Illinois community in which it was started. In the early days, the group was called the Greene County Home Bureau and had an impressive 320 members. Soon the group was challenged as World War II led to shortages of sugar and other household necessities.

The women rose to the challenge with programs to teach area homemakers to endure the hardships of war by sewing clothing, growing victory gardens and preserving the bounty of the gardens. Early meetings were held in the First Baptist Church in Carrollton, Illinois.

Today, the Association, which was renamed in the 1960s, is proud to have its own building with offices, a meeting room and a kitchen. *Between Greene Leaves*, a collection of hundreds of old and new family recipes from extension members, was first published in 1984. Proceeds from its sales allow the group to continue helping Greene County residents build a better life.

Using a spoon, stir in the flour mixture until combined. Then stir in the zucchini and walnuts.

Transfer the batter to the prepared pan. Bake for 1 hour, or until a toothpick inserted in the center comes out clean. Cool the cake in the pan on a wire rack before spreading on the frosting.

TO MAKE THE CREAM-CHEESE FROSTING: In a medium bowl, use an electric mixer to beat together the cream cheese and margarine until well-combined. Beat in the orange rind and orange juice. Then beat in enough of the powdered sugar to make a frosting of spreading consistency. Spread the frosting on top of the cake.

Makes 16 servings.

★ PER SERVING: 308 CALORIES, 5.8 G. TOTAL FAT, 1.1 G. SATURATED FAT, 2 MG. CHOLESTEROL, 252 MG. SODIUM

ELEGANT LEMON ROLL

Adapted from *Sassafras! The Ozarks Cookbook*
JUNIOR LEAGUE OF SPRINGFIELD

A tender lemon cake roll encases a creamy filling in this fancy-enough-for-company dessert. The filling tastes so rich, you'll find it hard to believe it's made with low-fat sweetened condensed milk and reduced-fat whipped topping.

CAKE

1 tablespoon + ⅔ cup sifted cake flour
1 teaspoon baking powder
  Pinch of salt
1 egg
¾ cup sugar
1 tablespoon oil
1 teaspoon lemon extract
6 egg whites
¼ cup powdered sugar

FILLING

1 can (14 ounces) low-fat sweetened condensed milk
⅓ cup lemon juice
1–2 teaspoons finely shredded lemon rind
5 drops yellow food coloring (optional)
1 cup thawed reduced-fat frozen whipped topping

TOPPING

¼ cup flaked coconut

TO MAKE THE CAKE: Preheat the oven to 375°. Lightly coat a jelly-roll pan with no-stick spray. Line the bottom of the pan with wax paper, then coat the wax paper with no-stick spray. Dust the wax paper with 1 tablespoon of the flour. Set aside.

Place the remaining ⅔ cup flour in a small bowl. Stir in the baking powder and salt.

In a large bowl, use an electric mixer to beat the egg on high speed for 1½ minutes, or until thick and lemon-colored. Slowly beat in ¼ cup of the sugar. Then beat on medium-high speed, scraping down the sides of the bowl often, for 2 minutes, or until the mixture is creamy and pale in color. Beat in the oil and lemon extract.

Wash and dry the beaters. In a medium bowl, beat the egg whites on high speed until they form soft peaks. Gradually add the remaining ½ cup sugar, beating until stiff peaks form.

Fold or gently stir the egg-white mixture into the oil mixture. Then fold or gently stir in the flour mixture.

Gently spread the batter evenly in the prepared pan. Bake for 10 minutes, or until no imprint remains when the cake is lightly touched in the center.

Lightly sift the powdered sugar on 1 side of a clean dish towel.

Immediately loosen the cake from the sides of the pan and invert it onto the towel. Remove the wax paper and roll up the towel and cake together, jelly-roll fashion, starting from a short end. Transfer to a wire rack, seam side down, and cool completely.

TO MAKE THE FILLING: In a large bowl, stir together the milk, lemon juice, lemon rind and food coloring (if using). Fold in the whipped topping.

Unroll the cake. Spread half of the filling on the cake to within ½" of its edges. Then roll up the cake without the towel. Transfer it to a serving platter. Spread the remaining filling over the cake roll.

TO MAKE THE TOPPING: Sprinkle the coconut over the cake roll. Carefully cover it with plastic wrap and refrigerate for 1 to 2 hours before serving. Store any remaining cake in the refrigerator.

TEST KITCHEN TIP: You can also use this cake to make a deliciously simple jelly roll. Prepare, bake and cool the cake as above but omit the filling and topping. Spread the cooled cake with ⅔ cup seedless red raspberry jam, then roll up the cake without the towel. Cover it with plastic wrap and refrigerate for 1 to 2 hours. Before serving, sift 2 tablespoons powdered sugar over the top of the cake. Store any remaining cake roll in the refrigerator.

Makes 10 servings.

★ PER SERVING: 271 CALORIES, 5.7 G. TOTAL FAT, 1.9 G. SATURATED FAT, 26 MG. CHOLESTEROL, 118 MG. SODIUM

Pumpkin and Spice Roll

Adapted from *Nutbread and Nostalgia*
JUNIOR LEAGUE OF SOUTH BEND

For a delightfully different holiday dessert, try this luscious cake roll. The perfectly spiced pumpkin cake is enhanced by a rich-tasting filling based on light cream cheese and butter-flavored sprinkles.

CAKE

1 tablespoon + ¾ cup all-purpose flour
2 teaspoons ground cinnamon
1 teaspoon baking soda
1 teaspoon ground ginger
½ teaspoon ground nutmeg
Pinch of salt
1 egg
1 cup sugar
⅔ cup canned pumpkin
1 teaspoon lemon juice
4 egg whites
½ cup finely chopped walnuts
¼ cup powdered sugar

FILLING

6 ounces light cream cheese, softened
2 tablespoons butter-flavored sprinkles
½ teaspoon vanilla
1 cup + 2 tablespoons powdered sugar

TO MAKE THE CAKE: Preheat the oven to 375°. Lightly coat a jelly-roll pan with no-stick spray. Line the bottom of the pan with wax paper, then coat the wax paper with no-stick spray. Dust the wax paper with 1 tablespoon of the flour. Set aside.

In a small bowl, stir together the remaining ¾ cup flour, cinnamon, baking soda, ginger, nutmeg and salt.

In a large bowl, use an electric mixer to beat the egg on high speed for 1½ minutes, or until thick and lemon-colored. Slowly beat in the sugar. Then beat on medium-high speed, scraping down the sides of the bowl often, for 2 minutes, or until the mixture is creamy and pale in color.

Stir in the pumpkin and lemon juice. Then fold or gently stir in the flour mixture.

Wash and dry the beaters. In a medium bowl, beat the egg whites on high speed until they form stiff peaks. Fold or gently stir the egg-white mixture into the pumpkin mixture.

Gently spread the mixture evenly in the prepared pan. Sprinkle the walnuts over the cake batter. Bake for 10 minutes, or until no imprint remains when the cake is lightly touched in the center.

Lightly sift the powdered sugar on 1 side of a clean dish towel.

Immediately loosen the cake from the sides of the pan and invert it onto the towel. Remove the wax paper and roll up the towel and cake together, jelly-roll fashion, starting from a short end. Transfer to a wire rack, seam side down, and cool completely.

TO MAKE THE FILLING: In a medium bowl, use an electric mixer to beat together the cream cheese, sprinkles, vanilla and 1 cup of the powdered sugar.

Unroll the cake. Spread the filling on the cake to within ½" of its edges. Then roll up the cake without the towel. Transfer it to a serving platter. Cover it with plastic wrap and refrigerate for at least 2 hours or up to 24 hours before serving.

Before serving, sift the remaining 2 tablespoons powdered sugar over the top of the cake. Store any remaining cake roll in the refrigerator.

Makes 16 servings.

★ PER SERVING: 163 CALORIES, 4.5 G. TOTAL FAT, 1.4 G. SATURATED FAT, 17 MG. CHOLESTEROL, 131 MG. SODIUM

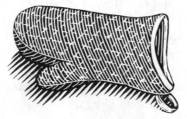

Ada's Gingerbread with Lemon Sauce

Adapted from *Cotton Country Cooking*
JUNIOR LEAGUE OF MORGAN COUNTY

Although we don't know Ada, we do know that her gingerbread recipe is delicious. It's tender, perfectly spiced and accented with a tart-sweet lemon sauce. We agree with Cotton Country Cooking *that this gingerbread is best served warm.*

GINGERBREAD

- 1 tablespoon + 2 cups all-purpose flour
- 1 cup sugar
- 3 tablespoons butter or stick margarine (not reduced-calorie), melted
- 2 tablespoons molasses
- 2 egg whites, lightly beaten
- 1 teaspoon baking soda
- 1 teaspoon ground cinnamon
- ½ teaspoon ground cloves
- ¼ teaspoon ground ginger
- ⅛ teaspoon salt
- 1 cup nonfat buttermilk

LEMON SAUCE

- ½ cup sugar
- 4 teaspoons cornstarch
- Pinch of salt
- Pinch of ground nutmeg
- 1 cup boiling water
- 2 tablespoons lemon juice
- 2 teaspoons butter or stick margarine (not reduced-calorie)
- ¼ teaspoon finely shredded lemon rind

TO MAKE THE GINGERBREAD: Preheat the oven to 400°. Lightly coat an 8″ × 8″ baking pan with no-stick spray, then sprinkle with 1 tablespoon of the flour. Shake the pan, tilting it back and forth, until it is coated with a light dusting of flour. Remove and discard the excess flour. Set the pan aside.

In a medium bowl, stir together the sugar, butter or margarine and molasses. Stir in the egg whites.

Place the remaining 2 cups flour in a medium bowl. Stir in the baking soda, cinnamon, cloves, ginger and salt.

Starting and ending with the flour mixture, stir the flour mixture and buttermilk alternately into the sugar mixture. Pour the batter into the prepared baking pan.

Bake for 35 minutes, or until a toothpick inserted in the center comes out clean. Let the gingerbread cool in the pan on a wire rack for 5 minutes.

TO MAKE THE LEMON SAUCE: In a small saucepan, stir together the sugar, cornstarch, salt and nutmeg. Gradually stir in the water. Cook, stirring, over medium heat until the mixture is thick and clear. Stir in the lemon juice, butter or margarine and lemon rind.

Serve the gingerbread warm with the lemon sauce.

Makes 9 servings.

★ PER SERVING: 295 CALORIES, 5 G. TOTAL FAT, 3 G. SATURATED FAT, 12 MG. CHOLESTEROL, 214 MG. SODIUM

RAISIN BARS

Adapted from *Family Creations*
GLADNEY FUND VOLUNTEER AUXILIARIES

A mere ¼ cup of mini chocolate chips provides a wealth of tasty buried treasure in these yummy bars. We reduced the amount of oil from the original recipe, but you'd never guess it from the taste.

       1 cup raisins
       1 cup water
      ⅓ cup canola oil
       1 cup sugar
       1 egg
    1¾ cups flour
      ¼ teaspoon salt
       1 teaspoon baking soda
       1 teaspoon ground cinnamon
      ½ teaspoon ground nutmeg
      ½ teaspoon ground allspice
      ¼ teaspoon ground cloves
      ¼ cup mini chocolate chips
      ¼ cup finely chopped walnuts
       2 tablespoons powdered sugar

Preheat the oven to 375°.

In a small saucepan, bring the raisins and water to a boil over high heat. Remove from the heat, stir in the oil and cool to lukewarm. Stir in the sugar and egg.

In a large bowl, stir together the flour, salt, baking soda, cinnamon, nutmeg, allspice and cloves. Add the raisin mixture and stir to combine. Stir in the chocolate chips and walnuts.

Coat a 13″ × 9″ baking pan with no-stick spray. Pour the batter into the pan and smooth the top with the back of a spoon. Bake for 20 to 25 minutes, or until the bars start to pull away from the sides of the pan.

Remove from the oven to cool. Dust lightly with the powdered sugar and cut into squares.

Makes 24.

★ PER BAR: 133 CALORIES, 4.8 G. TOTAL FAT, 0.4 G. SATURATED FAT, 9 MG. CHOLESTEROL, 60 MG. SODIUM

Cocoa Brownies

Adapted from *Cane River's Louisiana Living*
SERVICE LEAGUE OF NATCHITOCHES

These moist cake brownies get their terrific chocolate flavor from cocoa powder, which has only 1 gram of fat per tablespoon. Watch the baking time closely—if the brownies are overbaked, they'll be dry.

1 tablespoon + ¾ cup all-purpose flour
⅓ cup butter or stick margarine (not reduced-calorie), softened
4 egg whites
1 teaspoon vanilla
1 cup sugar
¼ cup unsweetened cocoa powder
Pinch of salt
¼ cup toasted and chopped pecans

Preheat the oven to 350°. Coat an 8″ × 8″ baking pan with no-stick spray, then sprinkle with 1 tablespoon of the flour. Shake the pan, tilting it back and forth, until it is coated with a light dusting of flour. Remove and discard the excess flour. Set the baking pan aside.

In a large bowl, use an electric mixer to beat together the butter or margarine, egg whites and vanilla. (Don't be concerned that the mixture is lumpy.) In a small bowl, stir together the remaining ¾ cup flour, sugar, cocoa powder and salt. Gradually add the sugar mixture to the butter mixture, beating until combined. Stir in the pecans. Spread the batter in the prepared pan. Bake for 25 to 30 minutes, or until the batter pulls away from the sides of the pan.

Use a sharp knife to score the surface into 2″ squares. Then cool completely in the pan on a wire rack. To serve, cut into squares.

Makes 16.

★ PER BROWNIE: 120 CALORIES, 5.1 G. TOTAL FAT, 2.5 G. SATURATED FAT, 10 MG. CHOLESTEROL, 53 MG. SODIUM

CHOCOLATE PUFFS

Adapted from *Treasures of the Smokies*
JUNIOR LEAGUE OF JOHNSON CITY

We substituted pureed prunes for some of the fat in the original recipe for these crinkle-topped cookies. A convenient way to get pureed prunes is to buy baby food strained prunes.

½ cup tub-style reduced-calorie margarine
¾ cup unsweetened cocoa powder
¼ cup pureed prunes
2 cups sugar
2 eggs, lightly beaten
½ cup fat-free egg substitute
2 teaspoons vanilla
3½ cups all-purpose flour
1 tablespoon baking powder
⅛ teaspoon ground cinnamon
⅓ cup powdered sugar

In a medium saucepan, melt the margarine over medium heat. Stir in the cocoa powder and prunes. Let stand at room temperature until cooled. Stir in the sugar, 1 cup at a time, beating well after each addition. Stir in the eggs, egg substitute and vanilla until well-mixed.

In a small bowl, stir together the flour, baking powder and cinnamon. Stir into the chocolate mixture and mix well. Cover and refrigerate for at least 12 hours.

Preheat the oven to 375°. Lightly coat 2 or 3 baking sheets with no-stick spray.

Place the powdered sugar in a shallow dish. Carefully drop a rounded tablespoon of the dough into the powdered sugar, then shape into a ball and roll to coat with powdered sugar. Transfer to a baking sheet. Repeat with the remaining dough and powdered sugar, leaving about 2″ between the cookies on the baking sheets.

Bake one sheet at a time for 10 minutes, or until almost no imprint remains when a cookie is lightly touched in the center. Transfer the cookies to a wire rack and let cool completely.

Makes 30.

★ PER PUFF: 133 CALORIES, 2.2 G. TOTAL FAT, 0.4 G. SATURATED FAT, 14 MG. CHOLESTEROL, 79 MG. SODIUM

GLAZED SOFTIES

Adapted from *Critics' Choice*
GUILD OF CORINTH THEATRE ARTS

These cookies are sweetened only with bananas, orange juice and a powdered-sugar glaze.

COOKIES

½ cup butter or stick margarine (not reduced-calorie), softened
2 cups mashed very ripe bananas
½ cup orange juice
4 egg whites, lightly beaten
2 teaspoons vanilla
1 teaspoon finely shredded orange rind
2 cups quick-cooking rolled oats
2 cups all-purpose flour
¾ teaspoon baking soda
¾ teaspoon ground nutmeg
⅛ teaspoon salt
¾ cup raisins (optional)

GLAZE

1½ cups powdered sugar
2 tablespoons orange juice

TO MAKE THE COOKIES: Preheat the oven to 350°.

In a large bowl, use an electric mixer to beat the butter or margarine until fluffy. Stir in the bananas and orange juice until well-mixed.

In a small bowl, use a fork to stir together the egg whites, vanilla and orange rind. Stir into the banana mixture.

In a medium bowl, stir together the oats, flour, baking soda, nutmeg and salt. Stir into the banana mixture. Stir in the raisins (if using).

Drop the dough by rounded tablespoons onto ungreased baking sheets, leaving about 2″ between the cookies.

Bake one sheet at a time for 20 minutes, or until the cookies are golden brown on the bottom. Cool for 1 minute on the cookie sheet. Transfer the cookies to a wire rack and let cool completely.

(continued)

TO MAKE THE GLAZE: In a small bowl, stir together the powdered sugar and orange juice; drizzle over the cookies.

Makes 40.

★ PER COOKIE: 102 CALORIES, 3 G. TOTAL FAT, 1.5 G. SATURATED FAT,
6 MG. CHOLESTEROL, 51 MG. SODIUM

....

FORGOTTEN COOKIES

Adapted from *300 Years of Carolina Cooking*
JUNIOR LEAGUE OF GREENVILLE

"Unforgettable" is a more accurate description of these light meringue chocolate-nut morsels. The whimsical name Forgotten Cookies refers to the technique of turning off the oven after baking and "forgetting" the cookies as they cool and dry for several hours.

> 2 egg whites
> ¾ cup sugar
> ½ cup mini chocolate chips
> ¼ cup finely chopped walnuts

Preheat the oven to 375°. Coat 2 large baking sheets with no-stick spray.

Using an electric mixer, beat the egg whites on high speed until soft peaks form. Add the sugar, 1 tablespoon at a time, and continue beating on medium speed until the egg whites form stiff peaks but are not dry (8 to 10 minutes total).

Fold in the chocolate chips and walnuts. Drop the dough by level tablespoons onto the prepared baking sheets, leaving about 2″ between the cookies.

Place in the preheated oven and turn off heat. Let the cookies remain in the oven until they cool to room temperature. (They may be left in the oven overnight and removed in the morning.) Store in an airtight container.

Makes 24.

★ PER COOKIE: 54 CALORIES, 2.1 G. TOTAL FAT, 0 G. SATURATED FAT,
0 MG. CHOLESTEROL, 5 MG. SODIUM

Chocolate-Nut Fingers

Adapted from *Critics' Choice*
GUILD OF CORINTH THEATRE ARTS

These distinctive cookies are like chocolate shortbread with a crispy meringue topping. Although ½ cup of butter may seem like a lot, the nutrition numbers show that it works out to only 4.7 grams of fat per cookie, which is low compared with many regular cookies.

1¾ cups all-purpose flour
⅓ cup sugar
3 tablespoons unsweetened cocoa powder
½ cup butter or stick margarine (not reduced-calorie), softened
1 teaspoon vanilla
2 egg whites + 2 egg whites
⅔ cup powdered sugar
¼ cup toasted and finely chopped walnuts

Preheat the oven to 375°.

In a small bowl, stir together the flour, sugar and cocoa powder.

In a medium bowl, use an electric mixer to beat together the butter or margarine, vanilla and 2 of the egg whites. Gradually beat in the flour mixture. (If necessary, knead the mixture until all the flour is incorporated.)

Coat an 11″ × 7″ baking pan with no-stick spray. Press the dough into the pan.

In a small bowl, stir together the powdered sugar, walnuts and the remaining 2 egg whites. Spread over the dough.

Bake for 20 minutes, or until the top is a deep golden brown. Cool in the pan on a wire rack before cutting.

Makes 24.

★ PER COOKIE: 100 CALORIES, 4.7 G. TOTAL FAT, 2.4 G. SATURATED FAT, 10 MG. CHOLESTEROL, 48 MG. SODIUM

ANISE BISCOTTI

Adapted from *Preserving Our Italian Heritage*
SONS OF ITALY FLORIDA FOUNDATION

Serve these golden, crunchy slices with nonfat ice cream for a refreshing dessert or with a glass of cold skim milk for a satisfying snack.

⅔ cup sugar
2 egg whites
1 egg
1 cup all-purpose flour
1 teaspoon anise seeds

Preheat the oven to 350°. Lightly coat an 8″ × 4″ loaf pan and a large baking sheet with no-stick spray; set aside.

In a medium bowl, use an electric mixer to beat together the sugar, egg whites and egg for 10 minutes. Gradually beat in the flour. Stir in the anise seeds.

Spoon the batter into the prepared pan. Bake for 30 to 35 minutes, or until a toothpick inserted in the center comes out clean. Cool in the pan on a wire rack for 10 minutes.

Remove the loaf from the pan. Cut the loaf into ½″ slices. Place the slices on their sides on the prepared baking sheet. Bake for 5 minutes; turn the slices over and bake for 5 minutes, or until golden.

TEST KITCHEN TIP: To make sure that you get an accurate toothpick test, carefully scrape away a tiny bit of the crust from the center of the loaf and then insert the toothpick.

Makes 16.

★ PER BISCOTTI: 66 CALORIES, 0.4 G. TOTAL FAT, 0.1 G. SATURATED FAT,
  13 MG. CHOLESTEROL, 11 MG. SODIUM

Sons of Italy Florida Foundation

When the Sons of Italy Florida Foundation decided to put together a cookbook, the Foundation was inundated with recipes from members throughout the state of Florida. Some were jotted quickly on a piece of paper, others were preserved on yellowing recipe cards in the handwriting of a favorite relative long deceased.

Some recipes were fresh versions of old Italian favorites, while others were a trip back in time—calling for dashes, pinches, handfuls, even "half an eggshell full" of ingredients. The result is an adventure. It's a trip through all the regions of Italy, with dishes both familiar and novel, old-fashioned and up-to-the-minute.

Preserving Our Italian Heritage placed second in the 1991 National Tabasco Community Awards Cookbook competition. More than 50,000 copies of the book have been sold, to benefit the Sons of Italy Florida Foundation. Established in 1988, the Foundation helps a wide variety of charitable, cultural, literary and educational causes. It even benefits scientific and medical research efforts, particularly research into Cooley's anemia.

Old-Fashioned Strawberry Shortcake

Adapted from *Albuquerque Academy à la Carte*
ALBUQUERQUE ACADEMY PARENTS' ASSOCIATION

This old-fashioned favorite, originally a Pennsylvania Dutch heirloom recipe, needed little revision to make it healthful. We used egg whites instead of a whole egg and substituted reduced-fat topping for whipped cream. The real key to success is using the ripest local berries you can find.

1¼ cups skim milk
2 teaspoons vinegar
2¼ cups all-purpose flour
2 teaspoons baking powder
Pinch of salt
½ cup + ⅓ cup sugar
2 tablespoons shortening
2 egg whites, lightly beaten
½ teaspoon baking soda
4 cups sliced strawberries
1 cup thawed reduced-fat frozen whipped topping

Preheat the oven to 325°. Lightly coat a 9″ round cake pan with no-stick spray.

In a small bowl, stir together the milk and vinegar.

In a large bowl, stir together the flour, baking powder, salt and ½ cup of the sugar. Use a pastry blender to cut in the shortening. Stir in the milk mixture, egg whites and baking soda until well-mixed but still slightly lumpy.

Pour into the prepared pan. Bake for 30 minutes, or until the top is golden and firm to the touch.

In a small bowl, stir together the strawberries and the remaining ⅓ cup sugar.

To serve, cut the shortcake into 6 wedges. Slice the wedges in half horizontally, making 2 layers. Turn the top layer upside down. Spoon some of the strawberries and juice over the bottom layer, then repeat over the top layer. Top each serving with some of the whipped topping.

TEST KITCHEN TIP: This shortcake is also delicious topped with slightly sweetened raspberries, blackberries, peaches or nectarines. Low-fat vanilla yogurt is a tasty substitute for the whipped topping.

Makes 6 servings.

★ PER SERVING: 387 CALORIES, 7.8 G. TOTAL FAT, 1.5 G. SATURATED FAT, 1 MG. CHOLESTEROL, 233 MG. SODIUM

LOW-FAT CRÈME ANGLAISE

Adapted from *West of the Rockies*
JUNIOR SERVICE LEAGUE OF GRAND JUNCTION

This silken sauce is sinfully good served warm over fresh fruit or chocolate angel cake (see the Test Kitchen Tip below).

    2 cups skim milk
    ¼ cup sugar
    ¼ cup fat-free egg substitute
    3 tablespoons cornstarch
    2 teaspoons vanilla

In a small saucepan, whisk together the milk, sugar, egg substitute and cornstarch. Cook over medium heat, whisking constantly, until thickened. Whisk in the vanilla. Serve warm.

TEST KITCHEN TIP: To make chocolate angel cake, stir 3 tablespoons unsweetened cocoa powder into the dry ingredients of an angel-cake mix, then prepare and bake according to the package directions.

Makes 12 servings.

★ PER SERVING: 41 CALORIES, 0 G. TOTAL FAT, 0 G. SATURATED FAT, 1 MG. CHOLESTEROL, 28 MG. SODIUM

Frozen Orange Dream Bars

Adapted from *Plain and Elegant*
WEST GEORGIA MEDICAL CENTER AUXILIARY

It's easy to change the flavor of these refreshing frozen treats by substituting your favorite gelatin flavor.

> 1 package (4-serving-size) sugar-free orange gelatin
> 1 cup boiling water
> 2 cups fat-free vanilla ice cream, softened

In a medium bowl, dissolve the gelatin in the water, then let stand until cooled to room temperature.

Stir in the ice cream. Spoon ¼ cup of the mixture into each of 12 small paper cups, then cover the cups with foil. Insert a wooden stick through the foil and into the ice-cream mixture. Freeze until firm. To serve, peel off the paper cups.

Makes 12.

★ PER BAR: 33 CALORIES, 0 G. TOTAL FAT, 0 G. SATURATED FAT,
0 MG. CHOLESTEROL, 41 MG. SODIUM

Nonfat Berry Freeze

Adapted from *Cane River's Louisiana Living*
SERVICE LEAGUE OF NATCHITOCHES

This cool sherbet treat is very simple to make. Just blend the ingredients until smooth, freeze until firm and enjoy!

> 1 package (10 ounces) frozen strawberries or raspberries, slightly thawed
> 1 container (8 ounces) fat-free plain yogurt
> ¼ cup sugar
> 1 tablespoon vanilla

OUR CAUSE

Service League of Natchitoches

Since 1714, when Louis Juchereau de St. Denis established it as the first permanent settlement in the Louisiana Purchase, Natchitoches has been a capital of gracious living. Even today, it's easy to imagine the peaceful, gracious life of bygone eras. Along the 35 miles of the Cane River Lake, the brick-paved streets are lined with colonial-era houses, beautifully preserved antebellum homes and working plantations.

The Service League of Natchitoches has been instrumental in preserving and improving the quality of life there since 1950. Sales of the group's first cookbook, *Cane River Cuisine*, funded the purchase and restoration of one of the town's historic antebellum mansions.

The League's new book, *Cane River's Louisiana Living*, shows off Natchitoches's historic houses and other sites and celebrates its heritage as a seat of fine Louisiana cooking. Proceeds from the book are earmarked for the League's scholarship funds for women.

In a blender or food processor, blend the strawberries or raspberries, yogurt, sugar and vanilla until smooth. Pour into individual sherbet or dessert dishes. Freeze for at least 3 hours, or until firm.

Makes 4 servings.

★ PER SERVING: 112 CALORIES, 0.2 G. TOTAL FAT, 0 G. SATURATED FAT, 1 MG. CHOLESTEROL, 45 MG. SODIUM

....

FRESH PEACH ICE CREAM

Adapted from *The Plaid Platter*
GREENWICH ACADEMY

Although fresh peaches give this homemade ice cream an outstanding flavor, we found that unsweetened frozen sliced peaches work well when fresh ones aren't in season. Just thaw the frozen slices, then mash. You'll need about 24 ounces of frozen peaches to give you 3 cups of mashed fruit.

> 3 cups mashed peaches
> 1 can (14 ounces) low-fat sweetened condensed milk
> ¾ cup evaporated skim milk
> ⅓ cup sugar
> 1 tablespoon vanilla
>   Pinch of salt
> 4 cups skim milk

In a large bowl, stir together the peaches, condensed milk, evaporated milk, sugar, vanilla and salt. Stir in the skim milk.

Transfer the mixture to a 4- or 5-quart ice-cream freezer and freeze according to the manufacturer's instructions. (For best texture, do not freeze for more than 2 hours before serving. Otherwise, the ice cream will become too hard to scoop.)

TEST KITCHEN TIP: If you don't have an ice-cream freezer, pour the peach mixture into a 13″ × 9″ baking pan. Cover and freeze for 6 hours, or until frozen. Before serving, break about a quarter of the frozen mixture into small chunks and transfer it to a food processor. Process on low speed just until smooth. Serve immediately. Process the remaining ice cream in batches.

Makes 3 quarts; 24 servings.

★ PER ½ CUP: 103 CALORIES, 0.7 G. TOTAL FAT, 0.5 G. SATURATED FAT, 3 MG. CHOLESTEROL, 49 MG. SODIUM

Fruit Sorbet

Adapted from *Delicious Developments*
FRIENDS OF STRONG MEMORIAL HOSPITAL

To get the perfect fluffy texture, prepare this quick-to-fix dessert immediately before serving. You can take your choice of fruit. Strawberries, blueberries or peaches work equally well.

> 1 package (16 ounces) unsweetened frozen fruit
> 1 cup fat-free plain yogurt
> ⅓ cup sugar
> 2 teaspoons lemon juice

Place the fruit in a blender or food processor. Blend with on/off pulses until chopped. Add the yogurt, sugar and lemon juice. Blend just until mixed. Serve immediately.

Makes 4 servings.

★ PER SERVING: 132 CALORIES, 0.2 G. TOTAL FAT, 0 G. SATURATED FAT, 1 MG. CHOLESTEROL, 46 MG. SODIUM

Low-Fat Banana Pudding

Adapted from *With Special Distinction*
MISSISSIPPI COLLEGE

To make individual parfaits, layer the vanilla wafers, bananas and pudding in 8 sherbet or dessert dishes. Coarsely crush 4 additional wafers and sprinkle some of the crumbs over each serving.

½ cup sugar
3 tablespoons all-purpose flour
3 egg whites, lightly beaten
½ cup fat-free egg substitute
1¾ cups skim milk
½ cup evaporated skim milk
1½ teaspoons vanilla
30 reduced-fat vanilla wafers
3 medium bananas, sliced

In a medium saucepan, stir together the sugar and flour.

In a small bowl, whisk together the egg whites and egg substitute. Whisk into the sugar mixture. Whisk in the skim milk and evaporated milk.

Cook over medium heat, whisking constantly, until the mixture just starts to thicken. To avoid curdling, remove from the heat immediately. Whisk in the vanilla.

Cover and refrigerate for at least 1 hour.

In a serving bowl, layer half of the vanilla wafers, half of the bananas and half of the pudding mixture. Repeat to use the remaining wafers, bananas and pudding. Cover and refrigerate for 2 to 4 hours.

Makes 8 servings.

★ PER SERVING: 211 CALORIES, 2.6 G. TOTAL FAT, 0.5 G. SATURATED FAT, 11 MG. CHOLESTEROL, 125 MG. SODIUM

CHOCOLATE DESSERT

Adapted from *300 Years of Carolina Cooking*
JUNIOR LEAGUE OF GREENVILLE

By replacing unsweetened chocolate with cocoa powder, we cut the fat in this scrumptious dessert but still ended up with devilishly good flavor.

> 1 cup all-purpose flour
> 2 teaspoons baking powder
> Pinch of salt
> 1¼ cups sugar
> 3 tablespoons + ¼ cup unsweetened cocoa powder
> ½ cup skim milk
> 2 tablespoons butter or stick margarine (not reduced-calorie), melted
> 1 teaspoon vanilla
> ½ cup packed brown sugar
> 1 cup water
> 2 cups fat-free vanilla ice cream

Preheat the oven to 350°. Coat an 11″ × 7″ baking pan with no-stick spray; set aside.

In a large bowl, stir together the flour, baking powder, salt, ¾ cup of the sugar and 3 tablespoons of the cocoa. Stir in the milk, butter or margarine and vanilla. Spread the batter in the prepared pan.

In a small bowl, stir together the brown sugar, the remaining ½ cup sugar and the remaining ¼ cup cocoa. Sprinkle over the batter. Very slowly pour the water over the cocoa topping.

Bake for 35 to 40 minutes, or until a toothpick inserted in the center comes out clean. Serve warm, topping each serving with a small scoop of the ice cream.

Makes 8 servings.

★ PER SERVING: 308 CALORIES, 3.5 G. TOTAL FAT, 0.5 G. SATURATED FAT, 0 MG. CHOLESTEROL, 166 MG. SODIUM

Sweet-Potato Pie

Adapted from *Cajun Men Cook*
BEAVER CLUB OF LAFAYETTE

As the recipe in Cajun Men Cook *points out, you can mash either cooked fresh or canned sweet potatoes to get the 2 cups you need for this spiced-just-right pie. If you use canned, be sure to get vacuum-packed sweets. They're lower in calories than the syrup-packed variety.*

PASTRY

1⅓ cups all-purpose flour
   Pinch of salt
¼ cup canola oil
3 tablespoons skim milk

FILLING

2 cups mashed cooked sweet potatoes
1 cup sugar
1 tablespoon butter-flavored sprinkles
¾ teaspoon ground cinnamon
½ teaspoon ground nutmeg
⅛ teaspoon ground cloves
4 egg whites, lightly beaten
1 cup evaporated skim milk
½ cup skim milk
1 teaspoon vanilla

TO MAKE THE PASTRY: Preheat the oven to 425°.

In a medium bowl, stir together the flour and salt. Add the oil and milk all at once. Using a fork, toss and stir lightly until the flour is moistened. Then, using your hands, gently shape the mixture into a ball.

Place the dough between two 12″-square pieces of wax paper. Gently roll it into a 12″ circle. Remove the top piece of wax paper. Then invert the dough onto a 9″ pie plate. Remove the remaining piece of wax paper and gently fit the dough into the pan. Fold the edges of the pastry under and flute them. Do not prick the pastry.

Line the pastry shell with a double thickness of heavy foil. Bake for 7 minutes. Remove from the oven, then remove the foil.

TO MAKE THE FILLING: In a large bowl, stir together the sweet potatoes, sugar, butter-flavored sprinkles, cinnamon, nutmeg and cloves. Stir in the egg whites, evaporated milk, skim milk and vanilla until well-combined.

Pour the filling into the partially baked pastry. Bake for 10 minutes. Reduce the heat to 350° and bake for 35 to 40 minutes, or until the filling is firm around the edge but still a little soft in the middle. (The center will get firm as the pie cools.)

Cool on a wire rack. Refrigerate until serving time. Store any remaining pie in the refrigerator.

TEST KITCHEN TIP: For variety, top each serving with a spoonful of reduced-fat vanilla yogurt or a little thawed reduced-fat frozen whipped topping.

Makes 8 servings.

★ PER SERVING: 357 CALORIES, 7.4 G. TOTAL FAT, 0.7 G. SATURATED FAT, 2 MG. CHOLESTEROL, 86 MG. SODIUM

SUGARLESS APPLE PIE

Adapted from *The Take Care Cookbook*
MID-FAIRFIELD HOSPICE

*Frozen apple juice concentrate sweetens the spicy apple filling in
this wonderful pie. For the pastry, we used some canola oil to
produce a tender crust with a minimum of saturated fat.*

PASTRY

2½ cups all-purpose flour
⅛ teaspoon salt
¼ cup butter or stick margarine (not reduced-calorie)
¼ cup canola oil
5–7 tablespoons skim milk

FILLING

⅔ cup frozen apple juice concentrate, thawed
2 tablespoons cornstarch
¾ teaspoon ground cinnamon
¼ teaspoon ground nutmeg
⅛ teaspoon ground cloves
5 cups peeled and sliced tart apples
1 tablespoon butter-flavored sprinkles

TO MAKE THE PASTRY: Preheat the oven to 400°.

In a medium bowl, stir together the flour and salt. Using a pastry
blender, cut in the butter or margarine.

In a cup, stir together the oil and 5 tablespoons of the milk.
Drizzle the oil mixture over the flour.

Using a fork, toss and stir lightly until the flour is moistened. If
necessary, add enough of the remaining 2 tablespoons milk to
moisten. Then, using your hands, gently shape the mixture into a
ball. Divide into 2 balls.

Place 1 ball of dough between two 12″-square pieces of wax
paper. Gently roll into a 12″ circle. Remove the top piece of wax
paper. Then invert the dough onto a 9″ pie plate. Remove the remaining piece of wax paper and gently fit the dough into the pan.

Place the remaining ball of dough between two 12″-square pieces
of wax paper. Gently roll into a 12″ circle. Set aside.

TO MAKE THE FILLING: In a medium saucepan, whisk together the apple juice concentrate, cornstarch, cinnamon, nutmeg and cloves. Cook over medium heat, whisking constantly, until the mixture begins to thicken and just comes to a boil. Remove from the heat and set aside.

Place the apples in the pastry-lined pie plate. Spoon the cornstarch mixture over the apples. Spoon the butter-flavored sprinkles over the top.

Invert the remaining dough circle over the apple filling. Fold the edges of the pastry under and flute. Use a sharp knife to cut 2 or 3 slits in the top crust. Bake for 40 minutes, or until the apples are tender and the crust is golden. Cool on a wire rack.

TEST KITCHEN TIP: For pie à la mode, top each wedge of pie with a small scoop of fat-free vanilla ice cream.

Makes 8 servings.

★ PER SERVING: 349 CALORIES, 13.2 G. TOTAL FAT, 1.7 G. SATURATED FAT, 15 MG. CHOLESTEROL, 111 MG. SODIUM

Fresh Blueberry Pie

Adapted from *Augusta Cooks for Company*
AUGUSTA COUNCIL

This luscious blueberry pie is really a cheesecake with a modest 8 grams of fat per serving.

CRUST

- 1¼ cups low-fat graham crackers crushed to fine crumbs
- 3 tablespoons powdered sugar
- 1 egg white, lightly beaten
- 2½ tablespoons tub-style reduced-calorie margarine, melted and cooled

FILLING

- 1 package (8 ounces) light cream cheese, softened
- 2 tablespoons skim milk
- ¾ cup sugar
- 3 teaspoons lemon juice
- 4 cups fresh blueberries
- 2 tablespoons cornstarch
- ¼ cup water
- 1 cup thawed reduced-fat frozen whipped topping (optional)

TO MAKE THE CRUST: Preheat the oven to 375°.

In a small bowl, stir together the cracker crumbs and powdered sugar.

In a cup, stir together the egg white and margarine. Add to the crumb mixture and stir until well-mixed.

Lightly coat a 9″ pie plate with no-stick spray. Pat the crumb mixture into the bottom and up the sides to form an even crust. Bake for 4 to 5 minutes, or until the edge of the crust is lightly browned. Cool on a wire rack.

TO MAKE THE FILLING: Use an electric mixer or a food processor to beat together the cream cheese, milk, ¼ cup of the sugar and 2 teaspoons of the lemon juice until smooth. Spread evenly in the cooled crust.

Spoon 3 cups of the blueberries over the cream-cheese mixture.

In a medium bowl, use a fork to mash the remaining 1 cup blueberries.

In a medium saucepan, stir together the cornstarch and the remaining ½ cup sugar. Gradually stir in the water until smooth. Stir
in the mashed blueberries and the remaining 1 teaspoon lemon juice.

Cook, stirring, over medium heat until the mixture comes to a
boil. Reduce the heat. Cook, stirring, for 1 minute more. Remove
from the heat and let stand at room temperature for 10 minutes. Stir
the blueberry mixture and spoon over the blueberries in the crust.
Cover and refrigerate for at least 2 hours.

Top each serving with a spoonful of the whipped topping (if
using). Store any remaining pie in the refrigerator.

Makes 8 servings.

★ PER SERVING: 266 CALORIES, 8.2 G. TOTAL FAT, 3.6 G. SATURATED FAT,
10 MG. CHOLESTEROL, 290 MG. SODIUM

NANNY'S CARAMEL PIE

Adapted from *Family Secrets*
LEE ACADEMY

Caramelized sugar gives this luscious cream pie a light golden color and subtle caramel flavor.

PASTRY

    1⅓ cups all-purpose flour
       Pinch of salt
    ¼ cup canola oil
    3 tablespoons skim milk

FILLING

    ⅓ cup all-purpose flour
       Pinch of salt
    1¼ cups sugar
    2 cans (12 ounces each) evaporated skim milk
    2 teaspoons vanilla
    1 tablespoon hot water
    2 teaspoons butter or stick margarine (not reduced-calorie)

MERINGUE

    3 egg whites
    1 teaspoon vanilla
    ¼ teaspoon cream of tartar
    ⅓ cup sugar

TO MAKE THE PASTRY: Preheat the oven to 450°.

In a medium bowl, stir together the flour and salt. Add the oil and milk all at once to the flour. Using a fork, toss and stir lightly until the flour is moistened. Then, using your hands, gently shape the mixture into a ball.

Place the ball of dough between two 12″-square pieces of wax paper. Gently roll into a 12″ circle. Remove the top piece of wax paper. Then invert the dough onto a 9″ pie plate. Remove the remaining piece of wax paper and gently fit the dough into the pan. Fold the edges of the pastry under and flute. Prick the pastry with a fork.

Line the pastry with a double thickness of heavy foil. Bake for 7 minutes. Remove from the oven, then remove the foil. Bake for 5 to 7 minutes more, or until the pastry is done. Cool on a wire rack.

OUR CAUSE

Lee Academy

The women of Clarksdale, Mississippi, pride themselves on their good home cooking. Of course, in the old days, before we worried about cholesterol and fat, that meant dishes that were fried or smothered in gravy. Today, the women of Clarksdale continue the tradition of good Southern cooking, but with a difference: In *Family Secrets* they've lightened the recipes to reflect the health concerns of the 1990s.

The family recipes in this book might explain why the students at Lee Academy are such achievers. The Clarksdale college preparatory school takes pride in the high academic achievement of its students. As important as academic success, though, is the school's emphasis on helping each child develop his own character. Self-discipline and a love of learning are watchwords at this small, special school. Money raised from the book, produced by faculty and parents, helps the school continue its record of excellence.

TO MAKE THE FILLING: In a medium bowl, stir together the flour, salt and ¾ cup of the sugar. Stir in the milk and vanilla until well-mixed.

Put the remaining ½ cup sugar in a heavy medium saucepan. Heat the sugar over medium heat until the sugar starts to melt. Reduce the heat to low; cook, stirring frequently, until the sugar is completely melted and a golden color. Immediately add the water, whisking constantly, until well-mixed. (A great deal of steam will rise; protect your stirring hand with an oven mitt or towel.)

Use a wire whisk to stir the milk mixture into the melted sugar. Cook over medium heat, whisking constantly, until the mixture begins to thicken and just comes to a boil. Cook for 1 to 2 minutes more. Stir in the butter or margarine until melted. Pour into the baked pastry shell.

TO MAKE THE MERINGUE: Preheat the oven to 350°.

Using an electric mixer, beat the egg whites on high speed until foamy. Add the vanilla and cream of tartar. Then beat on medium

(continued)

speed until the egg whites form soft peaks. Add the sugar, 1 table-spoon at a time, and continue beating on medium speed until the egg whites form stiff peaks but are not dry.

Spread the meringue over the filling in the pastry shell, making sure the meringue is sealed to the edge of the pastry all around.

Bake for 15 to 17 minutes, or until golden. Cool on a wire rack. Cover and refrigerate until serving time. Store any remaining pie in the refrigerator.

TEST KITCHEN TIP: When you add the milk mixture to the melted sugar, the sugar will immediately harden. Don't be con-cerned—it will melt again as the mixture cooks and thickens.

Makes 8 servings.

★ PER SERVING: 386 CALORIES, 8.2 G. TOTAL FAT, 1.2 G. SATURATED FAT, 6 MG. CHOLESTEROL, 132 MG. SODIUM

MOTHER'S ANGEL PIE

Adapted from *With Special Distinction*
MISSISSIPPI COLLEGE

This dessert is also delicious with a lemon topping. To make it, just fold 1 cup thawed reduced-fat frozen whipped topping into 8 ounces reduced-fat lemon yogurt; spread this mixture over the dessert in place of the whipped topping and cocoa powder.

4 egg whites
1 teaspoon vanilla
Pinch of salt
1 cup powdered sugar
½ cup sugar
⅛ teaspoon cream of tartar
2 cups thawed reduced-fat frozen whipped topping
2 teaspoons unsweetened cocoa powder

Line a 9″ pie plate with parchment paper. Coat the paper with no-stick spray.

In a large bowl, use an electric mixer to beat together the egg whites, vanilla and salt on high speed until soft peaks form.

Sift together the powdered sugar, sugar and cream of tartar 4 times. Gradually add the sugar mixture to the egg whites, beating for 7 minutes, or until the sugar is almost dissolved and stiff peaks form.

Pour into the prepared pie plate. Place in a cold oven. Turn the oven on to 350°. Bake for 45 to 50 minutes, or until deep golden brown.

Cool in the pie plate on a wire rack (dessert may dip some in the center as it cools). Then invert onto a serving plate and carefully peel off the paper.

Cover completely with the whipped topping. Sift the cocoa powder over the top.

TEST KITCHEN TIP: To make sure that the sugar is almost dissolved in the beaten egg whites, rub a little of the egg-white mixture between your fingers. The mixture should feel almost smooth and shouldn't have any large sugar crystals.

Makes 8 servings.

★ PER SERVING: 140 CALORIES, 4 G. TOTAL FAT, 0 G. SATURATED FAT,
0 MG. CHOLESTEROL, 40 MG. SODIUM

APPLE PHYLLO PACKAGES

Adapted from *From Generation to Generation*
SISTERHOOD OF TEMPLE EMANU-EL

Crisp, flaky phyllo wrapped around an apple-raisin filling produces an enlightened apple dumpling. Look for phyllo dough in the frozen dessert section of your supermarket.

4 medium Granny Smith apples or other tart apples, chopped
¼ cup raisins
¼ cup sugar
2 tablespoons low-fat graham crackers crushed to fine crumbs
½ teaspoon ground cinnamon
¼ teaspoon ground nutmeg
8 sheets phyllo dough
1 tablespoon skim milk
1 tablespoon powdered sugar

Preheat the oven to 400°. Lightly coat a large baking sheet with no-stick spray; set aside.

Place the apples in a large bowl.

In a small bowl, stir together the raisins, sugar, cracker crumbs, cinnamon and nutmeg. Add to the apples and toss until coated.

Place 1 sheet of the phyllo dough on a damp towel (keep the remaining sheets covered). Lightly coat the phyllo with no-stick spray. Repeat layering and spraying the dough 3 more times, using 3 more of the sheets of phyllo dough. Using a sharp knife, cut the stack into large quarters.

Spoon about ⅔ cup of the apple mixture in the center of 1 stack of phyllo. Fold the opposite corners of the phyllo over the apple mixture, wrapping the filling like a bundle. Place the bundle, seam side down, on the prepared baking sheet. Repeat with the remaining 3 stacks of phyllo.

Using the remaining phyllo and filling, repeat the layering, spraying, cutting and filling to make 4 more bundles. (You will have a total of 8 bundles.)

Brush the phyllo bundles with the milk and prick the top of each bundle 2 or 3 times with a sharp knife.

Bake for 20 minutes, or until golden brown. Let cool slightly, then sprinkle with the powdered sugar and serve warm.

TEST KITCHEN TIP: Phyllo dough dries out very quickly, so be sure to keep the phyllo covered with a damp cloth or paper towel and a piece of plastic wrap. Remove each sheet only when you're ready to use it.

Makes 8 servings.

★ PER SERVING: 87 CALORIES, 0.4 G. TOTAL FAT, 0.1 G. SATURATED FAT, 0 MG. CHOLESTEROL, 9 MG. SODIUM

....

LEMON PUDDING CAKE

Adapted from *Charleston Receipts*
JUNIOR LEAGUE OF CHARLESTON

This low-calorie dessert is actually two treats in one—a tangy lemon pudding topped with a spongelike cake.

½ cup sugar
3 tablespoons all-purpose flour
2 egg yolks, lightly beaten
1 cup skim milk
3 tablespoons lemon juice
2 teaspoons finely shredded lemon rind
2 egg whites

Preheat the oven to 350°. Lightly coat a 1-quart casserole or soufflé dish with no-stick spray; set aside.

In a large bowl, stir together the sugar and flour.

In a small bowl, stir together the egg yolks, milk, lemon juice and lemon rind. Add to the flour mixture and stir just until combined.

Place the egg whites in a clean small bowl. Beat with an electric mixer on high speed until the egg whites form stiff peaks. Gently fold the whites into the lemon mixture.

Spoon the batter into the prepared casserole. Place the casserole in a shallow baking pan, then pour very hot tap water into the pan to a depth of 1″.

(continued)

OUR CAUSE

Junior League of Charleston

Charleston Receipts is the oldest Junior League cookbook still in print. Since it was first published in 1950, more than 647,000 copies have been sold, resulting in nearly $900,000 for the many causes supported by the dynamic Junior League of Charleston, South Carolina.

The proceeds from that first cookbook were given to the Charleston Speech and Hearing Center. In 1991 the League was awarded the Distinguished Service Award from the American Speech-Language-Hearing Association for its contributions over the years to the fields of speech-language pathology and audiology.

Aside from a supplement added to the book in 1951 and a revised index, *Charleston Receipts* remains unchanged. It's filled with 750 recipes plus sketches by Charleston artists and verses in Gullah, a Creole language spoken by about 200,000 African-Americans living in the low country of South Carolina and Georgia.

In 1990 the cookbook was honored with inclusion in the Walter S. McIlhenny Hall of Fame for Community Cookbooks. Proceeds from the current printing go to the Low Country Children's Center and other Charleston agencies.

Bake for 35 minutes, or until a knife inserted in the center of the cake portion comes out clean. Serve warm.

Makes 4 servings.

★ PER SERVING: 174 CALORIES, 2.7 G. TOTAL FAT, 0.9 G. SATURATED FAT, 108 MG. CHOLESTEROL, 63 MG. SODIUM

FESTIVE MENUS

FESTIVE MENUS

·····················

*P*lease be our guest for a tasty trip around the USA.
You won't have to use your frequent-flier airline miles or log any road time in the family van. In fact, you won't even have to leave your kitchen.

To sample the best of regional community cooking, just consult the 19 menus that follow. You'll discover a range of entertaining styles—from casual to special occasion—planned around seasonal and holiday themes.

You can picnic on a grassy meadow in Madison County, Iowa, with a Covered-Bridge Picnic Lunch or linger over a Southern-Style Sunday Dinner. Score points with A Chili Bowl for Super Bowl or gather friends for a stylish summertime San Francisco Garden Party. It's an appetizing agenda, with many delicious stops along the way.

To make the journey hassle-free, we've included amounts for all condiments and fresh accompaniments. In addition, a one-serving nutritional analysis lets you easily work these menus into your daily eating plan. The portion size for all the featured recipes is one serving.

AMISH BARN-RAISING BREAKFAST

Fancy Egg Scrambles (page 178)
Honey Whole-Wheat Bread (page 56)
Apple butter
Orange slices
Fresh brewed coffee

For each serving, plan on 1 tablespoon apple butter and 1 medium orange.

★ PER SERVING: 527 CALORIES, 13.7 G. TOTAL FAT, 3.8 G. SATURATED FAT, 231 MG. CHOLESTEROL, 941 MG. SODIUM

COVERED-BRIDGE PICNIC LUNCH

Country Chicken Pie (page 108)
Ginger Beets (page 219)
Romaine lettuce with fat-free dressing
Old-Fashioned Strawberry Shortcake (page 256)

For each serving, plan on 1 cup torn romaine leaves with 2 tablespoons fat-free dressing.

★ PER SERVING: 889 CALORIES, 20.2 G. TOTAL FAT, 3.3 G. SATURATED FAT, 50 MG. CHOLESTEROL, 815 MG. SODIUM

GULF-COAST NEW YEAR'S DAY DINNER

Texas Caviar (page 12)
Baked tortilla chips
Shrimp Gumbo (page 78)
Steamed rice
Buttermilk Cornbread (page 36)
Lemon Pudding Cake (page 275)

For each serving, plan on 10 tortilla chips and ½ cup rice.

★ PER SERVING: 702 CALORIES, 7.4 G. TOTAL FAT, 1.6 G. SATURATED FAT, 248 MG. CHOLESTEROL, 1,058 MG. SODIUM

GEORGIA PATIO PARTY

Seafood Casseroles (page 153)
Romaine lettuce salad
Dijon-Honey Dressing (page 208)
Fresh Peach Ice Cream (page 260)
Iced tea with fresh mint

For each serving, plan on 2 cups torn romaine leaves.

★ PER SERVING: 404 CALORIES, 8.8 G. TOTAL FAT, 2.1 G. SATURATED FAT, 165 MG. CHOLESTEROL, 847 MG. SODIUM

A Texas Hometown Hoedown

Deep-Dish Taco Squares (page 84)
Marinated Vegetable Salad (page 193)
Watermelon wedges
Chocolate Puffs (page 250)

For each serving, plan on 1 medium watermelon wedge.

★ PER SERVING: 447 CALORIES, 7 G. TOTAL FAT, 1.8 G. SATURATED FAT,
42 MG. CHOLESTEROL, 1,057 MG. SODIUM

Supper on Lake Michigan

Apple-Glazed Barbecued
  Chicken (page 110)
Strawberry-Nut Salad (page 184)
Baked or roasted potato
Fresh Blueberry Pie (page 268)

For each serving, plan on 1 medium potato.

★ PER SERVING: 696 CALORIES, 14.4 G. TOTAL FAT, 4.5 G. SATURATED FAT,
56 MG. CHOLESTEROL, 511 MG. SODIUM

Alabama Catfish Cookout

Grilled catfish
Creole Sauce for Fish (page 142)
Orange Salad with Honey Vinaigrette (page 200)
Steamed rice
Sweet-Potato Pie (page 264)

For each serving, plan on 3 ounces catfish and ½ cup rice.

★ PER SERVING: 718 CALORIES, 14.1 G. TOTAL FAT, 1.7 G. SATURATED FAT,
51 MG. CHOLESTEROL, 198 MG. SODIUM

VERMONT MAPLE-SUGARING POTLUCK

Pot Roast with Apple Cider (page 90)
Tossed salad with fat-free dressing
Yogurt Rolls (page 54)
Warm maple syrup
Apple Phyllo Packages (page 274)

For each serving, plan on 2 cups tossed salad, 2 tablespoons fat-free dressing and 1 roll spread with 1 tablespoon pure maple syrup.

★PER SERVING: 670 CALORIES, 11.2 G. TOTAL FAT, 3.4 G. SATURATED FAT, 82 MG. CHOLESTEROL, 602 MG. SODIUM

OCTOBERFEST

Sausage and Barley Soup (page 70)
Mushroom-Sauced Noodles (page 167)
Steamed broccoli
Easy Sour-Cream Coffee Cake (page 49)

For each serving, plan on ½ cup broccoli.

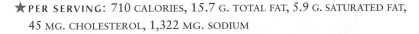

★PER SERVING: 710 CALORIES, 15.7 G. TOTAL FAT, 5.9 G. SATURATED FAT, 45 MG. CHOLESTEROL, 1,322 MG. SODIUM

NEW ENGLAND AUTUMN HARVEST

Appetizer Potato Pancakes (page 22)
Apple-Orchard Pork Chops (page 93)
Bow-tie noodles
Apricot-Glazed Carrots (page 226)
Pumpkin and Spice Roll (page 244)

For each serving, plan on 1 cup cooked noodles.

★PER SERVING: 827 CALORIES, 19.6 G. TOTAL FAT, 5.2 G. SATURATED FAT, 12 MG. CHOLESTEROL, 431 MG. SODIUM

Down-Home Shrimp Dinner

Garlic-Scented Broiled Shrimp (page 147)
Basil-Balsamic Potato Salad (page 190)
Corn on the cob with freshly ground pepper
Zucchini Bread (page 46)
Minted Fruit Salad (page 185)

For each serving, plan on 1 ear of corn.

★ PER SERVING: 465 CALORIES, 8.4 G. TOTAL FAT, 1.2 G. SATURATED FAT, 232 MG. CHOLESTEROL, 378 MG. SODIUM

Italian St. Joseph's Day Table

Yellow-Pepper Soup (page 67)
Grilled Eggplant with Marinara
  Sauce (page 224)
Light Fettuccine (page 166)
Italian Cake (page 238)

For each serving, plan on 1 serving of each dish.

★ PER SERVING: 713 CALORIES, 22.6 G. TOTAL FAT, 2 G. SATURATED FAT, 13 MG. CHOLESTEROL, 1,131 MG. SODIUM

Boston Bean-Town Bash

Triple-Bean Bake (page 174)
Cranberry-Orange Salad (page 197)
Whole-Wheat Nut Bread (page 48)
Sugarless Apple Pie (page 266)

For each serving, plan on 1 serving of each dish but 2 servings of the beans.

★ PER SERVING: 913 CALORIES, 17.8 G. TOTAL FAT, 2.2 G. SATURATED FAT, 15 MG. CHOLESTEROL, 681 MG. SODIUM

Southern-Style Sunday Dinner

Country Captain Chicken (page 118)
Pineapple Coleslaw (page 189)
Low-Fat Banana Pudding (page 262)

For each serving, plan on 1 serving of each dish.

★ PER SERVING: 751 CALORIES, 14.5 G. TOTAL FAT, 3.1 G. SATURATED FAT,
123 MG. CHOLESTEROL, 584 MG. SODIUM

Mardi Gras Gala

Cajun Fish (page 134)
Creole Lima Beans (page 218)
Assorted fresh greens
New Orleans Salad Dressing (page 212)
Nonfat Berry Freeze (page 258)

For each serving, plan on 1 cup of greens.

★ PER SERVING: 412 CALORIES, 7.5 G. TOTAL FAT, 1 G. SATURATED FAT,
25 MG. CHOLESTEROL, 607 MG. SODIUM

Heartland Block Party

Salmon Party Log (page 13)
Wheat crackers
Skewered Pasta and Vegetables (page 16)
Jan's Chicken Casserole (page 119)
Raw vegetable tray
Fresh fruit basket

*For each serving, plan on 7 crackers, lots of raw vegetables and 1
piece of fresh fruit.*

★ PER SERVING: 517 CALORIES, 12.8 G. TOTAL FAT, 4.9 G. SATURATED FAT,
81 MG. CHOLESTEROL, 798 MG. SODIUM

OREGON GRILLED-SALMON SUPPER

Stuffed Cherry Tomatoes (page 14)
Sweet-and-Spicy Grilled Salmon (page 141)
New potatoes with snipped fresh herbs
Sweet corn
Grapes

For each serving, plan on 4½ ounces small new potatoes (grilled or steamed and served with fresh basil, chives, tarragon or other snipped herbs), 1 cup corn or 1 ear corn on the cob and 1 cup grapes.

★ PER SERVING: 573 CALORIES, 9.9 G. TOTAL FAT, 2 G. SATURATED FAT, 69 MG. CHOLESTEROL, 550 MG. SODIUM

SAN FRANCISCO GARDEN PARTY

Fresh Artichokes with
** Mustard Sauce (page 214)**
Cioppino (page 74)
Sourdough bread
Fruit Sorbet (page 261)

For each serving, plan on 1 bread slice.

★ PER SERVING: 495 CALORIES, 4.2 G. TOTAL FAT, 0.5 G. SATURATED FAT, 71 MG. CHOLESTEROL, 1,069 MG. SODIUM

A CHILI BOWL FOR SUPER BOWL

Texas Cowboy Stew (page 79)
Hard roll
Creamy Caesar Salad (page 196)
Cocoa Brownies (page 249)

For each serving, plan on 1 hard roll and 1 brownie.

★ PER SERVING: 512 CALORIES, 14.5 G. TOTAL FAT, 5.7 G. SATURATED FAT, 74 MG. CHOLESTEROL, 603 MG. SODIUM

DIRECTORY

W e chose the recipes in *Healthy Favorites from America's Community Cookbooks* from a cross-section of community cookbooks nationwide. The organizations that publish those books raise money for good causes. If you would like to help support their causes by ordering any of their books, write to the addresses below. Postage and handling are included in the prices listed. If additional state sales tax is required, it is noted in the entry.

A Cook's Tour of the Azalea Coast
Auxiliary to the New Hanover–
    Pender County Medical Society
P.O. Box 5303
Wilmington, NC 28403

Send a check for $17.95 payable to *A Cook's Tour of the Azalea Coast*
Proceeds benefit: Health education and medical needs of the community and "Straight Talk," a hot line for teenagers
Recipe: Johnnycakes, page 40

Albuquerque Academy à la Carte
Albuquerque Academy Parents'
    Association
6400 Wyoming Boulevard, N.E.
Albuquerque, NM 87109

Send a check for $16.95 payable to *Albuquerque Academy*
Proceeds benefit: Albuquerque Academy Parents' Association Student Aid
Recipes: Old-Fashioned Strawberry Shortcake, page 256; Sausage and Barley Soup, page 70; Tender Scones, page 34; Tortellini with Tomatoes and Herb Dressing, page 192

Amazing Graces
Texas Conference United Methodist
    Ministers' Spouses Association
12955 Memorial Drive
Houston, TX 77079

Send a check for $17.45 payable to *Texas Conference Ministers' Spouses Association* (Texas residents add $1.23 state sales tax)
Proceeds benefit: Lakeview Conference Center, Nancy Oliphint Playground
Recipe: Oatmeal Bread, page 58

A Place Called Hope
Junior Auxiliary of Hope
P.O. Box 81
Hope, AR 71801

Send a check for $17.95 payable to *Junior Auxiliary of Hope*
Proceeds benefit: Junior Auxiliary of Hope Children's Fund projects
Recipes: Meatball Stroganoff, page 92; Oven-Baked Cottage Fries, page 234

A Shining Feast
First Baptist Church of Shreveport
543 Ockley Drive
Shreveport, LA 71106

Send a check for $20.00 payable
to *First Baptist Church Cookbook*
Proceeds benefit: Hunger relief
Mission Project
Recipes: Creole Lima Beans, page
218; Orange Salad with Honey Vinaigrette, page 200; Sweet-Potato
Muffins, page 38; Yogurt Rolls, page
54

A Taste of Aloha
Junior League of Honolulu
1802A Keeaumoku Street
Honolulu, HI 96822

Send a check for $21.63 payable
to *JLH Commerical Publications*
(Hawaii residents add $.80 state sales
tax)
Proceeds benefit: Projects to end domestic violence and to promote positive parenting
Recipe: Filet Charlemagne, page 88

A Taste of New England
Junior League of Worcester
71 Pleasant Street
Worcester, MA 01609

Send a check for $20.95 payable
to *Junior League of Worcester*
Proceeds benefit: Programs supported
by the League, including Good Start
(training for first-time parents) and
scholarships for young women
Recipe: Lemon-Ginger Chicken, page
120

Augusta Cooks for Company
Augusta Council of the Georgia
   Association for Children and
   Adults with Learning Disabilities
P.O. Box 3231, Hill Station
Augusta, GA 30914-3231

Send a check for $17.95 payable
to *Augusta Cooks for Company*
(Georgia residents add $.96 state
sales tax)
Proceeds benefit: The Michael A.
Steed Scholarship Fund for Learning
Disability Students and Teachers
Recipes: Fresh Blueberry Pie, page
268; Lemon Bread, page 42; Senate
Bean Soup, page 68; Stuffed Cherry
Tomatoes, page 14

The Authorized Texas Ranger
   Cookbook
Harris Farms Publishing Company
P.O. 191
Hamilton, TX 76531

Send a check for $21.95 payable
to *Harris Farms Publishing Company*
(Texas residents add $1.47 state sales
tax)
Proceeds benefit: A portion of the
proceeds go to the Texas Ranger
Museum and Hall of Fame in Waco.
Recipes: Corn-Casserole Soufflé, page
227; Headquarters Hash, page 85;
Low-Fat Mexican Casserole, page
127; Texas Cowboy Stew, page 79

Bay Leaves
Junior Service League of Panama City
P.O. Box 404
Panama City, FL 32402

Send a check for $15.95 payable to *Bay Publications* (Florida residents add $.98 state sales tax)
Proceeds benefit: Service projects of the League
Recipe: Cherry-Sauced Pork Chops, page 99

The Best of the South
Newton General Hospital Auxiliary
5126 Hospital Drive
Covington, GA 30209

Send a check for $17.95 payable to *Newton General Hospital Auxiliary* (Georgia residents add $.75 state sales tax)
Proceeds benefit: Newton General Hospital Equipment Fund
Recipe: Broccoli and Carrot Crudités, page 8

Between Greene Leaves
Greene County Homemakers
    Extension Association
R.R. 1, Box 216
Carrollton, IL 62016

Send a check for $10.50 payable to *Greene County Homemakers Extension Association* (Illinois residents add $.54 state sales tax)
Proceeds benefit: Continuing education for homemakers and 4-H members in Greene County
Recipe: Spiced Zucchini Cake, page 240

Beyond the Bay
Junior Service League of Panama City
P.O. Box 404
Panama City, FL 32402

Send a check for $17.95 payable to *Bay Publications* (Florida residents add $1.05 state sales tax)
Proceeds benefit: Service projects of the League
Recipes: Lamb Chops with Herbs, page 103; Light Crab Quiche, page 144; Molasses Beef Stew, page 80; Shrimp-Stuffed Peppers, page 152

Cafe Oklahoma
Junior Service League of Midwest
    City
P.O. Box 10703
Midwest City, OK 73140

Send a check for $19.45 payable to *Cafe Oklahoma* (Oklahoma residents add $1.27 state sales tax)
Proceeds benefit: Junior Service League of Midwest City
Recipes: Barbecue Pig in the Greens, page 204; Buttermilk Cornbread, page 36; Quick Breakfast Pizza, page 177

Cajun Men Cook
Beaver Club of Lafayette
P.O. Box 2744
Lafayette, LA 70506

Send a check for $19.90 payable to *Beaver Club*
Proceeds benefit: Various civic projects
Recipes: Pasta with Tomatoes and Herbs, page 162; Roma Meat Roll, page 86; Sweet-Potato Pie, page 264

California Kosher
Women's League of Adat Ari El
    Synagogue
12020 Burbank Boulevard
North Hollywood, CA 91607

Send a check for $22.45 payable to *Women's League of Adat Ari El Synagogue* (California residents add $1.65 state sales tax)
Proceeds benefit: The expansion of Jewish education and community activities of the League, including its interfaith food pantry and programs for the developmentally disabled
Recipe: Vanilla Cheesecake, page 236

Campsite to Kitchen
Outdoor Writers Association of America
Tradery House
4210 B.F. Goodrich Boulevard
P.O. Box 18408
Memphis, TN 38118

Send a check for $20.95 payable to *The Wimmer Companies, Inc.* (Tennessee residents add $1.32 state sales tax)
Proceeds benefit: Outdoor Writers Association of America
Recipes: Cajun Fish, page 134; Garlic-Scented Broiled Shrimp, page 147; Herb and Parmesan Walleye, page 136; Shrimp-and-Crab Cakes, page 146

Cane River's Louisiana Living
Service League of Natchitoches
P.O. Box 2206
Natchitoches, LA 71457

Send a check for $23.45 payable to *Service League of Natchitoches*
Proceeds benefit: Scholarships for women
Recipes: Cocoa Brownies, page 249; Nonfat Berry Freeze, page 258; Spicy Shrimp-and-Corn Chowder, page 76; Zucchini Bread, page 46

Carolina Blessings
Children's Home Society of North Carolina
P.O. Box 14608
Greensboro, NC 27415-4608

Send a check for $17.95 payable to *Children's Home Society of North Carolina* (North Carolina residents add $1.08 state sales tax)
Proceeds benefit: All programs of Children's Home Society of North Carolina
Recipe: Spicy Oyster-Artichoke Soup, page 73

Celebrating California
Children's Home Society of California
7695 Cardinal Court
San Diego, CA 92123-3399

Send a check for $20.95 payable to *Children's Home Society of California* (California residents add sales tax per county)
Proceeds benefit: Child care, family support, shelter care, foster-family care, group-home care and adoption services
Recipe: Grilled Cornish Hens with Strawberry Marinade, page 124

Celebrations on the Bayou
Junior League of Monroe
P.O. Box 7138
Monroe, LA 71211

Send a check for $23.45 payable to *Cotton Bayou Publications* (Louisiana residents add $.80 state sales tax)
Proceeds benefit: YWCA battered women's shelter, adolescent pregnancy prevention, education mini-grants
Recipe: Minted Fruit Salad, page 185

Changing Thymes
Austin Junior Forum
P.O. Box 26628
Austin, TX 78755 0628

Send a check for $20.45 payable
to *AJF Publications*
Proceeds benefit: Selected charitable
nonprofit organizations in the
Greater Austin community
Recipe: Fried Rice, page 158

Charleston Receipts
Junior League of Charleston
51 Folly Road
Charleston, SC 29407

Send a check for $13.50 payable
to *Junior League of Charleston*
Proceeds benefit: Projects of the
League, including funding and volun-
teering time to establish a parenting
coalition and organizing of confer-
ences and seminars to prevent child
abuse
Recipe: Lemon Pudding Cake, page
275

Coastal Cuisine, Texas Style
Junior Service League of Brazosport
P.O. Box 163
Lake Jackson, TX 77566

Send a check for $19.95 payable
to *Junior Service League of
Brazosport* (Texas residents add
$1.40 state sales tax)
Proceeds benefit: Educational and
service projects of the Junior Service
League in the Brazosport community
Recipes: Cheese and Broccoli Soup,
page 64; Chicken Rumaki, page 25;
John's Famous Beans, page 173; Sea-
soned Red Potatoes, page 232

Cooking in the Litchfield Hills
Pratt Nature Center
163 Papermill Road
New Milford, CT 06776

Send a check for $18.95 ($16.95
for each additional book) payable to
The Pratt Nature Center (Connecticut residents add $.96 state sales tax)
Proceeds benefit: Funding for
environmental education and outdoor
educational programming
Recipes: Apricot-Glazed Carrots,
page 226; Pasta with Tender Kale,
page 164; Pot Roast with Apple
Cider, page 90; Steamed Mussels
Bistro-Style, page 149

Cooking with Class
Parents' Council of Charlotte Latin
  School
9502 Providence Road
Charlotte, NC 28277

Send a check for $20.00 payable
to *CLS Parents' Council* (North Carolina residents add $1.02 state sales
tax)
Proceeds benefit: Various projects of
the Parents' Council
Recipes: Lazy Lasagna, page 170;
Potato Skins, page 24; Quick Swiss
Soufflé, page 180

Cooks Extraordinaires
Service League of Green Bay
P.O. Box 372
Green Bay, WI 54305

Send a check for $18.95 payable
to *Service League of Green Bay* (Wisconsin residents add $.80 state sales
tax)

Proceeds benefit: Various projects benefitting the children of Brown County, Wisconsin
Recipes: Apple-Orchard Pork Chops, page 93; Deep-Dish Taco Squares, page 84; Egg Rolls, page 20

Cotton Country Cooking

Junior League of Morgan County
P.O. Box 486
Decatur, AL 35602-0486

Send a check for $18.45 payable to *Cotton Country Cooking* (Alabama residents add $.60 state sales tax)
Proceeds benefit: HANDS—Home for Adolesents in Need of Direction and Supervision
Recipes: Ada's Gingerbread with Lemon Sauce, page 246; Blueberry Bread, page 44; Creole Sauce for Fish, page 142; Sweet-and-Sour Pork, page 94

Country Treasures

Virginia Farm Bureau
P.O. Box 27552
12580 West Creek Parkway
Richmond, VA 23261

Send a check for $13.50 payable to *Virginia Farm Bureau*
Proceeds benefit: Virginia Tech two-year agricultural scholarship program and Virginia Foundation for Agriculture in the Classroom
Recipes: Baked Sweet Potatoes and Apples, page 232; Corn Pudding, page 228; Lentil-Barley Bake, page 172; Mushroom Swiss Steak, page 87

Cranbrook Reflections

Cranbrook House and Gardens
   Auxiliary
380 Lone Pine Road
P.O. Box 801
Bloomfield Hills, MI 48303

Send a check for $23.45 payable to *Cranbrook Reflections* (Michigan residents add $.80 state sales tax)
Proceeds benefit: The preservation and restoration of Cranbrook House, a National Historic Landmark, and its surrounding gardens
Recipe: Marinated Pork Loin, page 100

Critics' Choice

Guild of Corinth Theatre Arts
P.O. Box 127
Corinth, MS 38834

Send a check for $12.50 payable to *Guild of Corinth Theatre Arts*
Proceeds benefit: Community theatre
Recipes: Chocolate-Nut Fingers, page 253; Fancy Egg Scrambles, page 178; Glazed Softies, page 251; Shrimp Stroganoff, page 148

Cucina Classica

Order Sons of Italy in America
New York Grand Lodge Foundation
2101 Bellmore Avenue
Bellmore, NY 11710-5605

Send a check for $18.00 payable to OSIA NY Grand Lodge Foundation
Proceeds benefit: Scholarships
Recipe: Barley-Vegetable Soup, page 69

Delicious Developments

Friends of Strong Memorial Hospital
Box 660
601 Elmwood Avenue
Rochester, NY 14642

Send a check for $23.45 payable to *Friends of Strong Memorial Hospital* (New York residents add $1.60 state sales tax)
Proceeds benefit: The Trauma Center at Strong Memorial Hospital
Recipes: Cornish Hens with Pineapple-Cornbread Stuffing, page 126; Crispy Snack Mix, page 29; Fruit Sorbet, page 261; Triple-Bean Bake, page 174

Desert Treasures
Junior League of Phoenix
P.O. Box 10377
Phoenix, AZ 85064

Send a check for $21.45 payable to *Junior League of Phoenix*
Proceeds benefit: Community projects
Recipe: Orange-Walnut Broccoli, page 220

Dinner Chimes
First Presbyterian Church
1621 East Garrison Boulevard
Gastonia, NC 28054

Send a check for $18.00 payable to *First Presbyterian Church*
Proceeds benefit: Foreign and home missions; charitable and church-sponsored organizations
Recipe: Pear and Celery Salad, page 188

Emory Seasons
Emory University Woman's Club
849 Houston Mill Road, N.E.
Atlanta, GA 30329

Send a check for $24.95 payable to *Emory Seasons* (Georgia residents add $1.10 state sales tax)

Proceeds benefit: Emory University Endowment Fund and other charitable projects serving the Emory community
Recipes: Artichoke Squares, page 21; Chicken Roll-Ups, page 113; Creamy Fresh Dill Dip, page 9; Pork Chop Dinner, page 96

Family Creations
Gladney Fund Volunteer Auxiliaries
Madison Square Station
P.O. Box 1152
New York, NY 10159

Send a check for $18.95 payable to *Gladney Fund Volunteer Auxiliaries*
Proceeds benefit: Gladney Center Adoption Programs
Recipes: Marinated Filet Mignon, page 91; Orzo and Pine-Nut Pilaf, page 161; Raisin Bars, page 248

Family Secrets
Lee Academy
415 Lee Drive
Clarksdale, MS 38614

Send a check for $17.45 payable to *Family Secrets*
Proceeds benefit: Lee Academy, a college preparatory school
Recipe: Nanny's Caramel Pie, page 270

Feast of Eden
Junior League of Monterey County
P.O. Box 2291
Monterey, CA 93942-2291

Send a check for $23.45 payable to *Junior League of Monterey County* (California residents add $1.30 state sales tax)
Proceeds benefit: Monterey County Children's Museum

Recipes: Grilled Eggplant with Marinara Sauce, page 224; Sautéed Halibut with Nectarine Salsa, page 137; Thai Asparagus, page 216; Zesty Crab-and-Artichoke Dip, page 6

Florida Flavors
Environmental Studies Council
P.O. Box 1657
Port Salerno, FL 34992-1657

Send a check for $18.95 payable to *Florida Classics Library* (Florida residents add $1.05 state sales tax)
Proceeds benefit: Environmental Studies Council
Recipes: Corn Rolls, page 35; Easy Sour-Cream Coffee Cake, page 49; Orange Duck with Wild-Rice Dressing, page 129; Spinach Lasagna, page 168

Florida's Finest
Junior League of South Brevard
    County
P.O. Box 361905
Melbourne, FL 32936-1905

Send a check for $19.70 payable to *Junior League of South Brevard County* (Florida residents add $1.08 state sales tax)
Proceeds benefit: Serene Harbor, Space Coast Early Intervention
Recipes: Cream of Cauliflower Soup, page 65; Tapioca Fruit Salad, page 186

Foods à la Louisiane
Louisiana Farm Bureau Federation
9516 Airline Highway
P.O. Box 95004
Baton Rouge, LA 70815

Send a check for $20.50 payable to *Louisiana Farm Bureau Federation* (Louisiana residents add $.68 state sales tax; East Baton Rouge Parish adds $1.36)
Proceeds benefit: Youth activities
Recipes: Baked Red Snapper, page 138; Broccoli-Cauliflower Casserole, page 222; Strawberry-Nut Salad, page 184

From Generation to Generation
Sisterhood of Temple Emanu-El
8500 Hillcrest
Dallas, TX 75225-4288

Send a check for $19.45 payable to *Sisterhood of Temple Emanu-El* (Texas residents add $1.40 sales tax)
Proceeds benefit: Community projects such as Service to the Blind, North Dallas Shared Ministries, Dallas Jewish Coalition for the Homeless, Youth Camp scholarships, Golden Acres Home for the Aged, Meals on Wheels and preschool scholarships
Recipes: Apple-Glazed Barbecued Chicken, page 110; Apple Phyllo Packages, page 274; Cream of Winter-Squash Soup, page 62; White-Bean and Garlic Dip, page 11

Georgia on My Menu
Junior League of Cobb-Marietta
    County
P.O. Box 727
Marietta, GA 30061

Send a check for $17.95 payable to *League Publications* (Georgia residents add $.80 state sales tax)
Proceeds benefit: Junior League of Cobb-Marietta County
Recipe: Cucumber and Tomato Salad with Sour-Cream Dressing, page 195

The Gulf Gourmet
Westminster Academy PTA
5003 Lawson Avenue
Gulfport, MS 39507

Send a check for $15.45 payable
to *The Gulf Gourmet* (Mississippi
residents add $.91 state sales tax)
Proceeds benefit: Projects and
programs at the Westminster Academy elementary school
Recipe: Seafood Casseroles, page 153

Heart and Soul
Junior League of Memphis
3475 Central Avenue
Memphis, TN 38111

Send a check for $25.95 payable
to *Junior League of Memphis Publications* (Tennessee residents add
$1.65 state sales tax)
Proceeds benefit: Community projects
assisting families and children
Recipe: Country Chicken Pie, page 108

Holy Cow, Chicago's Cooking!
Church of the Holy Comforter
P.O. Box 168
Kenilworth, IL 60043

Send a check for $20.20 payable
to *Women of the Church of the Holy
Comforter* (Illinois residents add
$1.32 state sales tax)
Proceeds benefit: Chicago area outreach organizations for the hungry,
homeless and families at risk
Recipe: Pomegranate Fruit Salad,
page 187

Holy Smoke
United Methodist Women
Peachtree Road United Methodist
    Church
3180 Peachtree Road, NE
Atlanta, GA 30305

Send a check for $18.50 payable
to *UMW, PRUMC* (Georgia residents
add $.90 state sales tax)
Proceeds benefit: UMW Mission Fund
Recipes: Chicken Tortilla Casserole,
page 107; Greek Spinach Pie, page
18; Paella Salad, page 206

Hospitality
Salem Hospital Aid Association
3 Weatherly Drive
Salem, MA 01970

Send a check for $22.95 payable to
Hospitality Cookbook (Massachusetts
residents add $1.00 state sales tax)
Proceeds benefit: Salem Hospital Aid
Association
Recipe: Roast Leg of Lamb with Herb
Crust, page 104

The Kitchen Connection
National Council of Jewish Women,
    Omaha Section
6005 Maple Street
Omaha, NE 68104

Send a check for $11.95 payable
to *NCJW—Omaha Section*
Proceeds benefit: Children and youth
projects
Recipe: Appetizer Potato Pancakes,
page 22

Lone Star Legacy
Austin Junior Forum
P.O. Box 26628
Austin, TX 78755-0628

Send a check for $20.45 payable
to *AJF Publications*
Proceeds benefit: Dayblo Family
Treatment Center, Austin Area Can-
delighters Childhood Cancer Foundation, AIDS Services of Austin,
Pediatric AIDS League and others
Recipe: Marinated Vegetable Salad,
page 193

Lone Star Legacy II
Austin Junior Forum
P.O. Box 26628
Austin, TX 78755-0628

Send a check for $20.45 payable
to *AJF Publications*
Proceeds benefit: Selected charitable
nonprofit organizations in the
Greater Austin community
Recipe: Green Beans and Tomatoes,
page 217

The Maine Collection
Portland Museum of Art Guild
7 Congress Square
Falmouth, ME 04105

Send a check for $21.45 payable
to *Portland Museum of Art Guild*
(Maine residents add $1.14 state sales
tax)
Proceeds benefit: The restoration of
the McLellan-Sweat House
Recipe: Watercress Salad Dressing,
page 210

*M. D. Anderson Volunteers
    Cooking for Fun*
M. D. Anderson Cancer Center
    Volunteers
1515 Holcombe Boulevard Box 115
Houston, TX 77030

Send a check for $18.00 payable
to *M. D. Anderson Volunteers Cooking for Fun*
Proceeds benefit: Volunteer services
Recipes: Italian Cake, page 238; Pep-
peronata, page 230; Spinach Balls,
page 19; Texas Caviar, page 12

Nothin' Finer
Chapel Hill Service League
P.O. Box 3003
Chapel Hill, NC 27515

Send a check for $19.90 payable
to *Chapel Hill Service League* (North
Carolina residents add $.96 state
sales tax)
Proceeds benefit: The League's community outreach programs
Recipes: Basil-Balsamic Potato Salad,
page 190; Chocolate Muffins, page
39; Ginger Beets, page 219; South-of-
the-Border Chicken, page 205

Nutbread and Nostalgia
Junior League of South Bend
P.O. Box 1452
South Bend, IN 46624

Send a check for $22.45 payable
to *Junior League of South Bend* (Indiana residents add $.95 state sales tax)
Proceeds benefit: Kidsfirst
Recipes: Jim's Favorite Baked Walleye, page 135; Mushroom-Sauced
Noodles, page 167; Orange Popovers
with Honey Butter, page 32; Pumpkin
and Spice Roll, page 244

Of Tide and Thyme
Junior League of Annapolis
19 Loretta Avenue
Annapolis, MD 21401

Send a check for $21.95 ($20.45
for each additional book) payable to
Junior League of Annapolis (Mary-
land residents add $.95 state sales tax)
Proceeds benefit: Various community
projects in Anne Arundel County
Recipe: Steak Salad, page 198

Only in California
Children's Home Society of California
7695 Cardinal Court
San Diego, CA 92123-3399

Send a check for $20.95 payable
to *Children's Home Society of California* (California residents apply
state sales tax per county)
Proceeds benefit: 10,000 children
and families who benefit from CHS
services
Recipe: Cioppino, page 74

Our Country Cookin'
Junior Social Workers of Chickasha
P.O. Box 355
Chickasha, OK 73023

Send a check for $16.95 payable
to *Our Country Cookin'* (Oklahoma
residents add $.67 state sales tax)
Proceeds benefit: Community needs
and projects
Recipe: Chocolate Cinnamon Rolls,
page 52

Pass It On
Delta Delta Delta National Fraternity
P.O. Box 5987
Arlington, TX 76005-5987

Send a check for $20.95 payable
to *Delta Delta Delta* (Texas residents
add $1.40 state sales tax)
Proceeds benefit: Collegiate and alumnae member programs and services
Recipe: Autumn Stir-Fry, page 233

Pass the Plate
Episcopal Church Women of Christ
   Church
P.O. Box 836
1601 Lucerne Way
New Bern, NC 28563

Send a check for $21.00 payable
to *Pass the Plate*
Proceeds benefit: Episcopal Church
Women of Christ Church Religious
Community Services, Thompson
Children's Home
Recipes: Broccoli Buffet Casserole,
page 221; Minted Peas, page 229;
Nancy's Breadsticks, page 51; New
England Clam Chowder, page 77

Peachtree Bouquet
Junior League of DeKalb County
P.O. Box 183
Decatur, GA 30031

Send a check for $17.45 payable
to *JLD Publications* (Georgia
residents add $.60 state sales tax)
Proceeds benefit: DeKalb Rape Crisis
Center and other community projects
Recipe: Fruited Curry Rice, page 156

*The Philadelphia Orchestra
   Cookbook*
West Philadelphia Committee for the
   Philadelphia Orchestra
P.O. Box 685
Bryn Mawr, PA 19010

Send a check for $19.00 payable
to *The Philadelphia Orchestra Cookbook* (Pennsylvania residents add
$.96 state sales tax)
Proceeds benefit: The Philadelphia
Orchestra
Recipe: Parsley-Parmesan Chicken,
page 117

The Plaid Platter
Greenwich Academy
200 North Maple Avenue
Greenwich, CT 06830

Send a check for $22.85 payable
to *Greenwich Academy Cookbook
Benefit*
Proceeds benefit: Greenwich
Academy Financial Aid Programs
Recipes: Fresh Peach Ice Cream, page
260; Shrimp Gumbo, page 78; Sweet-
and-Spicy Stuffed Chicken, page 123

Plain and Elegant
West Georgia Medical Center
   Auxiliary
1514 Vernon Road
P.O. Box 1567
LaGrange, GA 30240

Send a check for $17.95 payable
to *WGMC Auxiliary* (Georgia resi-
dents add $.75 state sales tax)
Proceeds benefit: Outreach to Frail
Elderly
Recipes: Apricot Salad, page 182;
Frozen Orange Dream Bars, page
258; Pineapple Coleslaw, page 189;
Savory Crab on Rice, page 143

Prairie Potpourri
Immanuel Medical Center Auxiliary
6901 North 72nd Street
Omaha, NE 68122

Send a check for $18.20 payable
to *Immanuel Medical Center Auxiliary* (Nebraska residents add $1.04
state sales tax)
Proceeds benefit: Immanuel Medical
Center Auxiliary Hospitality House
Recipe: Fresh Artichokes with Mustard Sauce, page 214

Presentations
Friends of Lied Center for Performing
   Arts
University of Nebraska–Lincoln
12th and R Streets
Lincoln, NE 68588-0151

Send a check for $24.90 payable
to *Presentations*
Proceeds benefit: Program and Per-
formance Fund, Lied Center for Per-
forming Arts
Recipes: Beef Club Salad, page 201;
Caraway Cottage Puffs, page 50;
Honey-Dijon Salmon, page 140;
White-Bean and Tuna Salad, page
207

Preserving Our Italian Heritage
Sons of Italy Florida Foundation
87 NE 44th Street, Suite 5
Ft. Lauderdale, FL 33334

Send a check for $17.95 payable
to *Sons of Italy Florida Foundation*
Proceeds benefit: Sons of Italy Florida
Foundation scholarship program and
various charities, including Cooley's
anemia
Recipe: Anise Biscotti, page 254

Rave Reviews
Junior League of North Little Rock
216 West Fourth Street
P.O. Box 9043
Main Street Station
North Little Rock, AR 72119-9043

Send a check for $16.95 payable to
Junior League of North Little Rock
Proceeds benefit: The League's community projects, grants and scholarships
Recipe: Red Beans and Rice, page
176

River Feast
Junior League of Cincinnati
3500 Columbia Parkway
Cincinnati, OH 45226

Send a check for $18.33 payable
to *Junior League of Cincinnati* (Ohio
residents add $.80 state sales tax)
Proceeds benefit: Projects of the
League
Recipes: Oven-Barbecued Chicken,
page 122; Parmesan Pita Chips, page
7

RSVP
Junior League of Portland
107 Elm Street, Suite 100R
Portland, ME 04101

Send a check for $18.45 payable
to *Junior League of Portland* (Maine
residents add $.90 state sales tax)
Proceeds benefit: Beacon Teen Center
child abuse and neglect prevention
program
Recipes: New Orleans Salad Dressing, page 212; Salmon Party Log,
page 13

Sassafras! The Ozarks Cookbook
Junior League of Springfield
2574 East Bennett
Springfield, MO 65804

Send a check for $21.45 payable
to *Sassafras!*
Proceeds benefit: Ozarks Food Har-
vest, Prime Time (a latchkey
program), Ronald McDonald House
and many more
Recipes: Cool-Cucumber Soup, page
60; Elegant Lemon Roll, page 242;
Pollo Arrollado, page 114

Savoring the Southwest
Roswell Symphony Guild
3201 North Main
P.O. Box 3078
Roswell, NM 88201

Send a check for $21.95 payable
to *Roswell Symphony Guild Publications* (New Mexico residents add
$1.21 state sales tax)
Proceeds benefit: Roswell Symphony
Orchestra
Recipe: Country Captain Chicken,
page 118

Sea Island Seasons
Beaufort County Open Land Trust
P.O. Box 75
Beaufort, SC 29901

Send a check for $17.95 payable
to *Sea Island Seasons* (South Carolina
residents add $.75 state sales tax)
Proceeds benefit: Support of the
Beaufort Open Land Trust
Recipe: Greek Cucumber-and-Yogurt
Soup, page 66

Settings
Junior League of Philadelphia
P.O. Box 492
Bryn Mawr, PA 19010

Send a check for $26.45 payable
to *Junior League of Philadelphia*
(Pennsylvania residents add $1.50
state sales tax)
Proceeds benefit: Projects of the Ju-
nior League
Recipe: Sweet-and-Spicy Grilled
Salmon, page 141

Simple Elegance
Our Lady of Perpetual Help Women's
   Guild
8151 Poplar Avenue
Germantown, TN 38183

Send a check for $19.45 payable
to *Our Lady of Perpetual Help
Women's Guild* (Tennessee residents
add $1.40 state sales tax)
Proceeds benefit: Assistance to Our
Lady of Perpetual Help Family Life
Center, St. Jude Children's Research
Hospital and the YWCA Women's
Abuse Shelter
Recipe: Dijon-Honey Dressing, page
208

Simply Simpático
Junior League of Albuquerque
2501 San Pedro NE, Suite 209
Albuquerque, NM 87110

Send a check for $16.95 payable
to *Simply Simpático*
Proceeds benefit: Women and
children in need
Recipe: Chinese Noodle and Meatball
Soup, page 61

Smoky Mountain Magic
Junior League of Johnson City
High South Publications
P.O. Box 1082
Johnson City, TN 37605

Send a check for $16.95 payable
to *High South Publications*
(Tennessee residents add $1.44 state
sales tax)
Proceeds benefit: Watauga Mental
Health Services, Children's Hospital
Recipes: Cheesy Carrot-Rice Ring,
page 157; Spanish Rice, page 160

Some Like It Hot
Junior League of McAllen
P.O. Box 2465
McAllen, TX 78502

Send a check for $19.95 payable
to *Junior League of McAllen*
Proceeds benefit: Various projects for
the children and youth in the community
Recipes: Light Fettuccine, page 166;
Oven Chicken Olé, page 116

Specialties of the House
Kenmore Association
1201 Washington Avenue
Fredericksburg, VA 22401

Send a check for $19.95 payable
to *Kenmore Association* (Virginia res-
idents add $.90 state sales tax)
Proceeds benefit: Restoration of the
Kenmore Museum and Gardens
Recipe: Yellow-Pepper Soup, page 67

Still Fiddling in the Kitchen
National Council of Jewish Women
30233 Southfield Road, Suite #100
Southfield, MI 48076

Send a check for $18.00 payable to
National Council of Jewish Women
Proceeds benefit: Meals on Wheels,
Baldwin School Homeless Shelter,
Space (support group for widows and
the divorced), Children of Israel and
more
Recipe: Grilled Lime Chicken and
Salsa, page 112

The Summerhouse Sampler
Historic Wynnton School
2303 Wynnton Road
Columbus, GA 31906

Send a check for $17.90 payable to *Wynnton/Summerhouse Sampler* (Georgia residents add $.90 state sales tax)
Proceeds benefit: Wynnton School projects
Recipe: Stir-Fried Pork with Broccoli and Sesame, page 98

The Take Care Cookbook
Mid-Fairfield Hospice
112 Main Street
Norwalk, CT 06851

Send a check for $17.00 payable to *Mid-Fairfield Hospice* (Connecticut residents add $.84 state sales tax)
Proceeds benefit: Mid-Fairfield Hospice
Recipes: Curried Pork-and-Apple Salad, page 202; Jan's Chicken Casserole, page 119; Sugarless Apple Pie, page 266; Whole-Wheat Nut Bread, page 48

Tastes in Plaid
Alamance County Historical Museum
4777 South NC 62
Burlington, NC 27215

Send a check for $18.95 payable to *Alamance County Historical Museum*
Proceeds benefit: Alamance County Historical Museum preservation projects
Recipes: Lemony Almond-Topped Fillets, page 133; Peachy Bran Muffins, page 37; Quick Shrimp Skillet, page 150; Seasoned Oyster Crackers, page 30

The Texas Experience
Richardson Woman's Club
P.O. Box 831963
Richardson, TX 75083-1963

Send a check for $20.00 payable to *The Texas Experience* (Texas residents add $1.36 state sales tax)
Proceeds benefit: Academic scholarships, preservation and maintenance of the historic Grissom House, Network of Community Ministries, American Heart Association and more
Recipe: Pasta with Carrots and Ham, page 171

300 Years of Carolina Cooking
Junior League of Greenville
17 West North Street
Greenville, SC 29601

300 Years of Carolina Cooking is out of print. To order a copy of the League's *Uptown Down South*, send a check for $17.20 payable to *Junior League of Greenville Publications*
Proceeds benefit: Community projects
Recipes: Chicken Spoon Bread, page 106; Chocolate Dessert, page 263; Forgotten Cookies, page 252; New England Brown Bread, page 47

Treasures of the Smokies
Junior League of Johnson City
High South Publications
P.O. Box 1082
Johnson City, TN 37605

Send a check for $16.95 payable to *High South Publications* (Tennessee residents add $1.44 state sales tax)
Proceeds benefit: Watauga Mental Health Services, Children's Hospital
Recipes: Chocolate Puffs, page 250; Cranberry-Orange Salad, page 197; Layered Mexican Dip, page 10; Skewered Pasta and Vegetables, page 16

Virginia Fare
Junior League of Richmond
102 W. Franklin Street
Richmond, VA 23220

Send a check for $23.95 payable
to *JLR Cookbooks* (Virginia residents
add $.90 state sales tax)
Proceeds benefit: Family Resource
Center/Literary Council
Recipes: Black-Bean and Corn Salad,
page 194; Mushroom Caps Stuffed
with Crab Imperial, page 28; Red
Pepper and Ricotta Puree with Linguine, page 165; Shrimp Pinwheels,
page 17

Welcome Home
Thomasville Civic Center Foundation
P.O. Box 1131
Thomasville, AL 36784

Send a check for $18.95 ($16.45
for each additional cookbook)
payable to *Thomasville Civic Center
Foundation* (Alabama residents add
$1.28 state sales tax)
Proceeds benefit: Thomasville Civic
Center building project
Recipe: Creole Cabbage, page 223

West of the Rockies
Junior Service League of Grand
    Junction
P.O. Box 3221
Grand Junction, CO 81502

Send a check for $20.95 payable
to *West of the Rockies* (Colorado res-
idents add $.54 state sales tax)
Proceeds benefit: Riverfront Project,
Young Parents, adult literacy
Recipes: Creamy Caesar Salad, page
196; Lamb Curry, page 102; Low-Fat
Crème Anglaise, page 257; Oriental
Chicken Wontons, page 26

What's Cooking in Delaware
American Red Cross in Delaware
910 Gilpin Avenue
Wilmington, DE 19806

Send a check for $19.00 payable
to *American Red Cross—Cookbook*
Proceeds benefit: Programs and activities of American Red Cross in
Delaware
Recipes: Great Turkey Burgers, page
128; Ranch Pepper Dressing, page
209; White-Bean Chili with Turkey,
page 81

Wild about Texas
Cypress Woodlands Junior Forum
P.O. Box 90020, Dept. 242
Houston, TX 77069

Send a check for $23.95 payable
to *Wild about Texas*
Proceeds benefit: Keep Pace, North-
west Assistance Ministries, Sooper
Puppy Tomball Emergency Assistance
Ministries, Forum Friends
Recipe: Friday-Night Flounder, page
132

With Special Distinction
Mississippi College
Box 4041
Clinton, MS 39058

Send a check for $22.35 payable
to *MC Cookbook* (Mississippi residents add $1.40 state sales tax)
Proceeds benefit: Restoration and
preservation of historic buildings on
the campus of Mississippi College
Recipes: Honey Whole-Wheat Bread,
page 56; Low-Fat Banana Pudding,
page 262; Mother's Angel Pie, page
273; Sirloin and Vegetable Soup,
page 72

INDEX

....

Note: <u>Underscored</u> page references indicate boxed text.

A

Anise
Anise Biscotti, 254
Appetizers. *See also* Dips
Appetizer Potato Pancakes, 22
Artichoke Squares, 21
Broccoli and Carrot Crudités, 8
Chicken Rumaki, 25
Crispy Snack Mix, 29
Egg Rolls, 20–21
Greek Spinach Pie, 18–19
Mushroom Caps Stuffed with Crab
    Imperial, 28
Oriental Chicken Wontons, 26–27
Parmesan Pita Chips, 7
Potato Skins, 24
Seasoned Oyster Crackers, 30
Shrimp Pinwheels, 17
Skewered Pasta and Vegetables, 16
Spinach Balls, 19
Stuffed Cherry Tomatoes, 14–15
Apples
Apple-Glazed Barbecued Chicken,
    110–11
Apple-Orchard Pork Chops, 93
Apple Phyllo Packages, 274–75
Baked Sweet Potatoes and Apples,
    233
Curried Pork-and-Apple Salad,
    202–3
Pomegranate Fruit Salad, 187
Sugarless Apple Pie, 266–67
Apricots
Apricot-Glazed Carrots, 226
Artichokes
Artichoke Squares, 21
Beef Club Salad, 201–2
Fresh Artichokes with Mustard
    Sauce, 214
Marinated Vegetable Salad, 193

Spicy Oyster-Artichoke Soup, 73
Steak Salad, 198
Zesty Crab-and-Artichoke Dip,
    4–6
Asian-style dishes
Autumn Stir-Fry, 233
Chinese Noodle and Meatball
    Soup, 61
Egg Rolls, 20–21
Fried Rice, 158
Oriental Chicken Wontons, 26–27
Quick Shrimp Skillet, 150
Stir-Fried Pork with Broccoli and
    Sesame, 98
Sweet-and-Sour Pork, 94
Thai Asparagus, 216
Asparagus
Thai Asparagus, 216

B

Balsamic vinegar
Basil-Balsamic Potato Salad, 190
Bananas
Bananarama, <u>239</u>
Glazed Softies, 251–52
Low-Fat Banana Pudding, 262
Tapioca Fruit Salad, 186
Barley
Barley-Vegetable Soup, 69
Lentil-Barley Bake, 172
Sausage and Barley Soup, 70
Basil
Basil-Balsamic Potato Salad, 190
Pasta with Tomatoes and Herbs,
    162
Beans
Black-Bean and Corn Salad,
    194–95
Creole Lima Beans, 218
Green Beans and Tomatoes, 217